MICROWAVE Diet COOKERY

Marcia Cone and Thelma Snyder

Photographs by Michael Geiger

SIMON AND SCHUSTER

New York London Toronto Syndey Tokyo

Copyright © 1988 by Thelma Snyder and Marcia Cone
All rights reserved
including the right of reproduction
in whole or in part in any form.
Published by Simon and Schuster
A Division of Simon & Schuster Inc.
Simon & Schuster Building
Rockefeller Center
1230 Avenue of the Americas
New York, NY 10020
SIMON AND SCHUSTER and colophon are registered trademarks
of Simon & Schuster Inc.
Designed by Karolina Harris
Illustrated by Glenn Wolff
Manufactured in the United States of America

Library of Congress Cataloging-in-Publication Data
Cone, Marcia.
    Microwave diet cookery/Marcia Cone and Thelma Snyder:
photographs by Michael Geiger.
    p. cm.
    Include index.
    ISBN 0-671-62388-5
    1. Low-calorie diet—Recipes.   2. Microwave cookery.   I. Snyder,
Thelma.   II. Title.
RM222.2.C577   1988
641.5′635—dc19   87-28904
                                                    CIP

Acknowledgments

*M*any people have mentioned the need for this type of book, but our friend Mary Redican was the first to suggest it. Our agent, Barney Karpfinger, enthusiastically promoted the idea; Susan Cioni was the most helpful among our tasters; Kitty Cone put aside her own work to give us computer time; Carole Lalli honed the manuscript into its present form; and Michael Geiger added the final visual touches with his photographs.

Contents

Introduction

*T*his is a cookbook for people who want to use a microwave oven to prepare good-tasting, low-calorie, healthful meals.

Here is a diet based on the proven methods of calorie counting, sound nutrition from the four basic food groups, and exercise. We offer no miracle foods or miracle method. What we do offer are the tremendous advantages of cooking with a microwave oven that you don't have with any other appliance. For example, you can cook all foods with less fat, prepare single portions with ease, and assemble a home-cooked dinner for four in thirty minutes or less. To some dieters that might seem miraculous.

Reducing cooking fat is a natural function for the microwave oven because foods don't stick to dishes during cooking. So, fat is really only added for flavor in some of our recipes. If you are the single dieter in your home, you will find it less burdensome to cook up a single serving for yourself in the microwave oven than in the conventional oven. And finally, because the microwave reduces cooking time dramatically, you'll be out of the kitchen and away from temptation, sooner.

The microwave is essential to this book, but the quality of the recipes we offer would not be possible without fresh ingredients. The unique flavors, textures, and aromas are due in large measure to the richness of nature's changing bounty. It was these raw materials, season by season, that kept us inspired, and it is our hope that the new menus, season by season, will keep you interested in cooking with fresh produce and give a lift to your diet.

The menus are designed for four servings, but almost every recipe is given as well in single or double servings. Our hope is that each one in the household, be it one, two, or more, will begin to reshape his or her eating habits whether or not he or she is concerned about weight control. We feel that the nondieters will enjoy the new dishes that emerge from your kitchen as much as you do, and that even if extra bread, rice, or vegetables are requested, there will still be a reduction in the amount of salt, sugar, and cholesterol that is eaten.

For you, the dieter, we suggest keeping a food diary for three days to a week before you begin, to discover those foods you are now eating in excess and when you are eating them. This can be helpful in understanding your eating patterns, in order to change them. (You may want to record the frequency and length of exercise sessions in the diary, too.) The majority of overeating is not done with the new foods we eat, no matter how delicious we find them, but with the old ones that we don't scrutinize, in the old familiar places and situations— at home, watching TV—that we don't think about.

Now for some more specifics about the microwave diet.

Microwave Diet Basics

800 calories per day are suggested to give a "quick start" for the first week, a little over 1,000 calories after that. If you want to lose weight, you should try not to exceed 1,000 to 1,200 calories per day if you are a woman; if you're a man, 1,200 to 1,400 calories per day is the limit.

We have designed our dinner menus to fit into the 800-calories-per-day goal that you'll need for the first week, because we want you to be encouraged with a quick weight loss in the beginning. This is when you will be most motivated and most willing to make sacrifices. After this initial weight loss, you can add more calories per week as suggested for your sex, by adding an extra fruit, bread, or snack. At that pace, you will lose weight slowly, but steadily.

Once your desired weight is achieved, perhaps you'll need to diet only during the week, and can indulge yourself on the weekend.

Making up those calories are 6 ounces of concentrated protein per day for women, 8 ounces for men. In her *Good Food Book,* Jane Brody says that "the average American eats two to four times more protein than is needed for good nutrition," and that too much protein can even increase the risk of certain health problems.

In our menus we have suggested an amount of concentrated protein to be more in line with what is really required. For dinner, this means 3 ounces of meat or poultry, 4 ounces of fish, or a suggested amount of complementary vegetable proteins such as found in Pasta e Fagioli (pasta and beans). To equal and substitute for the concentrated complete protein found in animal flesh, legumes* (any type) must be combined with a grain such as the wheat in pasta or bread, rice, kasha, bulgur, corn, barley, or sesame seeds.

The remaining 2 to 4 ounces are allotted between breakfast and lunch. You'll

* Legumes are peanuts, kidney beans, chick-peas, navy, pinto and lima beans, lentils, and split peas.

find that only four menus of the eighteen menus in each season contain red meat. The rest revolve around poultry, fish, and vegetables, which are lower in cholesterol and better for your heart and arteries.

3 servings of fruit and 2 servings of vegetables per day. Take advantage of fruits and vegetables! You'll never encounter more vitamins and minerals per calorie than with these important groups. And because of the short amount of cooking time and the minimal amount of water needed, there is nothing like microwave cooking to retain the bright appearance and nutrient value of produce.

In our diet plan, some sort of fruit is always suggested as a dinner dessert and the fruits in all the menus are interchangeable with each other.

We have tried to complement the vegetables so that you receive the maximum absorption of nutrients: For instance, you receive more iron from spinach or watercress when they are served with vitamin C (oranges, tomatoes).

2 servings bread or grains per day. Rice, oatmeal, kasha, or slices of bread are sources of fiber that will fill you up and keep your digestive system occupied for longer, so you will feel full.

1 tablespoon monounsaturated or polyunsaturated fat per day. All the recent information tells us that to reduce the risk of heart disease we should reduce saturated fats, and so our recipes call for olive oil (monounsaturate) and liquid safflower, corn, sesame, or sunflower oils (polyunsaturates).

1 teaspoon sugar per day. We use sugar and no artificial sweeteners so that you can train your taste buds toward less sweetness in foods. But as we have indicated in the snack section, it is better to have just one cookie one day, than to binge sometime down the road because you feel totally deprived.

We don't call for any salt. Since salt could be a cause of high blood pressure, we have taken a clue from other cultures and used a heavier hand with spices and herbs. For salt, we have substituted fresh basil, parsley, ginger, hot peppers, cuminseed, and the like. It is a good idea to check the potency of your dried spice before you begin, for they can lose their flavor over time. Some, like cuminseed and coriander, can be best preserved in the freezer.

Dinner menus begin with a light soup. It has also been found that those who begin their meals with soup consume 80 less calories per day, and that can add up to 560 per week or close to 2,400 per month. (That's over a pound a month without even trying.) With this in mind, we have designed each dinner menu to begin with soup, followed by a main course and then a dessert. We think serving three courses will give you the sense that you have consumed more, which will ultimately be more satisfying.

13

Most dinners can be prepared in thirty minutes according to a "Plan of Action." We always feel that it is better not to mull over the dinner possibilities at 5:00 or 5:30 P.M., but to follow a planned-out guideline. Some people may work faster or slower than we suggest, but our time estimates are pretty close.

In an effort to speed you in and out of the kitchen, we have tried to coordinate preparation and cooking time. You'll see that dessert is sometimes prepared after dinner, while the dishes are being cleared, or that the soup is served before the main dish has finished cooking. This is partly to feed you more quickly, but at the same time it elongates the meal in order to give your stomach the twenty minutes research indicates is necessary to signal your brain that you are nearly full.

We dovetail various menus so that the remainder of the cut-up broccoli that went into last night's soup can be used in the vegetable platter the next night. We suggest preparing some foods the night before serving them, while you're cleaning up the evening meal.

Lunch suggestions are included with each season. These will help you plan your daily calorie count and show you how to use dinner leftovers. Breakfast suggestions are in a separate chapter.

Drink 8 glasses of water per day. This flushes your system of the water it retains and helps you to feel full. If you can't get that much water down, choose one of the low-calorie beverages that are suggested throughout the book.

Liquids are an important part of your diet because they help to cleanse your system and, sometimes, give you that full feeling without adding excess calories. It is essential that you choose beverages that are low in calories, but not necessarily high in artificial sweeteners. The latter won't help you to reeducate your taste buds away from sugary drinks but will continue to fuel your craving for them, so that in a weak moment a cloyingly sweet soft drink will taste every bit as good as its artifically sweetened counterpart. On the other hand, if you retrain yourself to choose beverages that are less sweet, your taste buds will reject something else much sweeter.

Have a 100-calorie snack every other day, once you've seen that you're doing well. This can be a piece of fruit, two cookies, or even a cocktail. Look through the suggestions in the sidebars and in "Snacks" (page 279).

Dieting without exercise is futile. The body does a strange thing when you begin to diet. It tries to adjust for the weight loss by burning calories (metabolism) at a slower rate. The way to counteract this is to exercise, which can "raise your metabolism by 20 to 30 percent,'' according to Brody's *Good Food Book.* ''The effect can last for 15 hours after the exercise'' and there are indications that exercise done within two to three hours after dinner will burn more calories than the same exercise done on an empty stomach, says Dr. David Levitsky of Cornell University. So the next time that a walk after dinner just seems too much of an effort, do it anyway . . . it will help you tremendously.

Ways to Exercise and Increase Your Metabolism

After consulting your doctor, do one of these moderate exercises for a half hour, three times a week. This should increase your metabolism, not to mention make a difference in your muscle tone. Those activities with an asterisk (*) are good aerobic exercises—best for your heart and lungs—and should be done continuously for the half hour for best effect.

	CALORIES BURNED PER HOUR FOR APPROXIMATELY 150-POUND PERSON
swimming (¼ mph)*	300 to 350
cycling (8 mph)	300 to 350
scrubbing floors*	300 to 350
walking 3.5 mph, level ground*	300 to 350
cycling 8 mph*	300 to 350
Ping-Pong	300 to 350
raking leaves, hoeing	300 to 350
calisthenics*	300 to 350
doubles tennis	300 to 350
ballet exercises*	300 to 350
golfing, carrying clubs	300 to 350
digging in the garden	360 to 420
disco dancing	360 to 420
roller-skating*	360 to 420
horseback riding (posting to trot)*	360 to 420

Compiled largely from Jane Brody's Good Food Book (New York: W. W. Norton, 1985).

Basic Ingredients

Keep these ingredients on hand so that you are prepared with the basics.

Pantry:

Dry skim milk
Evaporated skim milk*
Onions
Garlic
Canned low-sodium chicken broth*
Clam juice*
Tomato juice*
White grape juice*
Olive oil
*Tomato paste in a tube (handy for
    thickening small amounts)**
Peppercorns
Hot pepper flakes
Paprika
Whole nutmeg
Dry vermouth or sherry
Low-sodium soy sauce
Long-grain rice
Whole wheat pasta or soba noodles
*Refrigerate after opening.

Refrigerator:

Carrots
Celery
Bean sprouts
Low-fat plain yogurt
Prepared mustard
Fresh lemons

Freezer:

Whole wheat pita
Grated fresh orange peel
Grated fresh lemon peel
Chopped fresh parsley

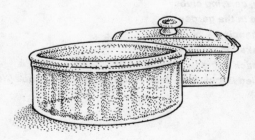

Suggested Utensils

▲ ▲ ▲ ▲ ▲ ▲ ▲ ▲ ▲ ▲ ▲ ▲

Dishes:

All dishware should be made of heatproof glass (to withstand the heat of the food while it is cooking), without any metal trim. Plastic cookware should be marked with a suitable-for-microwave seal.

1-quart covered casserole
2-quart covered casserole
3-quart covered casserole
10-inch Pyrex pie plate
2-quart rectangular baking dish
8-ounce oval ramekins
Individual cook-and-serve dishes made of glass or ceramic with nonmetallic trim:
  dinner plate
  1½-cup soup bowl or mug
  6- or 7-ounce custard cups
Large Pyrex mixing bowl

▼ ▼ ▼ ▼ ▼ ▼ ▼ ▼ ▼ ▼ ▼ ▼

▲ ▲ ▲ ▲ ▲ ▲ ▲ ▲ ▲ ▲ ▲ ▲

Equipment:

Ice cream scoops
  large (¼ cup)
  small (⅛ cup)
7-inch serving plates
  (to make the food seem like more)
Food processor or blender
Parchment paper

▼ ▼ ▼ ▼ ▼ ▼ ▼ ▼ ▼ ▼ ▼ ▼

Terms

▲ ▲ ▲ ▲ ▲ ▲ ▲ ▲ ▲ ▲ ▲ ▲

Covering:

"Cover tightly" means to cover with a casserole lid or plastic wrap that has been folded back slightly on one side.

  "Cover with wax paper" means to lay the wax paper loosely on top of a dish.

  If no term is mentioned in the recipe this indicates that a cover is not necessary.

▼ ▼ ▼ ▼ ▼ ▼ ▼ ▼ ▼ ▼ ▼ ▼

▲ ▲ ▲ ▲ ▲ ▲ ▲ ▲ ▲ ▲ ▲ ▲

Power Settings:

HIGH is full power for your oven.
MEDIUM will be 50 percent (5) on a full-powered oven or about 70 percent (7) on a smaller, lower-powered oven.
DEFROST will be 30 percent (3) on a full-powered oven or about 50 percent (5) on a smaller, lower-powered oven.
LOW will be 10 percent (1) on a full-powered oven or 20 percent (2) on a smaller, lower-powered oven.

▼ ▼ ▼ ▼ ▼ ▼ ▼ ▼ ▼ ▼ ▼ ▼

SPRING MENUS

*L*ayers of thick winter woolens will soon be shed for sleeker spring styles. If you still haven't been able to get rid of the pounds accumulated during the holiday dinners, this is the time to make a new start.

Prepare yourself by stocking the refrigerator with these seasonal vegetables that are virtually free from calories. At the beginning of each week, wash, trim, and cut up the vegetables and store them in plastic bags in the refrigerator, and snack on them to stave off hunger:

▲ ▲ ▲ ▲ ▲ ▲ ▲ ▲ ▲ ▲ ▲

- ◆ **broccoli, cut into spears**
- ◆ **radishes, whole**
- ◆ **iceberg lettuce, cut into wedges**
- ◆ **celery**

▼ ▼ ▼ ▼ ▼ ▼ ▼ ▼ ▼ ▼ ▼

If you need a more substantial snack, lightly dip raw vegetables into premade Creamy Mustard Dressing (page 290), but remember to add this to your daily calories.

Here are other spring incentives:

▲ ▲ ▲ ▲ ▲ ▲ ▲ ▲ ▲ ▲ ▲

- ◆ **Don't get angry at yourself for not taking off that weight this winter. Just take things one week at a time. Promise yourself that once you reach your ideal weight you will only have to be dieting during the week and not on the weekends.**
- ◆ **List some spring events coming up—a special dinner at work, a wedding—where you want to look smashing. Cut out a magazine picture of an outfit you would like to wear and tape it to your bedroom mirror with a sign that says: IF I LOSE FIFTEEN POUNDS, I WILL LOOK GREAT IN THIS.**
- ◆ **Take a few minutes in the morning each day to calm yourself. Sit down with a cup of coffee, relax, and picture yourself in that outfit. Athletes use this approach when trying to perfect a tennis stroke or other skill—it's called "patterning" or "visualization."**
- ◆ **Promise yourself a massage for your slimmer body this spring.**
- ◆ **It's time to get out and exercise again. Develop an outdoor exercise program of jogging, bike riding, playing tennis, or walking.**

▼ ▼ ▼ ▼ ▼ ▼ ▼ ▼ ▼ ▼ ▼

Each person has a control system—or set point—for the amount of fat in the body. It is the equilibrium that your body is drawn to, whether you want it or not. It is controlled by the number of calories that are burned in an hour. Dieting cannot change it; in fact, cutting down on calories may signal your body to burn less calories than usual to maintain that equilibrium.

So what's the answer? Exercise. Even a half hour's walk on a regular basis can be helpful. "Routine exercise can boost a dieter's sluggish 40-calorie-an-hour metabolic rate to 70 or 80 calories an hour," says Gabe Merkin, M.D., author of *Getting Thin* (Little, Brown and Company, 1983). "Just a half hour a day will keep you burning calories at a faster rate all day long."

This menu is ideal for a day when you know you'll be coming home late. If you take 10 minutes the night before to prepare and chill the terrine, you'll be all set.

WATERCRESS CONSOMMÉ

SVELTE TERRINE DE POISSON
WITH CREAMY HERB DRESSING

WHOLE WHEAT MELBA TOAST (2, 32 CALORIES)

SPICED ORANGES

Plan of action

10 MINUTES THE NIGHT BEFORE
15 MINUTES BEFORE SERVING

1. Prepare the terrine and creamy dressing the night before.
2. On the serving day, prepare and cook the spiced oranges and set them aside.

3. Prepare and cook the soup.
4. While the soup is heating, arrange the terrine slices on serving plates.
5. Serve the soup and then the terrine with toast.

Watercress Consommé

SERVINGS: 4 ◆ 33 CALORIES PER 1-CUP SERVING ◆ COOKING TIME: 8 TO 10 MINUTES

4 cups chicken broth
2 cups chopped watercress

¼ cup low-fat plain yogurt
Freshly ground pepper

Combine the broth and watercress in a 2-quart casserole. Cover tightly and cook on HIGH for 8 to 10 minutes, or until heated through. Garnish each serving with 1 tablespoon yogurt sprinkled with pepper.

◆ *For 1 Serving:* Combine 1 cup broth and ½ cup chopped watercress in a 1½-cup microwaveproof bowl. Cover tightly and cook on HIGH for 2 to 3 min-

utes, or until hot. Garnish with 1 tablespoon yogurt and a pinch black pepper.

23

Svelte Terrine de Poisson with Creamy Herb Dressing

SERVINGS: 4 FOR DINNER, OR 8 FOR LUNCH ◆ 234 CALORIES PER 2-SLICE DINNER SERVING, INCLUDING 4 TABLESPOONS CREAMY HERB DRESSING I ◆ 117 CALORIES PER 1-SLICE LUNCH SERVING, INCLUDING 2 TABLESPOONS DRESSING ◆ COOKING TIME: 4 TO 6 MINUTES

1 pound fresh or frozen, defrosted, flounder or sole fillets

1 tablespoon (1 packet) unflavored gelatin

3 tablespoons cold water

2 cups low-fat plain yogurt

¼ cup fresh lemon juice

2 tablespoons chopped fresh parsley

2 tablespoons chopped fresh chives or green onion tops

1 tablespoon chopped fresh dill, or 1 teaspoon dried

½ teaspoon cayenne pepper

4 cups trimmed spinach leaves

16 cherry tomatoes, or 4 medium tomatoes, sliced

1 cup Creamy Herb Dressing I (page 288)

Fold each fillet in thirds, envelope fashion, and place them seam side down around the outer rim of a 9- or 10-inch pie or cake plate, leaving the center open. Cover with a paper towel and cook on HIGH for 3 to 5 minutes, or until the fish flakes under the pressure of a fork. Drain the fish and finely flake it with a fork.

In a large glass bowl stir the gelatin into the cold water. Heat the mixture for 30 to 45 seconds on HIGH, or until the gelatin is dissolved; stir well. Stir in the yogurt, lemon juice, herbs, and pepper. Add the flaked fish and stir well to blend.

Line a loaf pan with plastic wrap and spoon in the mixture, spreading it evenly on top. Cover and refrigerate the terrine for 3 hours or overnight.

To serve: Unmold the terrine from the dish and cut it into 8 slices. Place 1 cup spinach leaves on each of 4 large serving plates, then place 2 slices of the fish terrine on top. Garnish with tomatoes and a ribbon of 4 tablespoons dressing down the center. Accompany each serving with 2 slices whole wheat melba toast.

◆ *Tips:* For serving at lunch, place 1 slice terrine on 2 slices of melba toast; serve with cucumber sticks and a piece of fruit.

If you're entertaining, 1 slice fish terrine with 2 tablespoons dressing makes an elegant sit-down first course. Your guests will feel that they are dining at a fine restaurant while consuming only 115 calories per serving. Or, you can cut each terrine slice into 6 squares to make 48 appetizer servings: Place each square on a cucumber slice and top with a dab of sauce. 17 calories per serving.

When you add a little vitamin C to your menu, with sources such as tomatoes or oranges, you can boost your iron absorption from vegetable sources—spinach, watercress—by 500 percent. That is why it is important to serve the fish terrine with tomatoes on top of the spinach leaves.

Spiced Oranges

SERVINGS: 4 ◆ 103 CALORIES PER ⅓-CUP SERVING ◆ COOKING TIME: 2 TO 3 MINUTES

½ cup dry vermouth or white grape juice
1 tablespoon sugar
4 whole cloves
½ teaspoon ground cinnamon
½ teaspoon vanilla extract
4 naval oranges, peeled and sliced crosswise into ¼-inch slices

Place all the ingredients except the orange slices into a 10-inch pie plate. Cook on HIGH for 2 to 3 minutes, or until heated, to blend the flavors. Add the orange slices and set aside the oranges in sauce until serving time. Serve warm or at room temperature.

CHINESE CABBAGE SOUP

PINEAPPLE CHICKEN TERIYAKI

ORANGE RICE

FRESH STRAWBERRIES WITH YOGURT OR
FROZEN STRAWBERRY DELIGHT (PAGE 47)

Menu

2

*262 calories
per serving*

Plan of action

32 MINUTES BEFORE SERVING

1. If serving Frozen Strawberry Delight, make that first and freeze it. Otherwise, just prepare the fresh strawberries right before serving.

2. Cook the Orange Rice.
3. While the rice is cooking, prepare the ingredients for the soup and chicken.
4. Cook the soup during the standing time for the rice.
5. Cook the chicken when the soup is finished.

6. Allow the chicken and rice to stand, covered, while eating the soup. Both chicken and rice should remain warm enough, but if not, reheat each on HIGH for 1 to 2 minutes.

Chinese Cabbage Soup

SERVINGS: 4 ◆ 26 CALORIES PER 1½-CUP SERVING ◆ COOKING TIME: 7 TO 8 MINUTES

4 cups chicken broth
2 cups thinly sliced Chinese cabbage

2 thin slices fresh peeled ginger
1 teaspoon low-sodium soy sauce

Combine all the ingredients in a 2-quart casserole. Cover tightly and cook on HIGH for 8 to 10 minutes, or until heated through.

◆ For 1 Serving: Combine 1 cup broth, ½ cup sliced cabbage, 1 slice ginger, and ¼ teaspoon soy sauce in a 1½-cup microwaveproof bowl. Cover tightly and cook on HIGH for 2 to 3 minutes.

Variation:

Chinese Cabbage Soup with Lemon: Add 1 teaspoon grated lemon peel and 1 teaspoon white vinegar.

Pineapple Chicken Teriyaki

SERVINGS: 4 ◆ 194 CALORIES PER SERVING WITH RICE ◆ COOKING TIME: 7 TO 8 MINUTES

1 teaspoon olive oil
2 garlic cloves, minced
4 green onions, thinly sliced
1 pound skinless, boneless chicken breasts, cut into ½-inch cubes
1 tablespoon freshly grated ginger
2 teaspoons grated orange peel

2 tablespoons dry vermouth
1 tablespoon low-sodium soy sauce
2 cups cubed fresh or canned unsweetened pineapple, drained
2 green or red bell peppers, cut into 1-inch squares
Dash freshly ground black pepper

Combine the oil, garlic, and onions in a 10-inch pie plate. Cook on HIGH for 1 minute. Stir in the chicken pieces, ginger, orange peel, vermouth, and soy sauce. Cover with wax paper and cook on HIGH for 3 minutes; stir well. Stir in the pineapple, red and green peppers and black pepper. Cover again and cook on HIGH for 3 to 4 minutes more, or until the chicken is opaque but tender. Serve the chicken and sauce over the rice.

◆ *For 1 Serving:* Combine ½ teaspoon oil, 1 small minced garlic clove, and 1 thinly sliced green onion in a 1½-quart casserole. Cook on HIGH for 30 seconds. Stir in 4 ounces of chicken cubes, 1 teaspoon grated ginger, 1 teaspoon grated orange peel, 1 tablespoon dry vermouth, and 1 teaspoon soy sauce. Cover with wax paper and cook on HIGH for 2 minutes. Stir in ½ cup pineapple; ½ of a green pepper, cubed; and a pinch black pepper. Cover again and continue to cook on HIGH for 1 to 2 minutes, or until heated through. See Basic Rice recipe for single serving.

Orange Rice

SERVINGS: 4 ◆ 135 CALORIES PER ½-CUP SERVING ◆ COOKING TIME: 10 TO 15 MINUTES

1 tablespoon grated orange peel
1 recipe Basic Rice (page 294)

Add the grated orange peel to the rice and water before cooking.

Fresh Strawberries with Yogurt

SERVINGS: 4 ◆ 42 CALORIES PER ½-CUP SERVING

2 cups whole fresh strawberries, washed, hulled, and halved
  Grated orange peel
½ cup low-fat plain yogurt

In each of 4 bowls place ½ cup strawberries. Stir in a pinch grated orange peel and garnish with 2 tablespoons yogurt on top.

Menu

3

518 calories
per serving

TANGY RADISH CONSOMMÉ

CONFETTI VEAL MEATBALLS

BASIC RICE (PAGE 294)

TOMATO SLICE SPRINKLED WITH
VINEGAR AND FRESH HERBS

GLAZED BANANA BOATS

Plan of action

30 MINUTES BEFORE SERVING

1. Cook the rice.
2. While the rice is cooking, prepare the ingredients for the soup and meatballs, and slice tomato.
3. Heat the soup and serve it. Let the rice stand.
4. While eating the soup, cook one batch of meatballs.
5. Cook the other batch of meatballs and serve with the rice and tomato.
6. Prepare and cook the bananas at the end of the meal.

Tangy Radish Consommé

SERVINGS: 4 ◆ 35 CALORIES PER 1-CUP SERVING ◆ COOKING TIME: 8 TO 10 MINUTES

4 cups chicken broth
16 red radishes, thinly sliced
    Dash hot pepper sauce
4 lemon slices

¼ cup chopped fresh chives or
    green onion tops
Freshly ground black pepper

Combine the broth, radishes, and hot pepper sauce in a 2-quart casserole. Cover tightly and cook on HIGH for 8 to 10 minutes, or until heated through.

Garnish each serving with a lemon slice, 1 tablespoon chives, and a grinding of pepper.

◆ *For 1 Serving:* Combine 1 cup broth, 4 thinly sliced radishes, and a pinch hot pepper sauce in a 1½-cup microwaveproof bowl. Cover tightly and cook on HIGH for 2 to 3 minutes, until heated through. Garnish with 1 tablespoon chopped chives, 1 lemon slice, and a dash pepper.

Confetti Veal Meatballs

MAKES: 20 ◆ 160 CALORIES PER 4 OUNCES (4 MEATBALLS) FOR DINNER; 80 CALORIES PER 2 OUNCES (2 MEATBALLS) FOR LUNCH ◆ COOKING TIME: 3 TO 5 MINUTES

Generous amounts of grated parsnips, carrots, and zucchini add a confettilike texture and also serve to stretch the veal and lower the calories. Parsnips especially add a delicate, sweet flavor.

1 pound ground veal
2 tablespoons chopped onion
½ cup grated parsnips
½ cup grated carrots
½ cup grated zucchini

1 egg, beaten
1 teaspoon fresh thyme, or ½ teaspoon dried
⅛ teaspoon grated nutmeg
Dash freshly ground black pepper
Dash salt

Combine all the ingredients in a medium mixing bowl, blending well. Form the mixture into *twenty* 1½-inch meatballs. Place 10 meatballs around the outer edge of a 10-inch pie plate and cover with wax paper. Cook on HIGH for 3 to 5 minutes, or until cooked through.

Transfer the meatballs to a serving plate and cook the remaining 10 meatballs in the same way.

◆ *For 2 Servings:* Cut the ingredient amounts in half and follow the basic recipe, cooking only one batch of 10 meatballs in a 10-inch pie plate.

Variations:

Veal Meatballs in Tomato Gravy: After transferring the cooked meatballs to the serving plate, stir 2 teaspoons tomato paste and 2 tablespoons skim milk into the cooking juices. Cook the

juices on HIGH for 2 minutes, or until bubbling, stirring once. Spoon the sauce over the meatballs. This sauce adds 5 calories per serving.

Veal Meatballs in Mushroom Sauce: Follow the Tomato Gravy variation, adding 6 sliced mushrooms with the tomato paste and milk. 11 calories.

◆ *Tips:* You may freeze the meatballs and rice on individual dishes. To reheat a frozen dinner serving, cover the dish with wax paper and cook on HIGH for 6 to 8 minutes or until the top of the wax paper feels very warm. To reheat a plate that has been refrigerated but not frozen, cover in the same way, and heat on HIGH for 2½ to 4 minutes.

For lunch, slice 2 meatballs and place them into 1 small or ½ large whole wheat pita pocket. Add ½ cup chopped lettuce or sprouts. 156 calories.

ENTERTAINING

Just because you're on a diet is no reason to cut back on socializing. In fact, you'll find that it is much easier to control your diet when you prepare the food. And when you serve tiny vealballs as appetizers, your guests won't even know that you're watching their diet, too.

Follow the basic Veal Meatballs recipe and make forty ¾-inch balls. Cook 20 meatballs at a time in a 10-inch pie plate, placing 12 around the outer rim and 8 in a ring on the inside, leaving the center open. Cover the plate with wax paper and cook on HIGH for 3 to 5 minutes, or until cooked through.

Serve the meatballs on toothpicks with a button mushroom or ¼ of a large mushroom cap. Dip them into Curry-Herb Dip (page 289). Each meatball with dip is about 24 calories.

Glazed Banana Boats

SERVINGS: 4 ◆ 189 CALORIES PER SERVING ◆ COOKING TIME: 3 TO 5 MINUTES

4 large ripe bananas, unpeeled, cut in half lengthwise
4 teaspoons lemon juice
4 teaspoons brown sugar
½ teaspoon ground cinnamon (optional)

Place the bananas, cut side up, in a 2-quart rectangular dish. Sprinkle evenly with lemon juice, brown sugar, and cinnamon. Cook, uncovered, on HIGH for 3 to 5 minutes, or until heated through. Serve warm.

◆ *For 1 Serving:* Cook 1 banana with ¼ of the remaining ingredients, placing the banana in a microwaveproof dish. Cook on HIGH for 45 seconds to 1½ minutes.

SHRIMP IN CLAM BROTH

PASTA PRIMAVERA

WHOLE WHEAT ITALIAN BREAD (1 SLICE, 75 CALORIES)

FRESH PINEAPPLE COCKTAIL

Menu

4

*443 calories
per serving*

Plan of action

25 TO 35 MINUTES BEFORE SERVING

1. Prepare and cook the pineapple dessert and set it aside.
2. Begin preparing the soup.
3. While the soup is cooking, cut up the vegetables for the primavera sauce.
4. Cook the pasta. Meanwhile, cook the primavera sauce.

5. While the pasta is cooking, peel and thinly slice the cooked shrimp.
6. Drain the pasta and set it aside. Keep the primavera sauce warm, with a cover.
7. Serve the soup, then the pasta and bread.

Make sure that the bread you serve is of a good quality and satisfying—and serve it the way the continental Europeans do—without butter!

Shrimp in Clam Broth

SERVINGS: 4 ◆ 88 CALORIES PER 1-CUP SERVING ◆ COOKING TIME: 8 TO 10 MINUTES

Cooking the shrimp in their shells adds flavor to the broth.

2 cups clam juice
2 cups chicken broth
8 large raw shrimp, unshelled
  Dash hot pepper sauce

Dash freshly ground black pepper
4 lemon slices
¼ cup chopped green onion tops

Pour the clam juice and chicken broth into a 2-quart casserole. Add the shrimp with shells, hot pepper sauce, and black pepper. Cover tightly and cook on HIGH for 8 to 10 minutes, or until heated through and the shrimp turn pink. Remove the shrimp, and peel and thinly slice.

To serve: Divide the soup between 4 bowls and add 2 sliced shrimp and a slice lemon to each bowl. Sprinkle with green onions.

◆ *For 1 Serving:* Combine ½ cup each clam juice and chicken broth, 2 unpeeled shrimp, and a dash each hot pepper sauce and black pepper in a 1½-cup microwaveproof bowl. Cover tightly and cook on HIGH for 3 to 4 minutes, or until the shrimp are pink. Remove the shrimp, peel, and thinly slice. Stir the sliced shrimp, 1 lemon slice, and 1 tablespoon chopped green onion into the heated soup and serve.

Pasta Primavera

SERVINGS: 4 ◆ 209 CALORIES PER ½-CUP SERVING ◆ COOKING TIME: 13 TO 18 MINUTES

So spicy and smooth that you won't feel as if you are dieting.

2 **quarts water**
4 **ounces thin dry spaghetti**
1 **teaspoon olive oil**
2 **garlic cloves, minced**
1 **cup chopped peeled fresh or canned plum tomatoes, undrained**
½ **cup chopped pimento, drained**
1 **tablespoon tomato paste**
2 **tablespoons chopped fresh basil, or 1 teaspoon dried**

¼ **cup grated Parmesan cheese**
½ **cup skim milk**
2 **cups asparagus tips, cut into 2-inch-long pieces (about 1 pound) (see tip)**
2 **small zucchini, cut into ¼-inch slices**
2 **cups thinly sliced mushrooms (about ¼ pound)**
¼ **teaspoon red pepper flakes**
Freshly ground black pepper

Bring the water to a boil on top of a conventional stove and cook the spaghetti until it is al dente, or still firm to the bite.

Meanwhile, in a 3-quart microwave casserole, combine the oil and garlic. Cook on HIGH for 1 to 2 minutes, or until the garlic is tender, but not brown. Stir in the tomatoes, pimento, tomato paste, and basil. Cook on HIGH for 5 minutes, stirring once. Stir in the grated cheese and skim milk. Stir in the asparagus tips. Cover tightly and cook on HIGH for 3 to 5 minutes, or until the asparagus is almost tender, stirring once. Add the zucchini, mushrooms, red and black peppers to taste; stir well. Cover again and cook on HIGH for 4 to 6 minutes, until heated through but not boiling, stirring once.

To serve: Drain the spaghetti and spoon ½ cup into each of 4 serving bowls. Spoon the primavera sauce over the pasta, dividing it evenly among the bowls. Serve immediately.

◆ *For 2 Servings:* Cut the recipe amounts and microwave oven cooking times in half. Use a 1½-quart casserole. Even when serving 1 person, it is more efficient to cook this recipe for 2 and refrigerate the remaining portion to eat within the next week.

◆ *Tip:* Reserve the asparagus stems to make Creamy Buttermilk and Asparagus Soup (page 34).

Asparagus are nature's "spring tonic." Not only are they low in calories, and a source of vitamins A and C, but they have a natural diuretic effect to stimulate a little spring cleaning.

Fresh Pineapple Cocktail

SERVINGS: 4 ◆ 71 CALORIES PER 1-CUP SERVING ◆ COOKING TIME: 1 TO 2 MINUTES

Heating the pineapple in a flavoring liquid speeds up the marinating process.

4 cups diced fresh pineapple or canned in
   unsweetened juices, drained
1 tablespoon lemon juice
2 tablespoons Triple Sec or orange juice
4 fresh mint sprigs

Place the pineapple in a 10-inch pie plate. Sprinkle with lemon juice and Triple Sec or orange juice. Cover with wax paper and cook on HIGH for 1 to 2 minutes. Set aside for 30 minutes, or until serving time.

To serve: Divide the pineapple and juices between 4 wine goblets. Top with a mint sprig.

Menu

5

337 calories
per serving

This menu takes advantage of clean grilling in the microwave oven on a browning dish. It also makes good use of the asparagus stalks left over from the preceding menu. To save time make the soup the night before and chill it.

CREAMY BUTTERMILK AND ASPARAGUS SOUP

GRILLED LAMB STEAKS WITH HERBED TOMATO TOPPING

PARSLIED NEW POTATOES

ZUCCHINI SALAD WITH CREAMY MUSTARD DRESSING

CARDAMOM-SPIKED CANTALOUPE HALVES

Plan of action

35 TO 40 MINUTES BEFORE SERVING

1. Prepare and cook the soup.
2. While the soup is cooking, prepare the potatoes for cooking.
3. Cook the potatoes. Meanwhile, prepare the salad.
4. Heat the browning dish and prepare the lamb for cooking.
5. Cook the lamb and prepare the tomatoes.
6. Cook the tomatoes.
7. Reheat the soup, if you are serving it warm. Leave the lamb on the browning dish until serving time. Reheat it on HIGH for 1 to 2 minutes on the browning dish. Serve with salad.
8. Prepare the cantaloupe and serve.

Creamy Buttermilk and Asparagus Soup

SERVINGS: 4 ◆ 36 CALORIES PER ½-CUP SERVING ◆ COOKING TIME: 8 TO 10 MINUTES

2 *green onions, cut into 1-inch pieces*
1½ *cups asparagus stems, trimmed and cut into 1-inch pieces (1 pound asparagus)*
2 *tablespoons water*

1 *cup buttermilk*
Dash hot pepper sauce
Pinch freshly grated nutmeg

Combine the green onions, asparagus, and water in a 1-quart casserole. Cover tightly and cook on HIGH for 5 to 7 minutes, or until tender, stirring once. Spoon the vegetables into the bowl of a food processor and puree. Add the buttermilk and blend.

Return the mixture to the casserole

and season with hot pepper sauce and nutmeg. Chill, or set aside if it is to be reheated right before serving. Reheat it on HIGH for 3 minutes.

Variation:

Curried Asparagus Soup: Add 1 teaspoon curry powder with the hot pepper sauce. 2 calories.

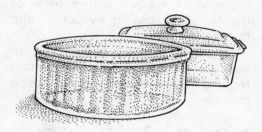

Grilled Lamb Steaks with Herbed Tomato Topping

SERVINGS: 4 ◆ 150 CALORIES PER SERVING ◆ COOKING TIME: 11 TO 16 MINUTES, INCLUDING HEATING BROWNING DISH

2 8-ounce leg of lamb steaks, 2½-inches thick (see Tip)
¼ teaspoon olive or vegetable oil

Herbed Tomato Topping:

1 teaspoon olive oil
1 garlic clove, minced
1 tablespoon chopped onion
½ pound tomatoes, preferably plum, cut into 1-inch pieces, or 1 cup canned, undrained

1 tablespoon chopped fresh basil
1 tablespoon chopped fresh parsley
Dash freshly ground black pepper

Place a browning dish, large enough to hold the steaks, in the microwave. Heat on HIGH for 6 to 9 minutes, or according to the manufacturer's instructions for grilled steaks.

Meanwhile, trim all the fat from the steaks. Cut each in half and remove the bone to form 4 round compact steaks.

Add the oil to the heated dish. Press the steaks onto the hot grill with a metal spatula. Cook on HIGH for 1 minute. Turn the steaks over and cook on HIGH for 1 to 2 minutes more, or until the desired doneness is reached. Remove the dish from the oven, but keep the steaks warm on the dish.

To make the topping, combine the oil, garlic, and onion in a 1-quart casserole. Cook on HIGH for 35 seconds to 1 minute, or until slightly tender. Add the remaining ingredients and cook on HIGH for 2 to 3 minutes, or until just heated through, stirring once. (Cooking without a cover allows some of the tomato juices to evaporate and thicken slightly.)

To serve: Place 1 lamb steak on each plate and top with ¼ cup tomato topping. Place a parslied potato on the side.

◆ *For 1 or 2 Servings:* Reduce the meat to the desired amount, but keep the amount of oil the same. Follow the same browning dish heating and steak-cooking instructions given in the basic recipe. To make 2 servings of sauce, combine ½ teaspoon olive oil, 1 small minced garlic clove, and 1½ teaspoons chopped onion in a 1-quart casserole. Cook on HIGH for 20 to 35 seconds, or until slightly tender. Add ¼ pound (½ cup canned, undrained) chopped fresh tomatoes, 1 tablespoon chopped fresh basil, 1 teaspoon chopped fresh parsley, and a pinch black pepper. Cook on HIGH for 1 to 1½ minutes, or until just hot; stir.

◆ *Tip:* Perhaps you can have your butcher trim the lamb for you.

Parslied New Potatoes

SERVINGS: 4 ◆ 45 CALORIES PER POTATO ◆ COOKING TIME: 4 TO 8 MINUTES

4 small (2-ounce) new potatoes, washed
¼ cup water
2 tablespoons chopped fresh parsley

Pierce each potato with a fork once. Combine the potatoes and water in a 1-quart casserole. Cover tightly and cook on HIGH for 4 to 8 minutes, or until fork tender. Let stand, covered, until serving time. Sprinkle with parsley before serving.

Zucchini Salad with Creamy Mustard Dressing

SERVINGS: 4 ◆ 39 CALORIES PER 1-CUP SERVING

This recipe may be considered a "free" vegetable addition and can be included in any meal plan.

1 pound small zucchini, washed and cut into
¼-inch-thick slices
2 green onions, thinly sliced
1 red radish, thinly sliced
2 tablespoons chopped fresh parsley

1 tablespoon lemon juice
¼ cup Creamy Mustard Dressing (page 290)
Dash freshly ground black pepper

Combine all the ingredients in a mixing bowl. Chill until serving time.

Cardamom-Spiked Cantaloupe Halves

SERVINGS: 4 ◆ 67 CALORIES PER ½ CANTALOUPE

2 cantaloupe, cut in half and seeded
Pinch ground cardamom
Lime wedges

Sprinkle the inside of each cantaloupe with the cardamom. Serve with lime wedges.

Menu

6

*353 calories
per serving*

CREAM OF CUCUMBER SOUP

GARLIC SHRIMP

ITALIAN BREAD (1 SLICE, 75 CALORIES)

MIXED GREENS WITH MUSTARD VINAIGRETTE

PINEAPPLE FREEZE WITH FRESH NUTMEG

Plan of action

1. Make the pineapple dessert and freeze it until serving time.
2. Prepare the soup up to the puree stage.
3. While the soup is cooking, assemble the ingredients for the shrimp and salad. Make the salad dressing.
4. Meanwhile, puree the soup and

25 TO 30 MINUTES BEFORE SERVING

continue to cook it.
5. Cook the shrimp.
6. While the shrimp are cooking, spoon the soup into serving bowls, and place the salad onto individual plates. Serve the soup.
7. Let the shrimp stand while eating the soup, then serve the shrimp with the salad.

Cream of Cucumber Soup

SERVINGS: 4 ◆ 54 CALORIES PER ¾-CUP SERVING ◆ COOKING TIME: 10 TO 15 MINUTES

1 garlic clove, minced
1 tablespoon white vinegar
2 medium cucumbers, peeled, halved, seeded, and sliced into ¼-inch pieces

1½ cups chicken broth
1 cup low-fat plain yogurt
Freshly ground black pepper

Combine the garlic and vinegar in a 2-quart casserole. Cook on HIGH for 35 seconds to 1 minute, or until tender. Stir in the cucumbers, reserving ½ cup for garnish. Cover tightly and cook on HIGH for 5 to 6 minutes, or until the cucumbers are tender. Pour the mixture into a food processor or

blender and puree until smooth.

Return the mixture to the cooking dish. Stir in the chicken broth. Cover tightly and cook on HIGH for 5 to 8 minutes, or until heated through, but not boiling.

To serve: Divide the soup among 4 bowls, topping each portion with ¼ cup yogurt, then 2 tablespoons reserved chopped cucumbers, and a grinding of fresh black pepper.

◆ *For 1 Serving:* Peel, halve, seed, and thinly slice ½ cucumber, setting aside 2 tablespoons for later. Combine 1 small minced garlic, 1 teaspoon white vinegar, and the remaining cucumber in a 1½-cup microwaveproof serving bowl. Cover tightly and cook on HIGH

for 1½ to 2½ minutes, or until the cucumber is tender. Spoon the mixture into a food processor or blender, along with ½ cup chicken broth. Puree until smooth. Pour it back into the cooking bowl and cook on HIGH for 1 to 2 minutes, until heated through. Top with ¼ cup yogurt, the reserved 2 tablespoons sliced cucumber, and a grinding of fresh black pepper.

Garlic Shrimp

SERVINGS: 4 ◆ 137 CALORIES PER 4-OUNCE SERVING ◆ COOKING TIME: 5 TO 8 MINUTES

This is a delightfully spicy dish. You can cook the shrimp with the shells on or off, but we prefer to leave the shells on to prolong the eating process, giving you a chance to become satiated.

For those in your family who aren't dieting, serve a little melted butter at the table for shrimp dipping.

1 teaspoon olive oil
4 garlic cloves, minced
2 tablespoons dry vermouth
1 teaspoon red pepper flakes (less if you don't want it spicy)
2 teaspoons paprika

1 pound raw fresh shrimp, shelled or unshelled
1 tablespoon fresh lemon juice
¼ cup chopped fresh parsley
Lemon wedges

Combine the oil and garlic in a 10-inch pie plate. Cook on HIGH for 1 to 2 minutes, or until tender. Stir in the vermouth, pepper flakes, and paprika, then add the shrimp and turn to coat evenly. Sprinkle with lemon juice. Cover tightly and cook on HIGH for 3 minutes; stir. Cover again and cook on HIGH for 1 to 3 minutes more, until the shrimp have turned pink.

To serve, sprinkle with parsley and serve with lemon wedges.

◆ *For 2 Servings:* Cut the ingredient amounts in half. Cook the oil and garlic in a 10-inch pie plate on HIGH for 30 seconds. After adding the spices, shrimp, and lemon juice, cover tightly and cook on HIGH for 2 minutes; stir. Cover again and cook on HIGH for another 1 to 2 minutes. Garnish with 2 tablespoons chopped parsley and serve with lemon wedges. Even if you want just 1 serving, it is more practical to make 2 servings and freeze or refrigerate the other half.

Mixed Greens with Mustard Vinaigrette

SERVINGS: 4 ◆ 44 CALORIES PER 1-CUP SERVING

4 cups mixed greens
½ cup Mustard Vinaigrette (page 288)

Combine all the ingredients in a salad bowl. Toss.

Pineapple Freeze with Fresh Nutmeg

SERVINGS: 6 ◆ 43 CALORIES PER ½-CUP SERVING ◆ COOKING TIME: 1 MINUTE

This is delicious when served frozen, or just as soon as it is made. Plan ahead to buy a fresh 2-pound pineapple, serving half that day in a fruit cup and freezing the other half for this recipe.

1 1-pound fresh pineapple
1 tablespoon sugar
½ cup low-fat plain yogurt

1 teaspoon Triple Sec or orange juice
  Freshly grated nutmeg

Remove the outer shell and core from the pineapple. Cut the flesh into ¼-inch slices, and then quarter these. Place the pieces in a single layer in a 2-quart rectangular dish. Freeze for 3 or 4 hours or overnight, until solid.

Place the dish tray with the pineapple pieces in the microwave and heat on DEFROST for 1 minute. Break up the pieces and spoon them into the processor. Pulse the processor on and off until the pineapple is chopped into small pieces. Add the remaining ingredients and continue to pulse at 15-second intervals until the mixture is blended and creamy. Serve immediately or place it into the freezer for later use.

Garnish each serving with freshly grated nutmeg.

◆ *Tip:* If the frozen pureed pineapple mixture is too solid, scoop out after freezing, place it in the microwave and heat on LOW for 1 to 2 minutes, or until slightly soft on the outside.

ENTERTAINING

We like to make several frozen fruit sorbets in one day and then, using a small ice cream scoop, serve a few flavors of each to add up to ½-cup servings. Try these com- *binations on a white dessert plate or in a wine goblet, garnished with a mint sprig or sage blossom:*

▲ ▲ ▲ ▲ ▲ ▲ ▲ ▲ ▲ ▲ ▲ ▲

◆ **Pineapple Freeze with Fresh Nutmeg (page 40) and Frozen Strawberry Delight (page 47)**
◆ **Orange-Pineapple Sorbet (page 261) and Banana Sorbet (page 190)**
◆ **Pink Grapefruit Sorbet (page 258) and Frozen Strawberry Delight (page 47)**

▼ ▼ ▼ ▼ ▼ ▼ ▼ ▼ ▼ ▼ ▼ ▼

MEXICAN TOMATO CALDO

LIME AND CILANTRO CHICKEN BREASTS
WITH SALSA AND AVOCADO

RUM FRUIT COCKTAIL

Menu

7

*314 calories
per serving*

Plan of action

1. Prepare the fruit cocktail and chill.
2. Cook the broth, or "caldo."
3. While the broth is cooking, prepare the chicken and salsa.
4. Cook the chicken. After turning the

25 TO 30 MINUTES BEFORE SERVING

chicken over, serve the broth. The chicken can stand in the oven after the second cooking time.

5. Prepare the chicken plates and serve.

Mexican Tomato Caldo

SERVINGS: 4 ◆ 27 CALORIES PER ¾-CUP SERVING ◆ COOKING TIME: 8 TO 10 MINUTES

Caldo is Spanish for a Mexican consommé. This particular one is light yet spicy, and fragrant with cilantro.

1½ cups beef broth
1 cup tomato juice
1 green pepper, chopped

Few dashes hot pepper sauce
2 tablespoons cilantro

Combine all the ingredients, except the cilantro, in a 2-quart casserole. Cover tightly and cook on HIGH for 8 to 10 minutes, or until heated through. Serve in mugs and sprinkle with fresh cilantro.

◆ *For 1 Serving:* Combine ¾ cup broth, ¼ cup tomato juice, ¼ chopped green pepper, and a dash hot pepper sauce in a mug. Cook on HIGH for 2 to 3 minutes. Garnish with 1 teaspoon chopped fresh cilantro.

"Soup consumption as a weight-loss strategy may help the obese dieter by slowing eating rate or reducing appetite through filling the stomach." *

This conclusion was made when the Department of Medicine at Baylor College, Houston, studied a group of 91 women and 31 men of approximately equivalent weight, who were at least greater than, or equal to, 130 percent of their ideal body weight. The subjects were divided into three groups: a control group, a traditional behavioral weight-loss group, and a soup/behavioral weight-loss group. The diet of the latter two groups was the same except that the soup group consumed part of their calories through at least 2 cups of soup per day.

During the year-long study, it was discovered that the traditional group lost an average of 13.8 pounds while the soup group lost an average of 15.1. According to the article, "soup intake was highly correlated with weight loss," and a self-administered questionnaire revealed that "group members were enthusiastic about the value of soup in their reducing plans."

* John P. Foreyt, Ph.D., et al., "Soup Consumption as a Behavioral Weight-Loss Strategy," *Journal of the American Dietetic Association,* Volume 86, Number 4, April 1986, p. 524.

Lime and Cilantro Chicken Breasts with Salsa and Avocado

SERVINGS: 4 ◆ 124 CALORIES PER 4-OUNCE SERVING OF CHICKEN, 84 CALORIES PER ¼ AVOCADO, 38 CALORIES PER ½ CUP SALSA ◆ COOKING TIME: 6 TO 8 MINUTES

4 4-ounce skinless, boneless chicken breasts
1 garlic clove, minced
2 green onions, thinly sliced
1 tablespoon fresh lime juice
    Freshly ground black pepper to taste

2 tablespoons chopped fresh cilantro, plus extra for garnish
1 avocado, peeled, pitted, and quartered
2 cups Fresh Tomato Salsa (see below)
    Lime wedges

Place the chicken breasts around the outer rim of a 10-inch pie plate, leaving the center open. Sprinkle with garlic, green onions, and lime juice. Cover with wax paper and cook on HIGH for 3 minutes. Turn the breasts over and rearrange, spooning any juices over the breasts. Cover again and cook on HIGH for 3 to 5 minutes, or until cooked through. Let stand for 5 minutes.

To serve: Slice each avocado quarter into 4 to 6 long thin slices and fan them out on the side of each of 4 plates. Spoon ½ cup salsa onto each plate beside the avocado to cover the other half of the plate. Slice the chicken breast into ¼-inch slices and arrange them on top of the salsa. Sprinkle the chicken with fresh cilantro and place a lime wedge on each plate.

◆ *For 1 Serving:* Place a 4-ounce boned chicken breast in an oval ramekin and sprinkle it with 1 small minced garlic clove, ½ chopped green onion, and 1 teaspoon lime juice. Cover tightly and cook on HIGH for 2 to 4 minutes. Serve with ¼ avocado, peeled and sliced, and ½ cup Fresh Tomato Salsa, arranging as described in the basic recipe. Garnish with cilantro and a lime wedge.

Fresh Tomato Salsa

MAKES: 2 CUPS ◆ 38 CALORIES PER ½ CUP

This salsa adds zip to many dishes. Just 1 tablespoon will dress up plain, sliced meat or steamed fish. Spread on cold sandwiches or scrambled eggs, too, and you'll never miss the salt or fat.

3 jalapeño peppers, quartered
2 large tomatoes, quartered

2 green onions, quartered
1 teaspoon wine or cider vinegar

Combine all the ingredients in the bowl of a food processor or blender and chop them well to blend; or chop by hand. Set aside.

Variation:

Salsa with Cilantro: Add 1 tablespoon chopped fresh cilantro.

Pour on the peppers! Jalapeños and hot pepper flakes are found in many of our recipes. The reason is twofold: so that you won't miss the accent of salt (which has been reduced or eliminated) and because these hot ingredients may literally melt away pounds. According to a study at Oxford Polytechnic in Headington, England, it seems that these peppers could temporarily speed up your metabolism by about 25 percent to burn up more calories!

Rum Fruit Cocktail

SERVINGS: 4 ◆ 41 CALORIES PER ½-CUP SERVING

1 cup fresh pineapple chunks
1 cup sliced strawberries
1 tablespoon rum
1 teaspoon aniseed

Combine all the ingredients in a medium bowl. Chill until serving time. Stir well again before serving. Divide the mixture and juices between 4 wineglasses.

If you want to serve the Cream of Asparagus Soup chilled, you may want to prepare it the night before.

CREAM OF ASPARAGUS SOUP (HOT OR COLD)

FISH IN A BAG

FRENCH BREAD (1 SLICE, 75 CALORIES)

MIXED GREENS WITH MUSTARD VINAIGRETTE

FROZEN STRAWBERRY DELIGHT

Plan of action

1. Make the strawberry dessert and place it in the freezer.
2. Prepare and cook the soup up to the pureeing point.
3. While the soup is cooking, make the salad.

20 TO 25 MINUTES BEFORE SERVING

4. Prepare the fish bags.
5. Puree and reheat the soup.
6. Serve the soup while cooking the fish.

Cream of Asparagus Soup

SERVINGS: 4 ◆ 44 CALORIES PER 1-CUP SERVING ◆ COOKING TIME: 10 TO 13 MINUTES

This soup is delicious hot or cold. We often prepare it the night before to chill, while we're in the kitchen cleaning up the dinner dishes. Then it can be served chilled, or reheated for the next night's dinner.

1 pound asparagus stalks, trimmed and cut into ½-inch pieces
2 cups chicken broth
2 green onions, thinly sliced
1 tablespoon fresh lemon juice

Dash cayenne pepper
1 tablespoon chopped fresh dill, or 1 teaspoon dried
Dash freshly ground black pepper
½ cup buttermilk or low-fat plain yogurt

Combine all ingredients, except buttermilk, in a 2-quart casserole. Cover tightly and cook on HIGH for 8 to 10 minutes, or until the asparagus is tender. Pour into a food processor or blender and puree until smooth.

45

Pour the mixture back into the cooking casserole. Stir in the buttermilk and heat on HIGH for 2 to 3 minutes. Continue to heat if serving hot, or refrigerate at this point for at least 1 hour to serve chilled.

Fish in a Bag

SERVINGS: 1 ◆ 126 CALORIES ◆ COOKING TIME: 2 TO 4 MINUTES

This recipe can be prepared for one or as many people as you wish, and is delicious and great for entertaining. If you wish, you may eliminate the parchment paper and use individual ramekins, cooking with a lid or plastic wrap cover.

1 4-ounce flounder or sole fillet
1 tablespoon lemon juice
1 tablespoon dry white wine
1 teaspoon chopped fresh mint leaves, or ¼ teaspoon dried
  Pinch freshly ground black pepper

Pinch cayenne pepper
1 green onion, thinly sliced
1 small tomato, cut into 4 ¼-inch slices
2 mushrooms, thinly sliced

Cut a 15-inch square of parchment paper. Place the fish fillet in the center of the paper. Sprinkle the fillet with the lemon juice, wine, mint, black and cayenne peppers, and green onion. Overlap the tomato slices on top of the fillet to cover it. Sprinkle the mushrooms on top of the tomato.

Fold two sides of the parchment paper over the fish fillet in a twofold letter fashion, with the folds along the long sides of the fillet. Grasp the two shorter open ends and pull them up to meet over the fillet, forming a triangle. Gently fold down the open ends to seal. (See illustration.) Place the package in the microwave and cook on HIGH for 2 to 4 minutes.

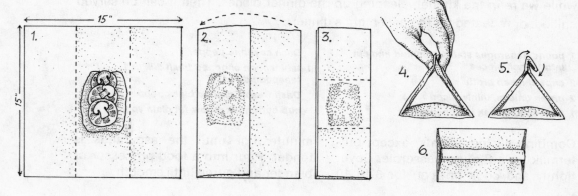

◆ *Notes:* When cooking more than one package, follow the times as shown.

If cooking more than 1 bag at a time, place them in a circle in the microwave, leaving at least a 1-inch space between them.

▲ ▲ ▲ ▲ ▲ ▲ ▲ ▲ ▲ ▲ ▲ ▲

2 packages: 3 to 6 minutes
4 packages: 6 to 8 minutes
6 packages: 8 to 10 minutes

▼ ▼ ▼ ▼ ▼ ▼ ▼ ▼ ▼ ▼ ▼ ▼

Mixed Greens with Mustard Vinaigrette

SERVINGS: 4 ◆ 44 CALORIES PER 1-CUP SERVING

4 cups mixed greens
½ cup Mustard Vinaigrette (page 288)

Combine all the ingredients in a salad bowl. Toss.

Frozen Strawberry Delight

SERVINGS: 8 ◆ 46 CALORIES PER ½-CUP SERVING ◆ COOKING TIME: 1 MINUTE

This ruby sorbet is beautiful when served in a white soup bowl with mint sprigs. Add 1 vanilla wafer or chocolate-covered strawberry and an extra 35 calories.

You can serve it immediately, or freeze it for 1 hour or for as long as you wish. If it appears to be too solidly frozen after that, place it in the microwave for 1 to 2 minutes on LOW to make the scooping out easier.

1 16-ounce bag frozen unsweetened strawberries
2 tablespoons sugar
½ cup low-fat plain yogurt

1 tablespoon Triple Sec or concentrated frozen orange juice
Fresh mint sprigs

Place the bag of frozen strawberries into the microwave and heat on DE-FROST for 1 minute, or until partially defrosted. Pour the strawberries into the food processor or blender and chop into small pieces. Add the remaining ingredients except mint and process until smooth. Garnish with the mint sprigs.

Menu

9

349 calories
per serving

As this is a more time-consuming menu, we suggest you cook it on the weekend. That will enable you to utilize the leftovers for lunches or dinners throughout the week.

LEMON EMERALD SOUP

ROAST TURKEY BREAST

KASHA STUFFING WITH MUSHROOMS AND PEPPERS

CELERY AND CARROT STICKS
(6 ½" - × - 3" STRIPS, 24 CALORIES)

STRAWBERRIES IN WINE

Plan of action

1. Cook and chill the strawberry dessert.
2. Cook the turkey. Meanwhile, chop and prepare the remaining ingredients for the soup, the kasha, and the vegetable sticks.
3. During the standing time of the turkey, cook the kasha for the stuffing.
4. During the standing time of the kasha, cook and serve the soup.

Lemon Emerald Soup

SERVINGS: 4 ◆ 33 CALORIES PER 1-CUP SERVING ◆ COOKING TIME: 8 TO 10 MINUTES

Thin, jewel-like strips of spinach float in a delicate lemon broth.

4 cups chicken broth
1 teaspoon lemon juice
2 cups thinly sliced spinach

¼ teaspoon freshly grated nutmeg
4 lemon slices

Combine the broth and lemon juice in a 2-quart casserole. Cover tightly and cook on HIGH for 5 minutes. Stir in the spinach and nutmeg. Cover again and cook on HIGH for 3 to 5 minutes, or until heated through. Top each serving with a lemon slice.

◆ *For 1 Serving:* Combine 1 cup chicken broth, ¼ teaspoon lemon juice, ½ cup thinly sliced spinach, a grating of fresh nutmeg, and 1 lemon slice in a 1½-cup microwaveproof serving bowl. Cover tightly and cook on HIGH for 2 to 3 minutes, or until heated through.

Roast Turkey Breast

MAKES: 2½ POUNDS MEAT ◆ 119 CALORIES PER 3-OUNCE DINNER SERVING (WITHOUT SKIN), 79 CALORIES PER 2-OUNCE LUNCH SERVING ◆ COOKING TIME: 1 HOUR 27 MINUTES TO 1 HOUR 32 MINUTES (7 MINUTES PER POUND ON HIGH, THEN 8 MINUTES PER POUND ON MEDIUM)

As with any poultry, the secret to keeping the calories low is to remove the skin, after cooking. A turkey breast is made up entirely of lower-calorie white meat, the dieter's delight.

1 6-pound turkey breast
½ lemon
½ teaspoon paprika

Place the turkey breast, skin side down, in a 2-quart rectangular dish. Cook, uncovered, on HIGH for 42 minutes. Turn the breast skin side up. Rub it with half a lemon and sprinkle it with paprika. Cook the breast, uncovered, on MEDIUM for 45 to 50 minutes, or until done. The juices should run clear, not red, from the meatiest area of the breast, and that area should reach 170°F before standing time.

Let the turkey stand tented with foil, for 10 to 20 minutes.

Kasha Stuffing with Mushrooms and Peppers

MAKES: 2 CUPS ◆ 129 CALORIES PER ½-CUP SERVING ◆ COOKING TIME: 8 TO 11 MINUTES

When buckwheat seeds are stripped of their outer shell they are called "buckwheat groats." There is no better source of vegetable protein than buckwheat.

When these groats are roasted, which serves to bring out their rich nutlike flavor, they are called "kasha." This recipe is a type of kasha pilaf, mixed with vegetables, that makes a healthy and satisfying stuffing for turkey.

1 teaspoon vegetable or olive oil
1 onion, chopped
1 green pepper, chopped

½ cup roasted buckwheat kernels
1½ cups chicken broth
¼ pound mushrooms, sliced

Combine the oil, onion, and green pepper in a 2-quart casserole. Cover tightly and cook on HIGH for 2 to 3 minutes, or until tender. Stir in the buckwheat kernels to coat them with the oil and vegetables. Stir in the broth.

Cover again and cook on HIGH for 5 to 7 minutes, or until the liquid is absorbed. Stir in the mushrooms. Cover again and cook on HIGH for 1 minute. Let stand for 5 minutes.

FAVORITE BREAD STUFFING

MAKES: 2 CUPS ◆ 72 CALORIES PER ½-CUP SERVING ◆ COOKING TIME: 6 MINUTES

If the kasha stuffing doesn't appeal to you, try this more traditional bread stuffing, which is even lower in calories.

1 cup thinly sliced celery
2 tablespoons chopped onion
4 slices whole wheat bread
1 cup chicken broth

¼ cup chopped fresh parsley
¼ teaspoon chopped fresh or dried tarragon leaves
¼ teaspoon chopped fresh or dried sage leaves
Dash freshly ground black pepper

Combine the celery and onion in a 1-quart casserole. Cover tightly and cook on HIGH for 3 minutes, or until almost tender. Stir in the remaining ingredients to blend well. Cover again and cook on HIGH for 3 minutes. Serve with turkey or chicken.

◆ *For 2 Servings:* Cut the ingredient amounts and cooking times in half and combine them in a 1-quart casserole.

Strawberries in Wine

SERVINGS: 4 ◆ 44 CALORIES PER ½-CUP SERVING ◆ COOKING TIME: 2 TO 3 MINUTES

½ cup dry white wine
1 tablespoon sugar
1 tablespoon orange juice

½ teaspoon vanilla extract
1 pint whole strawberries, washed and hulled
Mint sprigs

Combine the wine, sugar, orange juice, and vanilla in a 1-quart casserole. Cook on HIGH for 2 to 3 minutes, or until boiling. Stir in the strawberries. Cover and refrigerate until serving time. Serve, chilled, in wine goblets. Garnish with a sprig of mint.

CHINESE CABBAGE SOUP WITH LEMON (PAGE 26)

SZECHUAN BEEF AND VEGETABLES

BASIC RICE (PAGE 294)

PINEAPPLE AND KIWI

Menu

10

*360 calories
per serving*

Plan of action

30 MINUTES BEFORE SERVING

1. Freeze the beef for the Szechuan beef, to make slicing easier.
2. Slice fruit for dessert and chill.
3. Begin cooking the rice.
4. Meanwhile, prepare the soup ingredients and begin the beef preparations.

5. While the rice stands, covered, cook the soup and finish preparing the beef dish.
6. Serve the soup.
7. Cook the beef dish and serve with the rice.

Brown rice may be substituted for white rice, but you'll need to add an extra 20 minutes to your preparation time. In our opinion, if you have the time you and your family will reap many nutritional benefits from the substitution. Because brown rice has its nutrition-rich bran still intact, it offers more vitamin E, more dietary fiber, and more protein than white rice.

Szechuan Beef and Vegetables

**SERVINGS: 4 ◆ 155 CALORIES PER BEEF SERVING, 93 CALORIES PER ½ CUP RICE
◆ COOKING TIME: 7 TO 8 MINUTES**

¾ pound beef top round steak

1 teaspoon sesame oil

1 garlic clove, minced

1 teaspoon cornstarch

1 teaspoon dry sherry or vermouth

1 tablespoon low-sodium soy sauce

1 teaspoon lemon juice

¼ cup beef broth

⅛ to ¼ teaspoon red pepper flakes

4 green onions, cut into 1½-inch pieces

1 red bell pepper, cut into 1-inch cubes

1 green bell pepper, cut into 1-inch cubes

¼ pound mushrooms, thinly sliced

Partially freeze the beef, then thinly slice across the grain on an angle, into slices about ⅛ inch thick. Cut the sliced pieces in half crosswise.

Combine the oil and garlic in a 10-inch pie plate. Cook on HIGH for 35 seconds. In a small dish combine the cornstarch, sherry or vermouth, soy sauce, lemon juice, and broth together, until smooth. Pour this mixture into the cooking dish and cook for 1½ minutes; stir.

Stir in the beef and red pepper flakes, coating well. Cover with wax paper and cook on HIGH for 2 minutes. Stir well and push the meat to the outside of the dish, leaving the center open. Spoon the green onion, bell peppers, and mushrooms into the center of the dish. Cover again and cook on HIGH for 2 minutes. Stir the vegetables and beef together. Cover again and cook on HIGH for 1 to 2 minutes more, or until the desired doneness of meat and vegetables is reached. Serve with ½ cup rice per person.

◆ *For 2 Servings:* Slice 6 ounces partially frozen top round steak into thin slices. Combine ½ teaspoon sesame oil and 1 small minced garlic clove into a 1-quart casserole. Cook on HIGH for 35 seconds. In a small dish combine ½ teaspoon each cornstarch, dry sherry, and lemon juice, and 2 teaspoons each soy sauce and beef broth. Stir into the garlic mixture. Cook on HIGH for 1 minute. Stir in the beef and a generous dash red pepper flakes. Cover with wax paper and cook on HIGH for 1 minute. Stir well and push the meat to the outside of the dish. Spoon 2 sliced green onions, 1 cubed green pepper, and 2 ounces sliced mushrooms into the center. Cover again and cook on HIGH for 1 minute. Stir the vegetables and beef together. Cover again and cook on HIGH for 30 seconds to 1 minute more, or until the desired doneness is reached.

Pineapple and Kiwi

SERVINGS: 4 ◆ 45 CALORIES PER ½-CUP SERVING, 61 CALORIES WITH STAR FRUIT

This is such a simple dessert, yet so visually and flavorfully attractive.

2 cups fresh or canned pineapple cubes packed in their own juices (see Tip)

1 kiwi, peeled and cut into 8 slices
4 slices Star Fruit (Carambola) (optional)

Place ½ cup pineapple into each serving dish, and top each with 2 pieces of kiwi. Garnish with Star Fruit.

◆ *Tip:* Drain the juices from the canned pineapple and save for the next menu.

This main course salad incorporates a meat protein, fruit, and vegetables, along with cottage cheese and yogurt in the dressing. With such a menu, we'd like you to treat yourself to a bonus dessert of two vanilla wafers (18½ calories each), or one of the other treats from the desserts and snacks on page 279.

CURRIED TOMATO-PINEAPPLE SOUP

TURKEY AND ORANGE SALAD WITH
CREAMY ORANGE DRESSING

BONUS DESSERT (50 CALORIES)

Plan of action

20 MINUTES BEFORE SERVING

1. Prepare and cook the soup.
2. Make the salad dressing.
3. Prepare the salad and set it aside until the soup is finished.

Curried Tomato-Pineapple Soup

SERVINGS: 4 ◆ 71 CALORIES PER 1-CUP SERVING ◆ COOKING TIME: 8 TO 10 MINUTES

This soup has a delightful flavor and it is a great way to use up the juices from the unsweetened pineapple chunks in Menu #10.

3 cups tomato juice
1 cup unsweetened pineapple juice

1 teaspoon curry powder
Pinch freshly ground black pepper

Combine all the ingredients in a 2-quart casserole. Cover tightly and cook on HIGH for 8 to 10 minutes, or until heated through. Serve in bowls or mugs.

◆ *For 1 Serving:* Combine ¾ cup tomato juice, ¼ cup pineapple juice, and ¼ teaspoon curry powder in a microwaveproof bowl or mug. Cook on HIGH for 2 to 3 minutes, or until hot.

Turkey and Orange Salad with Creamy Orange Dressing

SERVINGS: 4 ◆ 292 CALORIES PER 1¼-CUP SERVING (OR 239 CALORIES WITHOUT PEANUTS)

This salad is spectacular when arranged on a colorful array of lettuce leaves. Try a curly endive, radicchio, and oak leaf or any other selection that may come from your garden or local market.

12 *ounces cooked skinless turkey (page 49), cut into ½-inch cubes*
1½ *cups thinly sliced celery*
2 *green onions, thinly sliced*
4 *naval oranges, peeled and divided into segments*

½ *cup Creamy Orange Dressing (page 291)*
¼ *cup chopped peanuts (optional)*
4 *cups different-colored lettuce*

Combine all the ingredients in a large bowl, except the lettuce and peanuts.

To serve: Line 4 serving plates with the lettuce. Divide the salad between the 4 plates. Sprinkle each serving with 1 tablespoon chopped peanuts, if desired.

◆ *For 1 Serving:* Combine 3 ounces cubed turkey, ⅓ cup sliced celery, ½ sliced green onion, 1 sectioned naval orange, and 2 tablespoons Creamy Orange Dressing. Serve on 1 cup lettuce leaves and sprinkle with 1 tablespoon chopped peanuts, if desired.

Variations:

Turkey and Apple Salad with Creamy Orange Dressing: Substitute 4 Granny Smith apples, cut into ½-inch chunks, for the naval oranges. 1 calorie.

Turkey Salad with Creamy Orange Dressing in Cantaloupe: Cut 2 medium cantaloupes in half and remove the seeds. Eliminate the naval oranges and lettuce leaves. Spoon the turkey salad into the cantaloupe halves and serve. 23 calories less.

Chopsticks are deftly wielded throughout the Orient, but to the less experienced occidental these utensils can make eating much slower. For someone trying to cut down on calories. the slower you eat the less you are likely to eat. Remember, it takes twenty minutes for your brain to receive the signal from your stomach that you are beginning to feel full, so eating slowly is a great advantage.

Except for the dessert, this meal lends itself well to chopsticks. Even the soba noodle soup is suited to it, where in Japan shoveling is encouraged to gather up all the noodles into your mouth.

TOFU SOBA SOUP

STEAMED VEGETABLE BOWLS WITH GINGER DRESSING

FLUFFY LEMON-STRAWBERRY ROLL

Plan of action

1. Prepare and cook the soup.
2. While the soup is cooking, prepare the dressing and ingredients for the vegetable bowls.
3. Serve the soup. Meanwhile, cook the vegetable bowls.

30 MINUTES BEFORE SERVING

4. Serve the vegetable bowls and dressing.
5. Make the dessert right before serving it.

Tofu Soba Soup

SERVINGS: 4 ◆ 167 CALORIES PER 1½-CUP SERVING ◆ COOKING TIME: 13 TO 17 MINUTES

This soup is a nutritious combination of whole wheat noodles or "soba" and soybean curd or "tofu." Soba is available at Asian food or specialty stores, and it is lower in calories than conventional pasta and gives a decidedly Japanese flavor to this soup.

2 cups chicken broth
2 cups beef broth
2 ounces whole wheat soba or high-protein angel hair pasta
1 tablespoon grated fresh ginger
1 teaspoon low-sodium soy sauce

1 teaspoon white vinegar
16 ounces tofu, cut into ¼-inch cubes
8 mushrooms, thinly sliced
2 green onions, thinly sliced

Pour the chicken and beef broths into a 3-quart casserole. Add the soba, ginger, soy sauce, and vinegar. Cover tightly and cook on HIGH for 8 to 10 minutes to bring to a boil.

After the broth comes to a boil, stir in the tofu. Cover again and cook on MEDIUM for 5 to 7 minutes, or until the noodles are tender.

To serve: Divide the sliced mushrooms and green onions between 4 serving bowls. Spoon 1½ cups of the soup and noodles into each serving bowl. Serve with chopsticks and a soup spoon.

◆ *For 1 Serving:* Pour ¼ cup each chicken and beef broths into a 1-quart casserole. Add ½ ounce soba, 2 tea-spoons ginger, ¼ teaspoon each soy sauce and vinegar. Cover tightly and cook on HIGH for 5 minutes, or until boiling. Stir in 4 ounces cubed tofu. Cover again and cook on MEDIUM for 5 to 6 minutes, or until the noodles are tender. Spoon the soup into a bowl and sprinkle with ½ chopped green onion and 2 thinly sliced mushrooms.

Steamed Vegetable Bowls with Ginger Dressing

SERVINGS: 4 ◆ 80 CALORIES FOR 12 VEGETABLE PIECES, INCLUDING 1 TABLESPOON DRESSING FOR DIPPING ◆ COOKING TIME: 2 TO 10 MINUTES

If you can fit four individual 6- to 7-inch-diameter bowls in your microwave oven, this recipe will be so much easier to cook and serve. The vegetables look so attractive in separate bowls, too. The vegetables are arranged with the shorter cooking ones in the center, so that no stirring is required.

¼ small head cabbage

8 whole mushrooms

4 plum tomatoes, quartered, or 16 cherry tomatoes, cut in half

½ pound broccoli, stems removed and cut into 16 flowerets

½ pound asparagus, trimmed into 2½-inch spears (reserve the remaining stalks for soup)

¼ pound string beans, trimmed

1 small (¼-pound) yellow squash, cut into ¼-inch slices

1 small (¼-pound) zucchini, cut into ¼-inch slices

¼ pound snow peas

1 recipe Ginger Oriental Dressing or Gingered Oriental Dressing with Mustard (page 287)

Cut the cabbage into quarters and each quarter in half. If the mushrooms are large, quarter them; if smaller, cut them in half.

Place the mushrooms and tomatoes in the center of each 6- or 7-inch microwaveproof bowl or large platter and arrange the other vegetables attractively around the outside. Cover tightly with plastic wrap that is turned back slightly on one corner. Follow

▲ ▲ ▲ ▲ ▲ ▲ ▲ ▲ ▲ ▲ ▲ ▲

1 bowl	HIGH	2 to 4 minutes
2 bowls	HIGH	3 to 6 minutes
3 bowls	HIGH	4 to 8 minutes
4 bowls	HIGH	6 to 10 minutes
1 12-inch platter	HIGH	5 to 10 minutes

▼ ▼ ▼ ▼ ▼ ▼ ▼ ▼ ▼ ▼ ▼ ▼

the cooking power and times above. The shortest times will give fairly crisp vegetables.

Hold the vegetables with chopsticks and dip them into the dressing.

Variation:

Crunchy Sunflower Vegetable Bowls: Before serving, sprinkle each vegetable bowl with 1 tablespoon toasted sunflower seeds. Add 51 calories for each tablespoon.

TOASTED SUNFLOWER SEEDS

MAKES: ¼ CUP ◆ 51 CALORIES PER 1 TABLESPOON SERVING ◆ COOKING TIME: 3 TO 4 MINUTES

¼ cup sunflower seeds

Spread the sunflower seeds out on a microwaveproof plate. Cook on HIGH for 3 to 4 minutes, or until warm and toasted.

Fluffy Lemon-Strawberry Roll

SERVINGS: 4 ◆ 69 CALORIES PER SERVING ◆ COOKING TIME: 2 TO 3 MINUTES

It is hard to believe that this lucious dessert is so low in calories!

2 eggs, separated
¼ teaspoon cream of tartar
1 teaspoon grated lemon peel, plus long thin slices lemon peel for garnish

1 tablespoon sugar
1 tablespoon water
1 cup sliced strawberries, plus 4 whole strawberries for garnish

Combine the egg whites and cream of tartar in a medium mixing bowl and beat until stiff but not dry. In a small bowl combine the yolks, lemon peel, sugar, and water, beating together well. Gently fold the yolk mixture into the whites.

Pour into a 9-inch pie plate and spread the top to make it smooth. Cook on HIGH for 1½ to 2½ minutes, or until set. Spoon the sliced strawberries in about a 3-inch row down the center of the set egg mixture. Fold each side of the egg soufflé over the strawberries in an envelope fashion.

To serve: Cut into 4 serving pieces and, using a spatula, lift each piece onto individual serving plates. Garnish each with a whole strawberry and a few pieces of lemon peel.

◆ *For Fewer Servings:* It is difficult to cut this recipe in half, so just make the whole recipe and share it with someone. If there is no one to share with, it is also very good cold the next day. Serve the remaining half with a glass of milk for a lunch of 284 calories.

Menu

13

360 calories
per serving

TOMATO CONSOMMÉ
WITH CELERY STICKS AND BREADSTICKS

CHICKEN DIJON

LEMONY BROCCOLI SPEARS

APPLE-ORANGE COMPOTE

Plan of action

25 TO 30 MINUTES BEFORE SERVING

1. Cook the compote and set it aside until serving time.
2. Prepare and cook the soup.
3. While the soup is cooking, assemble and prepare the ingredients for the chicken and broccoli.

4. Cook the chicken.
5. Allow the chicken to stand, covered. Cook the broccoli.
6. Serve the soup while the broccoli is cooking.

Tomato Consommé

SERVINGS: 4 ◆ 38 CALORIES PER 1-CUP SERVING, PLUS 46 CALORIES PER 2 BREADSTICKS ◆ COOKING TIME: 8 TO 10 MINUTES

2 cups tomato juice
2 cups beef broth
1 tablespoon chopped fresh parsley

Dash hot pepper sauce
4 celery sticks
8 4½"-x-½" breadsticks

Combine all the ingredients except the celery and breadsticks in a 2-quart casserole. Cover tightly and cook on HIGH for 8 to 10 minutes, or until heated through. Serve in mugs with 1 celery stick and 2 breadsticks each.

◆ *For 1 Serving:* Pour ½ cup tomato juice, ½ cup beef broth, 1 teaspoon chopped fresh parsley, and a small dash of hot pepper sauce into a microwaveproof mug. Cook on HIGH for 2 to 3 minutes, or until heated through. Serve with a celery stick and 2 breadsticks.

Chicken Dijon

SERVINGS: 4 ◆ 155 CALORIES PER SERVING ◆ COOKING TIME: 7 TO 9 MINUTES

1 teaspoon olive oil
2 garlic cloves, minced
2 green onions, thinly sliced
2 tablespoons dry wine or vermouth
1 tablespoon fresh lemon juice

4 tablespoons Dijon mustard
1 teaspoon freshly chopped tarragon, or ¼ teaspoon dried
Dash freshly ground black pepper
4 4-ounce skinless, boneless chicken breasts

Combine the oil, garlic, and green onions in a 10-inch pie plate. Cook on HIGH for 1 minute. Stir in the wine, lemon juice, mustard, tarragon, and pepper. Roll the chicken breasts in this mixture and place the breasts around the outer rim of the dish. Cover with wax paper and cook on HIGH for 3 minutes.

Turn the breasts over and spoon some of the sauce over the breasts. Cover again and cook on HIGH for 3 to 5 minutes more, or until the chicken is opaque but still tender. Serve each chicken breast with the juices spooned on top.

◆ *For 1 Serving:* Combine ¼ teaspoon olive oil, ½ minced garlic clove, and ½ sliced green onion in an 8-ounce oval ramekin or cereal bowl. Cook on HIGH for 35 seconds. Stir in ½ tablespoon dry white wine, 1 teaspoon lemon juice, 1 tablespoon mustard, ¼ teaspoon freshly chopped tarragon or a pinch dried, and a pinch freshly ground pepper. Place a 4-ounce chicken breast on top. Cover tightly and cook on HIGH for 2 to 4 minutes, or until opaque but still tender. Serve the chicken with its juices.

Lemony Broccoli Spears

SERVINGS: 4 ◆ 20 CALORIES PER 3½-OUNCE SERVING ◆ COOKING TIME: 4 TO 8 MINUTES

1 pound broccoli, trimmed and cut into stalks
2 tablespoons water
2 teaspoons grated lemon peel

Place the broccoli stalks on a round 10-inch pie plate, arranging them like the spokes of a wheel, with the flowerets toward the center. Sprinkle with the water and lemon peel. Cover tightly and cook on HIGH for 4 to 8 minutes, or until tender or tender-crisp, depending on your taste.

◆ For 1 Serving: Place ¼ pound trimmed broccoli into an 8-ounce oval microwaveproof ramekin, or cereal bowl. Sprinkle with 1 tablespoon water and ½ teaspoon grated lemon peel. Cover tightly and cook on HIGH for 2 to 4 minutes, or until cooked to tender or tender-crisp.

Apple-Orange Compote

SERVINGS: 4 ◆ 101 CALORIES PER ½-CUP SERVING ◆ COOKING TIME: 5 TO 7 MINUTES

2 medium apples (Granny Smith), peeled and sliced into ¼-inch slices
2 naval oranges, peeled and divided into segments
½ cup white grape juice
1 tablespoon lemon juice
1 tablespoon Triple Sec or orange juice
⅛ teaspoon ground cinnamon
   Freshly grated nutmeg

Combine all the ingredients in a 2-quart casserole. Cover tightly and cook on HIGH for 2 minutes; stir. Cook on HIGH for 3 to 5 minutes more, or until the apples are tender. Serve the mixture warm or at room temperature.

◆ For 2 Servings: Cut the ingredient amounts in half. Combine in a 1-quart casserole. Cover tightly and cook on HIGH for 2 minutes; stir. Cook on HIGH for 1 to 3 minutes more.

SPICY TOMATO SOUP WITH CRUDITÉS

SEAFOOD RISOTTO

AMARETTO CHEESECAKES WITH STRAWBERRY SAUCE

Menu

14

*514 calories
per serving*

Plan of action

30 TO 40 MINUTES BEFORE SERVING

1. Make the cheesecakes and speed chill them in the freezer, or prepare and chill the night before.
2. While the cheesecakes are baking, prepare the ingredients for the risotto.
3. Remove the cheesecakes from the microwave and cook the risotto.

4. While the risotto is cooking, cut up the crudités for the soup and make the strawberry sauce.
5. During the standing time of the risotto, cook the soup.
6. Serve the soup, then the risotto. The risotto will keep warm, when covered, for up to 30 minutes.

Spicy Tomato Soup with Crudités

SERVINGS: 4 ◆ 49 CALORIES PER ½-CUP SERVING ◆ COOKING TIME: 7 TO 10 MINUTES

4 cups tomato juice
2 green onions, thinly sliced
½ teaspoon celery seeds
Dash hot pepper sauce

Dash Worcestershire sauce
Celery sticks
Radishes
Cucumber sticks

Combine the tomato juice, onion, celery seeds, hot pepper, and Worcestershire sauce in a 2-quart casserole. Cover tightly and cook on HIGH for 7 to 10 minutes, or until heated through. If you wish, the same mixture can be poured into 4 mugs, covered, and heated for the same amount of time.

Serve the soup with the celery sticks, radishes, and cucumber sticks.

◆ *For 1 Serving:* Combine 1 cup tomato juice, ½ thinly sliced green onion, a dash celery seed, and a drop hot pepper and Worcestershire sauces in a microwaveproof cereal bowl or mug. Cook on HIGH for 1 to 2 minutes. Serve with cut-up vegetables.

Seafood Risotto

SERVINGS: 4 ◆ 302 CALORIES PER GENEROUS 1-CUP SERVING ◆ COOKING TIME: 17 TO 23 MINUTES

Eating this Italian rice dish when you're on a diet seems like a dream come true. There is nothing more satisfying than the glistening combination of rice flavored with chicken broth, onion, seafood, and a touch of Parmesan.

   You can allow this rice to stand between 5 and 30 minutes after cooking is finished and it will still remain hot.

1 teaspoon olive oil	4 ounces raw peeled shrimp (see Note)
1 medium onion, chopped	4 ounces scallops
1 cup raw Arborio or long-grain rice	1 pound mussels, cleaned
2 tablespoons grated Parmesan cheese	¼ cup chopped fresh parsley
1¾ cups chicken broth	

Combine the oil and onion in a 3-quart casserole. Cook on HIGH for 1 minute. Stir in the rice, cheese, and broth. Cover tightly and cook on HIGH for 6 to 8 minutes, or until the broth boils. Stir in the shrimp and scallops. Cover again and cook on MEDIUM for 5 minutes; stir.

   Place the mussels on top of the rice. Cover again and cook on HIGH for 5 to 9 minutes, or until the mussels are all opened. Let stand, covered, for 5 minutes.

   To serve: Divide the risotto among 4 large soup bowls. Sprinkle with the fresh parsley.

◆ *Note:* You may use all shrimp or all scallops if you wish.

◆ *For 2 Servings:* Combine ½ teaspoon oil and ½ chopped onion, in a 2-quart casserole. Cook on HIGH for 1 minute. Stir in ½ cup rice, 1 tablespoon cheese, and 1 cup broth. Cover tightly and cook on HIGH for 4 to 7 minutes, or until the broth boils. Stir in 2 ounces each of shrimp and scallops. Cover tightly and cook on MEDIUM for 4 minutes. Place ½ pound cleaned mussels on top. Cover again and cook on HIGH for 5 to 7 minutes, or until the mussels are opened and the rice is tender but not mushy. Let stand, covered, for 5 minutes. Serve in big bowls.

Amaretto Cheesecakes with Strawberry Sauce

SERVINGS: 4 ◆ 137 CALORIES PER SERVING, INCLUDING THE SAUCE ◆ COOKING TIME: 8 TO 12 MINUTES

8 ounces part skim milk ricotta
1 egg, beaten
1 tablespoon grated lemon peel
1 tablespoon sugar

1 tablespoon amaretto, or 1 teaspoon almond flavoring
½ cup Strawberry Sauce (see below)

Combine all the ingredients except the sauce in a large glass mixing bowl, and stir until well blended. Place the bowl in the microwave and cook on HIGH for 1 minute; stir. Cook on HIGH for 1 minute more.

Pour the mixture into 4 individual 6- or 7-ounce custard cups. Place these in the microwave in a circle, leaving at least a 1-inch space between the cups. Cook on MEDIUM for 6 to 10 minutes, or until a knife inserted into the center comes out clean. Speed chill in the freezer for 15 minutes.

To serve: Unmold each cheesecake. Spoon 2 tablespoons Strawberry Sauce on top of each.

Strawberry Sauce

MAKES: 1 CUP ◆ 18 CALORIES PER 2 TABLESPOONS ◆ COOKING TIME: 4 TO 6 MINUTES

This may also be served over sherbet or fresh pineapple.

1 pint fresh strawberries, hulled
1 tablespoon sugar

½ teaspoon vanilla extract
Pinch cardamom powder

Combine all the ingredients in a 2-quart casserole. Cover with wax paper. Cook on HIGH for 4 to 6 minutes, stirring after 3 minutes, or until the mixture boils and the berries begin to fall apart.

Pour the mixture in the bowl of a food processor or blender, or force the berries through a sieve to puree. Chill until serving time.

15

409
calories
per
serving

Unlike most of the other menus, we suggest that you serve the fruit cup as a first course. This order seems to make sense in coordinating the recipe cooking times; and serving the fruit first will begin to satisfy you before you get started on the main course.

Because this menu also takes slightly longer than the rest of the menus, we suggest that you make it on the weekend or the night before your dinner. Reheating small portions of the veal mixture will take no time at all.

FOUR FRUIT CUP

VEAL CUBES WITH VEGETABLES PRINTEMPS

NEW RED POTATOES

Plan of action

45 MINUTES BEFORE SERVING

1. Prepare and cook the veal dish.
2. While the veal is cooking, prepare and chill the fruit cup.
3. Prepare the potatoes for cooking, rubbing the peeled part of the po-

tatoes with a cut lemon if they are to stand very long.
4. Serve the fruit cup while the potatoes are cooking.

Four Fruit Cup

SERVINGS:4 ◆ 65 CALORIES PER 1-CUP SERVING

1 cup melon balls
1 cup halved strawberries
1 cup orange segments

1 cup fresh pineapple chunks or unsweetened chunks, drained
Mint leaves

Combine all the ingredients, except the mint, in a mixing bowl. Chill. Serve in stemmed sherbet glasses or in small bowls with mint leaves.

Veal Cubes with Vegetables Printemps

SERVINGS: 4 ◆ 258 CALORIES PER GENEROUS-CUP SERVING ◆ COOKING TIME: 37 TO 38 MINUTES

This is a light meat-and-vegetable stew that is served on a bed of flavorful dark greens.

1 teaspoon olive oil
1 garlic clove, minced
2 tablespoons chopped onion
1 pound veal stew meat, cut into ½-inch cubes
1 tablespoon tomato paste
2 tablespoons dry white wine
½ cup beef broth
1 tablespoon lemon juice

2 tablespoons chopped fresh parsley
¼ cup chopped fresh basil
¼ teaspoon red pepper flakes
1 cup fresh or frozen peas
¼ pound snow pea pods, trimmed
½ pound mushrooms, quartered
1 bunch watercress, or 2 bunches arugula or dandelion leaves

Combine the oil, garlic, and onion in a 2-quart casserole. Cook on HIGH for 35 seconds or 1 minute, or until slightly tender. Stir in the veal to coat. Cover tightly and cook on HIGH for 5 minutes; stir.

Stir in the tomato paste, wine, broth, lemon juice, parsley, 2 tablespoons basil, and the pepper flakes. Cover tightly and cook on HIGH for 5 minutes; stir. Cover again and cook on MEDIUM for 15 minutes.

Stir in the peas. Cover again and cook on MEDIUM for 10 minutes, or until the meat is tender. Stir in the pea pods and mushrooms. Cook on HIGH for 2 minutes. Let stand, covered, for 5 to 10 minutes.

To serve: Line each serving plate with about 10 watercress, arugula, or dandelion leaves. Spoon a generous cup full of stew onto each plate and sprinkle with the remaining 2 tablespoons basil leaves.

◆ For Fewer Servings: Rather than cut this recipe in half, we think it is more practical to make the whole thing and freeze the remainder for portioning out later.

New Red Potatoes

SERVINGS: 4 ◆ 86 CALORIES PER 2 POTATOES ◆ COOKING TIME: 6 TO 10 MINUTES

1 pound (8) small red potatoes
¼ cup water

Scrub the potatoes and peel a strip around the center of each. Combine the potatoes and water in a 2-quart casserole. Cover tightly and cook on HIGH for 6 to 10 minutes, or until fork tender.

Menu

16

441 calories per serving

NEW ORLEANS TOMATO BROTH

CAJUN FISH STEAKS

LEMON RICE (PAGE 238)

SPINACH, TOMATO, AND MUSHROOM SALAD

FRESH ORANGE WITH LEMON CREAM

Plan of action

30 TO 40 MINUTES

1. Cook the rice. Meanwhile, prepare the ingredients for the broth and fish. Wash the spinach.
2. Remove the rice from the microwave for standing time and cook the soup.
3. While the soup is cooking, prepare the salad and dessert. Chill them both.
4. Serve the soup. Meanwhile, cook the fish.

New Orleans Tomato Broth

SERVINGS: 4 ◆ 39 CALORIES PER 1-CUP SERVING ◆ COOKING TIME: 10 TO 13 MINUTES

2 tablespoons chopped onion
1 cup thinly sliced celery
2 cups clam juice
2 cups chicken broth

¾ teaspoon paprika
½ teaspoon cayenne pepper
¼ teaspoon dried thyme leaves

Combine the onion and celery in a 2-quart casserole. Cover tightly and cook on HIGH for 2 to 3 minutes, or until almost tender. Stir in the remaining ingredients. Cover again and cook on HIGH for 8 to 10 minutes, or until heated through.

Cajun Fish Steaks

SERVINGS: 4 ◆ 136 CALORIES PER 4-OUNCE SERVING ◆ COOKING TIME: 7 TO 10 MINUTES

**1 pound swordfish, halibut, or cod steaks, ½
   to ¾ inch thick
2 to 4 teaspoons Cajun Mix (see box)
2 teaspoons fresh lemon juice**

Cut the fish steaks into 4-ounce portions, removing the skin. Rub both sides of the steaks with the Cajun Mix. Arrange the steaks around the outside of a 9- or 10-inch pie plate, with the thicker sections toward the outside. Sprinkle with lemon juice. Cover with wax paper and cook on MEDIUM for 7 to 10 minutes, or until the fish flakes when pressed with a fork. Let stand for 3 minutes. Spoon the cooking juices over the top to serve.

◆ *For 1 Serving:* Rub both sides of a 4-ounce fish steak with ½ to 1 teaspoon Cajun Mix. Place the steak into an oval ramekin and sprinkle with lemon juice. Cover with wax paper and cook on MEDIUM for 2 to 3 minutes.

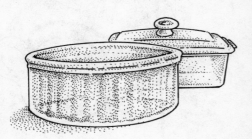

CAJUN MIX

MAKES: ABOUT ½ CUP ◆ 1 CALORIE PER TEASPOON

This spicy seasoning mix is as good on chicken and steaks as it is on fish. There are no calories worth counting here.

**1 tablespoon paprika
1 teaspoon garlic powder
1 teaspoon cayenne pepper
1 teaspoon black pepper
½ teaspoon crushed dried thyme leaves
½ teaspoon crushed dried oregano leaves**

Combine all the ingredients in a custard cup. Keep in an attractive small jar, covered, for future use.

Spinach, Tomato, and Mushroom Salad

SERVINGS: 4 ◆ 40 CALORIES PER 1¼-CUP SERVING

½ **pound spinach, washed and trimmed
(about 4 cups)**
1 **cup sliced tomatoes**
1 **cup sliced mushrooms**
¼ **cup Mustard Vinaigrette (page 288)**

Toss all the ingredients in a large bowl
and chill until serving time.

Fresh Orange with Lemon Cream

SERVINGS: 4 ◆ 92 CALORIES PER SERVING

½ **cup low-fat ricotta cheese**
4 **teaspoons sugar**
1 **teaspoon grated lemon peel**
2 **medium naval oranges, peeled and cut into
segments**
Mint sprigs

In a small bowl beat the ricotta, sugar,
and lemon peel together until smooth
and creamy.

To serve: Spoon 2 tablespoons of
the ricotta cream into the center of
each of 4 dessert plates. Arrange half
an orange in a fan around the cream.
Garnish with mint sprigs.

MUSSELS OR CLAMS CAPRI

CRUSTY FRENCH BREAD (2 SLICES, 150 CALORIES)

TOASTED PIGNOLI AND SPINACH SALAD

MELON CRESCENTS WITH STRAWBERRY SAUCE

Menu

17

*384 calories
per serving*

Plan of action

1. Prepare the strawberry sauce and chill.
2. Toast the pignoli for the salad.
3. Clean and cook the mussels or clams.
4. While the mussels are cooking, prepare the salad.

20 TO 25 MINUTES BEFORE SERVING

5. Serve the mussels with French bread, then serve the salad.
6. Cut up the melon and serve the dessert.

Mussels or Clams Capri

SERVINGS: 4 ◆ 110 CALORIES PER ¾ POUND (11 TO 12 CLAMS OR MUSSELS) WITH ¼ CUP BROTH ◆ COOKING TIME: 7 TO 9 MINUTES

Fresh oregano, one of the first herbs to bear green leaves in the spring, graces this sunny seaside dish. It is not quite a soup, but there is enough broth so that 2 pieces of bread are needed to sponge it all up.

1 teaspoon olive oil
2 garlic cloves, minced
2 green onions, thinly sliced
½ to 1 teaspoon red pepper flakes
3 pounds mussels or clams, well scrubbed

2 tablespoons chopped fresh oregano, or 1 teaspoon dried
1 tablespoon fresh lemon juice
¼ cup chopped fresh parsley
¼ cup dry white wine

Combine the oil, garlic, green onions, and pepper flakes in a 3-quart casserole. Cook on HIGH for 35 to 45 seconds, or until slightly tender. Stir in the mussels or clams, coating them with the mixture.

Add the remaining ingredients. Cover tightly and cook on HIGH for 5 minutes; stir. Cover again and cook on HIGH for 1 to 3 minutes, or until all the mussels are opened. Discard any that don't open.

Divide the clams or mussels among 4 soup bowls and pour some broth into each bowl. Dip the clams or mussels into the broth as you eat them and then mop up the rest with the crusty bread.

◆ *For 1 Serving:* Combine ¼ teaspoon olive oil, 1 minced small garlic clove, ½ chopped green onion, and ¼ teaspoon red pepper flakes in a 1-quart casserole. Stir in ¾ pound mussels or clams. Add 1 tablespoon each chopped fresh parsley and white wine, 2 teaspoons chopped fresh oregano or ¼ teaspoon dried, and 1 teaspoon lemon juice. Cover tightly and cook on HIGH for 2½ minutes; stir. Cover again and cook on HIGH for 30 seconds to 1½ minutes, or until all the mussels are opened.

Toasted Pignoli and Spinach Salad

SERVINGS: 4 ◆ 57 CALORIES PER 1¼-CUP SERVING ◆ COOKING TIME: 2 MINUTES

2 tablespoons pignoli or pine nuts
½ pound spinach leaves, washed and trimmed (about 4 cups)
1 cup sliced mushrooms

2 whole pimentos, rinsed and thinly sliced
¼ cup Mustard Vinaigrette (page 288)

Place the pignoli on a small microwaveproof plate. Cook on HIGH for 2 minutes to toast and bring out their flavor. Combine the pignoli and remaining ingredients in a medium bowl. Toss and serve.

Melon Crescents with Strawberry Sauce

SERVINGS: 4 ◆ 67 CALORIES PER SERVING

1 large ripe cantaloupe
1 recipe Strawberry Sauce (page 63)

Quarter the melon and remove the seeds and rind. Slice each quarter into ¼-inch-thick crescents and fan out between 4 serving plates. Spoon ¼ cup sauce at the base of each fan. Chill until serving time.

MINTED CANTALOUPE WITH STRAWBERRIES

CHEESE AND ASPARAGUS OMELET

HONEY-BRAN MUFFINS
WITH STRAWBERRY JAM (PAGE 298)

COFFEE

Menu

18

*411 calories
per serving*

Plan of action

1. Make jam and refrigerate.
2. Cut up and chill the fruit.
3. Mix up the muffin batter and set aside.
4. Prepare and cook the omelet.

10 MINUTES THE NIGHT BEFORE OR EARLIER
20 TO 25 MINUTES BEFORE SERVING

5. While the omelet is cooking, spoon the muffin mixture into cups.
6. During the omelet's standing time, cook the muffins.

When you sit down to eat fruit for breakfast or brunch, choose it in its whole form, rather than as a juice. Whole grapefruit or oranges will give you more roughage to encourage your digestive system. It will also keep you satisfied for longer than an equivalent amount of fresh juice.

Minted Cantaloupe with Strawberries

SERVINGS: 4 ◆ 41 CALORIES PER SERVING

1 large cantaloupe, quartered and seeded
1 cup sliced strawberries
4 mint sprigs

Pile ¼ cup fresh strawberries on each melon quarter and garnish with fresh mint. Chill until serving time.

71

Cheese and Asparagus Omelet

SERVINGS: 4 ◆ 172 CALORIES PER SERVING ◆ COOKING TIME: 7 TO 10 MINUTES

20 medium asparagus tips, 1½ inches in
    length (about 1 cup)
 6 eggs, beaten
 1 tablespoon grated Parmesan cheese

½ cup low-fat cottage cheese
1 tablespoon chopped fresh chives
Freshly ground black pepper

Place the asparagus tips in a 9-inch glass pie plate. Cover tightly and cook on HIGH for 2 minutes (to cook partially). Remove the asparagus from the dish and set them aside.

Pour the beaten eggs into the pie plate. Cover with plastic wrap and cook on HIGH for 2 minutes. Stir the outer edges into the less cooked inner sections. Stir in the cheeses to blend well.

Arrange the asparagus tips on the eggs, spacing them evenly around the rim of the dish with the tips pointing toward the center. Cover again and cook on MEDIUM for 3 to 6 minutes, until the eggs are almost set in the center. Let stand, covered, for 2 minutes.

To serve: Cut the omelet into 4 wedges and sprinkle with chives.

◆ Tip: Save the asparagus stalks for soup.

Honey-Bran Muffins

MAKES: 6 ◆ 190 CALORIES PER MUFFIN ◆ COOKING TIME: 2 TO 3 MINUTES

You can approach making these muffins in two ways: Bake the whole batch at once and freeze the remainder, reheating them later; or bake a muffin fresh every day for a week from the batter that you have kept covered and refrigerated.

1 cup bran flakes
2 tablespoons vegetable oil
⅔ cup buttermilk
1 cup whole wheat flour
2 tablespoons honey

1½ teaspoons baking powder
1 egg, beaten
¼ cup raisins
¼ teaspoon grated nutmeg
½ teaspoon ground cinnamon

Combine all the ingredients in a large bowl and stir until just mixed. Place 2 cupcake liners in one or up to six 5- or 6-ounce custard cups or a microwave muffin pan.

Spoon the batter into the prepared

cups, filling them just half full. If cooking more than 1 in custard cups, place them at least 1 inch apart in the microwave; if cooking more than 3, arrange them in a circle.

Follow these cooking times:

▲ ▲ ▲ ▲ ▲ ▲ ▲ ▲ ▲ ▲ ▲ ▲

1 muffin	HIGH	*30 seconds*
2 muffins	HIGH	*1 minute*
4 muffins	HIGH	*1½ minutes, rearranging once*
6 muffins	HIGH	*2½ to 3 minutes, rearranging once*

▽ ▽ ▽ ▽ ▽ ▽ ▽ ▽ ▽ ▽ ▽ ▽

Refrigerate any remaining batter and keep up to 1 week, stirring just before you cook any muffins.

◆ *Tip:* Reheat 1 frozen muffin by wrapping it in a paper towel and heating on HIGH for 15 seconds.

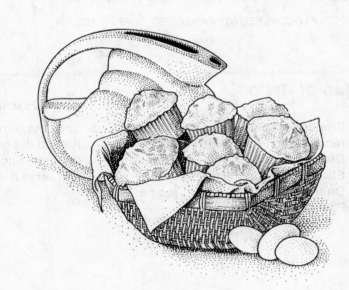

Mother's Day Lunch or Dinner for 8

For an extra treat, serve a 3-ounce glass of champagne before the meal or with the strawberry dessert and add 63 calories.

442 calories
per serving
for lunch

1 SVELTE TERRINE DE POISSON WITH CREAMY HERB DRESSING (PAGE 24)	
(1 SLICE WITH 2 TABLESPOONS DRESSING)	117
PASTA PRIMAVERA (PAGE 32)(¼-CUP SERVING)	105
FRENCH BREAD (1 SLICE)	70
FROZEN STRAWBERRY DELIGHT (PAGE 47) (½-CUP SERVING)	46
CHOCOLATE-COVERED STRAWBERRIES RECIPE (PAGE 134)	41

Plan of Action

20 MINUTES THE DAY BEFORE
25 MINUTES ON THE SERVING DAY

1. Prepare 1 recipe Svelte Terrine, 2 recipes each Frozen Strawberry Delight and Chocolate-Covered Strawberries on the day before.
2. On the serving day, cook 1 recipe Pasta Primavera.

3. Slice the terrine and serve it.
4. Reheat the pasta on HIGH for 2 to 4 minutes. Slice 1 loaf French bread and serve it with the pasta.

Lunch Suggestions

*A*ll of the following lunch suggestions are approximately 200 calories. Many of them turn one of the leftover dinner menus into a nutritious midday meal.

Whole Foods Sliced Turkey Pita

2 ounces sliced Roast Turkey Breast (page 49) in	79 calories
1-ounce whole wheat pita with	95 calories
Sliced radishes and alfalfa sprouts	10 calories
½ cup skim milk	44 calories
TOTAL	228 calories

Turkey and Fruit Pocket

2 ounces sliced Roast Turkey Breast (page 49) in	79 calories
1-ounce whole wheat pita with	95 calories
½ apple, sliced and tucked inside	40 calories
1 cup alfalfa sprouts	10 calories
1 tablespoon Creamy Orange Dressing (page 291), spooned on top	16 calories
Mineral water or seltzer	
TOTAL	240 calories

Tuna Salad Sandwich with Herb Dressing

2 ounces water-packed tuna combined with	72 calories
2 tablespoons Creamy Herb Dressing II (page 288) in	22 calories
1-ounce whole wheat pita with	95 calories
½ cup chopped lettuce leaves	5 calories
½ cup skim milk	44 calories
TOTAL	238 calories

Confetti Cottage Cheese Salad

¾ cup low-fat cottage cheese mixed with	123 calories
Sliced radishes, cucumbers, shredded carrots, and pepper slices	20 calories
3 melba toasts	45 calories
Mineral water or seltzer	
TOTAL	**188 calories**

Cilantro Chicken and Salsa Sandwich

2 ounces sliced leftover Lime and Cilantro Chicken Breasts (page 43) in	112 calories
1-ounce pita with	95 calories
2 tablespoons Fresh Tomato Salsa (page 43), on top	4 calories
½ cup skim milk	44 calories
TOTAL	**255 calories**

Curried Meatball Sandwich

2 Confetti Veal Meatballs (page 29), sliced and stirred with	80 calories
2 tablespoons Curry-Herb Dip (page 289) in	22 calories
1-ounce pita with	95 calories
Sliced radishes and watercress on top	10 calories
½ cup skim milk	44 calories
TOTAL	**251 calories**

Inside-Out Turkey Sandwich

½ cup Favorite Bread Stuffing (page 50) formed into a patty to cover	80 calories
2 ounces sliced Roast Turkey Breast (page 49) wrapped in 1 romaine leaf	81 calories
½ cup skim milk	44 calories
TOTAL	**205 calories**

Dijon Chicken and Pepper Pocket

2 ounces sliced Chicken Dijon (page 59), in	124 calories
1-ounce pita with	95 calories
1 green pepper, sliced and tucked inside	20 calories
2 tablespoons Creamy Mustard Dressing (page 290)	
on top (optional)	22 calories
½ cup skim milk	44 calories
TOTAL	**305 calories**

Svelte Terrine de Poisson with Curry Sauce

1 slice Svelte Terrine de Poisson (page 24), with	97 calories
2 tablespoons Curry-Herb Dip (page 289), on top	22 calories
2 melba toasts	30 calories
Cucumber sticks	
1 orange, nectarine, or ½ banana	53 calories
Mineral water or seltzer	
TOTAL	**202 calories**

77

SUMMER MENUS

*T*here is no time like the summer to be dieting. The fresh fruit gives us its natural sweetness, and we can gorge ourselves on just-picked garden-grown vegetables scented with fresh herbs.

The heat is often an appetite suppressant, too, causing us to reach for a cool drink rather than something to eat. Look for the low-calorie drinks that appear in this section.

On the other hand, summer is also a time when it is difficult to hide any bulges you've been collecting over the winter months, and that can be the strongest incentive of all to want to take off a few pounds.

So if you're trying to tighten up some of those spongy areas, here are some easy-to-follow muscle toners.

▲ ▲ ▲ ▲ ▲ ▲ ▲ ▲ ▲ ▲ ▲

- ◆ *To firm the inner thighs:* Grab a thick thesaurus or dictionary. Sit on the edge of a straight-backed chair with your hands holding the sides of the seat. Put the book between your knees and press it as hard as you can for 3 seconds. Relax and repeat this six times.
- ◆ *For a firmer abdomen:* Lie on your back with your hands behind your head. Lift your left knee and touch it with your right elbow, exhaling as you do. Next, straighten out your left leg and bend your right knee, and touch it with your left elbow. Do this sixteen times in a moderate, even rhythm.
- ◆ *For firmer upper arms:* Hold two big novels—Russian sagas are good—in each hand. Place your feet 12 inches apart and bend over at the waist, bending your knees slightly. Bring the books together right above the floor, then raise your straight arms, like the wings of a bird, until the books are parallel to the floor. Repeat this motion ten times.

▼ ▼ ▼ ▼ ▼ ▼ ▼ ▼ ▼ ▼ ▼

Here are some other summer tips to help you lose those extra pounds.

▲ ▲ ▲ ▲ ▲ ▲ ▲ ▲ ▲ ▲ ▲ ▲

◆ Put down your fork between each bite. This will slow down your eating, and give your brain a chance to get the message from your stomach that you are full. It also gives you a chance to enjoy your food and think about what you're eating.

◆ Don't bring all the serving dishes to the table, but prepare the plates in the kitchen. This way you won't be tempted to easily reach for seconds, but will have to get up and go into the kitchen, which might give you pause.

◆ Assign someone else to clear the table, so that you don't chomp on the leftovers as you toss them out or put them away. If there is no one but you, leave the dishes at the table a minute and fix yourself a glass of herbal ice tea. Go into another room and enjoy your drink, perhaps with a book or in front of the television. This will signal you that dinner is over. Later, when you go back to clear the table, there's won't be such a temptation to eat what is left.

◆ Eating should be a visual pleasure, as well as a flavor experience, to be completely satisfying. With all the fresh summer produce, keep in mind the variety of colors that will be available to you this season and scatter them through each meal. Here are some colorful suggestions that won't break your calorie bank:

fresh raspberries strewn over cooked chicken or a chicken salad
honeydew, cantaloupe, and watermelon balls or cubes for appetizer or dessert
peaches and strawberries for dessert
steamed green beans garnished with chopped pimento
all sorts of colorful lettuce to fill up the plate

▼ ▼ ▼ ▼ ▼ ▼ ▼ ▼ ▼ ▼ ▼ ▼

We like to whir a quarter of a cantaloupe to puree into a beautiful apricot-colored sauce and serve with Very Berry Roll (page 116) or Grilled Cornish Hens (page 112).

CREAM OF AVOCADO SOUP

HUACHINANGO CON JUGO DE NARANJA
(RED SNAPPER WITH ORANGE SAUCE)

RICE WITH GREEN OR RED PEPPER

MANGO ''ICE CREAM''
OR MANGO SLICES WITH CREAM

Plan of action

20 TO 25 MINUTES BEFORE SERVING
IF PREPARING THE MANGO ''ICE CREAM,'' DO IT THE NIGHT BEFORE

1. If not serving the Mango ''Ice Cream,'' prepare the mango slices.
2. Cook the rice. Meanwhile, chop the pepper and prepare the fish.
3. Prepare the soup now or while the fish is cooking.
4. Cook the fish during the standing time of the rice.
5. Serve the soup.

Cream of Avocado Soup

SERVINGS: 4 ◆ 129 CALORIES PER ½- TO ¾-CUP SERVING

1 medium ripe avocado, peeled and seeded
½ cup low-fat skim milk
1 tablespoon lemon juice

1 cup chicken broth
¼ cup dry sherry
Lemon wedges

Cut the avocado into 1-inch chunks. Combine the avocado, skim milk, lemon juice, broth, and sherry in the bowl of a food processor or blender. Puree until smooth. Chill until serving time. Garnish with lemon wedges.

Huachinango con Jugo de Naranja

SERVINGS: 4 ◆ 141 CALORIES PER SERVING ◆ COOKING TIME: 6 TO 9 MINUTES

2 garlic cloves, minced
2 green onions, thinly sliced
¼ cup chopped fresh parsley
½ cup orange juice

4 4-ounce red snapper fillets
4 green olives, sliced (omit these on restricted salt diet)

Combine the garlic, green onions, parsley, and orange juice in a 9-inch glass pie plate. Cook on HIGH for 2 to 3 minutes, or until the garlic is tender and the juice comes to a boil.

Stir well and place the fish fillets, skin side down, around the outer rim of the dish with the thicker edges toward the outside. Top each fillet with olive slices. Cover with a paper towel and cook on HIGH for 4 to 8 minutes, or until the fish flakes under light pressure of a fork.

To serve: Place 1 fillet with its juices and ½ cup rice on each plate.

◆ *For 1 Serving:* Combine 1 small minced garlic clove, ½ chopped green onion, 1 tablespoon chopped parsley, and 2 tablespoons orange juice in an 8-ounce oval ramekin. Cook on HIGH for 35 seconds to 1 minute. Add a 4-ounce red snapper fillet, skin side down. Top with 1 sliced green olive. Cover with a paper towel and cook on HIGH for 1½ to 3 minutes, or until done. For 2 servings, double the ingredients and cooking times given for 1 serving.

Rice with Green or Red Pepper

SERVINGS: 4 ◆ 139 CALORIES PER SERVING

1 recipe Basic Rice (page 294)
1 green or red bell pepper, seeded and chopped

Prepare the rice and add the pepper at the end of cooking, before standing time. This will steam the pepper, giving it a slight crunch.

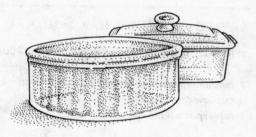

Mango "Ice Cream"

SERVINGS: 4 OR 8 ◆ 76 CALORIES PER 2-SCOOP SERVING (½ CUP)

This dessert is so creamy, rich, and unbelievably good for you.

1 1-pound ripe mango, peeled and seeded
1 tablespoon sugar
¼ cup low-fat plain yogurt

1 tablespoon orange juice
½ teaspoon vanilla extract

Cut the mango into 1-inch chunks and place it in a bag in the freezer for 1 hour, or until partially frozen. When partially frozen, combine it with the remaining ingredients in the bowl of a food processor or blender and puree until smooth.

You may serve it at this point, by spooning it into wineglasses, or freeze it for 1 to 2 hours and serve it in scoops like ice cream.

Mango Slices with Cream

SERVINGS: 4 ◆ 83 CALORIES PER SERVING

1 1-pound mango, peeled and seeded
½ cup low-fat plain yogurt
1 tablespoon sugar
½ teaspoon vanilla extract

Cut the mango into long thin slices. Fan one-quarter of the slices out on each dessert plate. Combine the yogurt, sugar, and vanilla in a small bowl. Spoon 2 tablespoons of the cream in a ribbon over each plate of mango slices.

CHILLED CANTALOUPE SOUP

FAJITAS WITH FLOUR TORTILLAS AND SALSA

CHILLED WATERMELON CUBES

Plan of action

1. Prepare the soup and chill it.
2. Heat the browning dish in the microwave.
3. While the browning dish is heating, rub the steak with Worcestershire sauce and make the salsa.
4. While the steak is cooking, shred the lettuce and slice the tomatoes.
5. Serve the soup.
6. Heat the tortillas right before serving with the steak.
7. Cut up the watermelon right before serving.

20 TO 25 MINUTES BEFORE SERVING

Chilled Cantaloupe Soup

SERVINGS: 4 ◆ 61 CALORIES PER ¾- TO 1-CUP SERVING

There is a fruit and yogurt drink in India called *lassi,* and there is nothing like it to restore and refresh on a painfully hot day. This chilled soup is much like that drink, and for a change, you may want to serve it in a tall glass with ice.

1 medium cantaloupe, peeled, halved, and seeded
¼ cup dry sherry

¼ cup low-fat plain yogurt
Pinch freshly grated nutmeg

Cut the cantaloupe into 1-inch cubes. Place the cantaloupe pieces in the bowl of a food processor or blender. Add the sherry and yogurt and puree until smooth. Chill until serving time.

To serve: Spoon the mixture into soup bowls or large ice tea glasses and serve with ice and ice tea spoons. Sprinkle the top with nutmeg.

◆ *For 1 Serving:* Combine 1 quarter peeled, seeded, and cubed canta-

86

loupe with 1 tablespoon each sherry and yogurt. Blend in a processor or blender until smooth. Chill it and serve with a sprinkling of fresh nutmeg.

REFRESHING LOW-CALORIE SUMMER DRINKS

These drinks are delicious and so cooling in summer, and each makes 1 tall serving.

Sparkling Cider:

¾ cup club soda
¾ cup apple juice
   Dash fresh lemon juice
   Calories: 88

Orange Juice Fizz:

¾ cup club soda
¾ cup orange juice
1 lemon slice
   Calories: 83

Hawaiian Bubbler:

1½ cups club soda
3 ice cubes made from the juice of unsweetened canned pineapple
   Calories: 48

Floating Cherry Cooler:

1½ cups club soda
3 small cherries, without stems, frozen in ice cubes
   Calories: 15

Florida Fizz:

¾ cup club soda
¾ cup grapefruit juice
   Fresh mint
   Calories: 74

Fajitas with Flour Tortillas and Salsa

SERVINGS: 4 ◆ 313 CALORIES PER SERVING ◆ COOKING TIME: 10 TO 17 MINUTES, INCLUDING HEATING THE BROWNING DISH

Half the steak is cooked and chilled for Menu #1.

½ pound London broil round steak, ¼ inch
  thick, trimmed (see Tip)
1 tablespoon Worcestershire sauce
4 6-inch flour tortillas

4 cups shredded lettuce
4 medium tomatoes, thinly sliced
1 cup Fresh Tomato Salsa (page 43)

Preheat the microwave browning dish on HIGH for 6 to 9 minutes, or according to the manufacturer's instructions for grilled meat.

Meanwhile, rub the steak with the Worcestershire sauce. Press the steak down onto the heated browning dish and cook on HIGH for:

▲ ▲ ▲ ▲ ▲ ▲ ▲ ▲ ▲ ▲ ▲ ▲

◆ **2 minutes on each side for rare**
  3 minutes on each side for medium
  4 minutes on each side for well

▼ ▼ ▼ ▼ ▼ ▼ ▼ ▼ ▼ ▼ ▼ ▼

Let the meat stand for 1 minute on the dish, and slice thinly across the grain on a diagonal.

Right before serving, wrap the tortillas in a paper towel and heat on HIGH for 30 seconds. Cut each tortilla into quarters.

To serve: Place the 4 quarters of the tortilla on each plate, with 3 ounces sliced steak, 1 cup shredded lettuce, 1 sliced tomato, and ¼ cup salsa. Wrap each piece of tortilla around some meat, lettuce, and tomato and dip into the salsa before eating.

◆ *For 2 Servings:* Cut the amount of meat in half and rub it with 1½ teaspoons Worcestershire sauce. Heat the browning dish as directed and cook the meat for the the time given in the basic recipe. Reduce the remaining ingredient amounts by half. Wrap 2 tortillas in paper towels and heat on HIGH for 15 seconds, before cutting each into quarters.

Chilled Watermelon Cubes

SERVINGS: 4 ◆ 57 CALORIES PER 1-CUP SERVING

4 cups cubed watermelon
 Lime wedges

Place 1 cup watermelon cubes into each of 4 wineglasses and serve with a lime wedge.

The actual preparation time for this menu is less than 30 minutes, but every item needs to be chilled. So before dinner, relax for a few minutes with a cool club soda drink until the food is chilled to the desired temperature, or cook the scallops the night before to chill them.

Menu

3

*463 calories
per serving*

CHILLED DILLED CUCUMBER SOUP

SCALLOP AND AVOCADO SALAD

FRESH BLUEBERRIES WITH ORANGE CREAM

Plan of action

40 TO 50 MINUTES BEFORE SERVING

1. Cook the scallops and chill them.
2. Make the soup and chill it.
3. Prepare the dessert and chill it.

4. Chop the ingredients for the salad and mix them together.
5. Serve the soup.

Chilled Dilled Cucumber Soup

SERVINGS: 4 ◆ 56 CALORIES PER ¾ CUP SERVING ◆ COOKING TIME: 4 TO 8 MINUTES

2 **tablespoons thinly sliced green onions**
2 **1-pound cucumbers, peeled, seeded, and thinly sliced**
1¼ **cups chicken broth**
½ **cup low-fat plain yogurt**

2 **tablespoons chopped fresh parsley**
2 **tablespoons chopped fresh dill, plus 4 sprigs for garnish**
1 **tablespoon lemon juice**
  Dash cayenne pepper

Combine the green onions and cucumbers in a 2-quart casserole. Cover tightly and cook on HIGH for 4 to 8 minutes, or until tender. Pour the mixture into the bowl of a food processor or blender. Add the remaining ingredients, except dill sprigs. Refrigerate or speed chill in the freezer for 15 minutes, stirring occasionally.

To serve: Pour the mixture into soup bowls and garnish with the dill sprigs.

◆ *For 1 Serving:* Combine 2 teaspoons thinly sliced green onion and

½ cucumber, peeled, seeded, and thinly sliced in a small microwave-proof bowl. Cover tightly and cook on HIGH for 2 to 3 minutes, or until tender. Pour into the food processor or blender and add 5 tablespoons chicken broth, 2 tablespoons yogurt, 1½ teaspoons each chopped fresh parsley and dill, 1 teaspoon lemon juice, and a pinch cayenne pepper. Puree and chill for 15 minutes.

Scallop and Avocado Salad

SERVINGS: 4 ◆ 309 CALORIES PER 1-CUP SERVING ◆ COOKING TIME: 3 TO 6 MINUTES

Cook the scallops in the morning or the afternoon in advance of completing the salad later in the day.

1 **pound raw scallops**
1 **tablespoon lime juice**
½ **cup thinly sliced green onions**
1 **pound avocado, peeled, seeded, and cut into ¼-inch cubes (about 1 cup)**
½ **cup finely chopped green pepper**

2 **tablespoons chopped fresh cilantro**
1 **to 2 tablespoons chopped pickled jalapeño peppers**
½ **cup Mustard Vinaigrette (page 288)**
4 **medium ripe tomatoes, cut from the tops into 4 wedges leaving bottoms attached**

Place the scallops around the outer rim of a 9-inch pie plate, leaving the center open. Sprinkle with lime juice. Cover with a paper towel and cook on MEDIUM for 3½ to 6 minutes, or until the scallops flake under the pressure of a fork. Chill for 1 hour or speed chill for 30 minutes in the freezer.

If using large sea scallops, cut each scallop into quarters before tossing with the remaining ingredients, except the tomatoes. (Smaller bay scallops don't need to be cut up.) Chill until serving time.

To serve: Place a tomato onto each plate and spread the wedges apart at the top. Spoon 1 cup salad into the center of each tomato.

◆ *For 1 Serving:* Place ¼ pound scallops in a microwaveproof cereal bowl, leaving the center open. Sprinkle with ½ teaspoon lime juice. Cover with a paper towel and cook on MEDIUM for 1½ to 2½ minutes, or until done. Chill for 1 hour. Cut sea scallops into quarters; bay scallops don't need to be cut. Toss them with 2 tablespoons thinly sliced green onions, ¼ peeled, seeded, and cubed avocado, 2 tablespoons finely chopped green pepper, 1½ teaspoons each chopped fresh cilantro and jalapeño pepper, and 2 tablespoons Mustard Vinaigrette. Spoon into the center of 1 tomato, cut into wedges.

Fresh Blueberries with Orange Cream

SERVINGS: 4 ◆ 98 CALORIES PER ½-CUP SERVING

½ cup low-fat ricotta or cottage cheese
4 teaspoons sugar
2 teaspoons grated orange peel

1 teaspoon vanilla extract
1 pint fresh blueberries

Combine the cheese, sugar, orange peel, and vanilla together in a small bowl. Stir until smooth and creamy.

To serve: Place ½ cup berries into 4 wine goblets or dessert plates and top each with 2 tablespoons orange cream.

Menu

4

380 calories
per serving

FRESH CHILLED TOMATO-BASIL SOUP

COLD STEAK SLICES WITH
ROSY GREEN PEPPERCORN SAUCE

INDIVIDUAL PLUM TARTS

Plan of action

15 TO 20 MINUTES BEFORE SERVING

1. Make the soup and chill it.
2. Make the dessert.
3. Mix the peppercorn sauce and

arrange the salad; chill it until serving time.
4. Serve the soup.

Fresh Chilled Tomato-Basil Soup

SERVINGS: 4 ◆ 60 CALORIES PER 1-CUP SERVING ◆ COOKING TIME: 5 TO 8 MINUTES

1 *garlic clove, minced*
2 *tablespoons chopped onion*
2 *pounds ripe tomatoes, peeled, seeded, and chopped; or 2 cups chopped canned, undrained*
2 *tablespoons tomato paste*
1 *cup chicken broth*

½ *cup buttermilk*
¼ *cup chopped fresh basil*
1 *tablespoon lemon juice*
1 *teaspoon grated orange peel*
  Dash freshly ground black pepper
  Pinch cayenne pepper

Combine the garlic and onion in a 2-quart casserole. Cover tightly and cook on HIGH for 1 to 2 minutes, until the onion is tender. Stir in the tomatoes and tomato paste. Cover with wax paper and cook on HIGH for 4 to 6 minutes, or until the mixture boils, stirring twice.

Pour into the bowl of a food processor or blender and puree. Return the mixture to the casserole and stir in the

remaining ingredients. Chill the mixture until serving time.

◆ *Fewer Servings:* It makes sense to prepare all 4 servings of this recipe and freeze the portion you won't be eating. If you want to make just 1 serving of a soup, choose one from another menu that can be easily made in single servings.

Cold Steak Slices with Rosy Green Peppercorn Sauce

SERVINGS: 4 ◆ 196 CALORIES PER SERVING

Try the sauce on cold chicken or fish.

Rosy Green Peppercorn Sauce:

2 pimentos, drained and rinsed
¼ cup chicken broth
2 tablespoons Dijon mustard
2 tablespoons green peppercorns

4 cups mixed greens
12 ounces steak from Fajitas (page 87), thinly sliced

Combine the pimentos, broth, and mustard in the bowl of a food processor or blender and puree. Stir in the peppercorns. Chill or serve at room temperature.

To serve: Line each plate with 1 cup mixed salad greens. Arrange 3 ounces of the steak slices, overlapping slightly, in a row on top of the greens, and spoon 2 tablespoons sauce down the center of the steak on each plate.

Individual Plum Tarts

MAKES: 1 ◆ 124 CALORIES ◆ COOKING TIME: 1 TO 2 MINUTES

These are the simplest little desserts to make, yet are so tasty because the natural juices come from the plum, with a little help from the liqueur.

Cleanup is minimal, because cooking and serving are done on the same plate.

1 large ripe damson plum, sliced into eighths
½ piece whole wheat bread, made into bread crumbs
1 tablespoon orange-flavored liqueur

1 teaspoon sugar
¼ teaspoon vanilla extract

Arrange the plum slices in a pinwheel on a 6-inch microwaveproof dessert plate or paper plate.

Combine the bread crumbs, liqueur, sugar, and vanilla in a small custard cup and sprinkle this over the top of the plums. Cook on HIGH for 1 to 2 minutes, or until the plum is cooked through, rotating after 30 seconds.

◆ Note: For more than one tart, increase the ingredients accordingly and follow these cooking times:

93

▲ ▲ ▲ ▲ ▲ ▲ ▲ ▲ ▲ ▲ ▲ ▲

2 tarts	HIGH	2 to 4 minutes
3 tarts	HIGH	2½ to 4½ minutes
4 tarts	HIGH	3 to 5 minutes

▼ ▼ ▼ ▼ ▼ ▼ ▼ ▼ ▼ ▼ ▼ ▼

Let the tart or tarts stand for 10 minutes before serving at room temperature.

Here's a delicious and inexpensive vegetarian meal.

CHILLED PARSLEY SOUP

MEXICAN STUFFED ZUCCHINI BOATS WITH SALSA

SOUTH OF THE BORDER WATERMELON ROUNDS

Plan of action

30 MINUTES BEFORE SERVING

1. Chill the whole watermelon until just before serving.
2. Prepare, cook, and chill the soup.
3. Prepare and cook the zucchini.
4. While the zucchini is cooking, prepare the salsa.

5. Serve the soup and then the zucchini.
6. Right before dessert, remove the rind from the watermelon, cut it into rounds, and serve it.

Chilled Parsley Soup

SERVINGS: 4 ◆ 80 CALORIES PER ¾-CUP SERVING ◆ COOKING TIME: 4 TO 5 MINUTES

1 bunch parsley, trimed and finely chopped (2 cups), plus 4 sprigs for garnish
1 garlic clove, minced

2 cups chicken broth
1 cup low-fat plain yogurt

94

Combine the parsley, garlic, and 2 tablespoons broth in a 1-quart casserole. Cover tightly and cook on HIGH for 4 to 5 minutes, or until the parsley is blanched and wilted. Spoon the mixture into the bowl of a food processor or blender, along with ¼ cup broth, and finely chop. Add the remaining broth and ¾ cup yogurt. Puree and chill.

To serve: Divide the soup among 4 soup bowls or cups. Top with the remaining ¼ cup yogurt in dollops on each bowl, and place a parsley sprig in the top like a flag.

◆ *For 1 Serving:* Combine ¼ cup chopped parsley, 1 small minced garlic clove, and 1 tablespoon broth in a 2-cup glass measure. Cook on HIGH for 1½ to 2 minutes. Chop finely in the processor or blender with 3 tablespoons additional broth. Add the remaining ¼ cup broth and 3 tablespoons yogurt. Puree and chill. Garnish with 1 tablespoon yogurt and a parsley sprig.

Mexican Stuffed Zucchini Boats with Salsa

SERVINGS: 4 ◆ 229 CALORIES PER 2 ZUCCHINI HALVES, PLUS 15 CALORIES FOR ¼ CUP SALSA ◆ COOKING TIME: 11 TO 17 MINUTES

We first tasted a dish similar to this in a Mexican restaurant and would not have ordered it if the waiter hadn't insisted. It was delicious. This is our low-calorie version.

4 small (¼-pound) zucchini, cut in half lengthwise
1 garlic clove, minced
2 tablespoons chopped onion
1 pound ripe tomatoes, seeded and cut into ¼-inch cubes, or 1 cup chopped canned, undrained
1 cup fresh or frozen corn kernels

1 jalapeño pepper, seeded and chopped
1⅓ cups low-fat cottage cheese
¼ teaspoon ground cumin
¼ teaspoon black pepper
4 ounces grated Monterey Jack cheese
1 cup Fresh Tomato Salsa (page 43)

Scoop out each zucchini half with a grapefruit knife, leaving a ¼-inch shell. Discard the inner pulp. Place the zucchini, cut side down, in a 2-quart rectangular dish. Cover with wax paper and cook on HIGH for 2 to 4 minutes, or until tender-crisp, rearranging after 2 minutes. Drain the dish and turn the halves over.

Combine the garlic and onion in a 2-

quart casserole. Cover with wax paper and cook on HIGH for 1 minute. Stir in the tomatoes, corn, and jalapeño pepper. Cover again and cook on HIGH for 3 to 5 minutes, or until heated through, stirring once. Stir in the cottage cheese, cumin, and black pepper and mix well. Spoon the mixture into the zucchini shells, heaping and rounding it on top. Sprinkle the tops with the grated cheese. Cook, uncovered, on MEDIUM for 5 to 7 minutes, or until the cheese is melted, repositioning them after 2 minutes. Serve with a side of salsa.

◆ *For 1 Serving:* Cut 1 small zucchini in half lengthwise and scoop out the center. Discard the pulp. Place it cut side down on a microwaveproof serving plate. Cover with wax paper and cook on HIGH for 1 minute. Combine ¼ teaspoon minced garlic and 2 teaspoons chopped onion in a 1-quart casserole. Cook on HIGH for 30 seconds. Stir in 1 chopped plum tomato or ½ large tomato (¼ pound), ¼ cup corn kernels, and ¼ chopped jalapeño pepper. Cover with wax paper and cook on HIGH for 1½ to 3 minutes. Stir in ⅓ cup cottage cheese and a pinch each of cumin and black pepper. Spoon the mixture into the zucchini halves. Sprinkle the top with 1 ounce grated Jack cheese. Cook, uncovered, on MEDIUM for 1 to 3 minutes, or until the cheese is melted. Serve with salsa.

South of the Border Watermelon Rounds

SERVINGS: 4 ◆ 74 CALORIES PER ROUND

The fresh fruit vendors in Mexico sell watermelon slices without the rinds that look like big pink wheels.

4 pounds watermelon

Cut the rind from the watermelon and slice into 4 rounds.

menu

340 CALORIES PER SERVING

CHINESE CABBAGE
SOUP WITH LEMON

SZECHUAN BEEF
AND VEGETABLES

RICE (½ CUP COOKED)

PINEAPPLE AND KIWI

SPRING MENU 10 *(page 51)*.

SUMMER MENU 9 (page 106):
Tomato-Orange Soup, Warm Chicken with Avocado and Cantaloupe Salad, Frozen Strawberry Delight.

L U N C H E S
Center: Svelt Terrine de Poisson with Curry Sauce *(page 77).*
L–r: Scallop Salad and Melon Slices *(page 140),*
          Shrimp and Cucumber Salad in Pita *(page 139),*
          Chilled Grilled Hen and Berries *(page 138),*
          Chilled Zucchini Boat and Salsa *(page 139).*

SUMMER MENU 16 *(page 127)*:
Steamed Whole Fish with Two Sauces (pictured with Dilled Cucumber Sauce), Summer Squash Salad with Mustard Vinaigrette, Corn Chowder with Chiles, Peach Sundae.

SUMMER MENU 12 *(page 114):*
Chilled Curried Summer Squash Soup, Tuna Provençale, Mixed Greens with Mustard Vinaigrette, Very Berry Roll.

WINTER BRUNCH MENU 18 *(page 262):*
Glazed Pink Grapefruit, Savory Veal Sausage Patties, Apricots Poached in White Wine, Cheese Polenta.

ORANGE AND SHREDDED ROMAINE SOUP

CREAMY CHICKEN SALAD WITH GRAPES

WHOLE WHEAT MELBA TOASTS (4, 64 CALORIES)

HONEYDEW MELON WITH LIME AND RASPBERRIES

Plan of action

1. Cook the chicken and chill it.
2. While the chicken is cooking, chop and prepare the remaining ingredients for the salad.
3. Cook the broth part of the soup. Meanwhile, chop up the remaining soup ingredients.

25 TO 30 MINUTES BEFORE SERVING

4. Proceed with the soup. Meanwhile, mix the salad together and chill it.
5. Assemble the dessert and chill it.
6. Serve the meal, beginning with the soup.

Orange and Shredded Romaine Soup

SERVINGS: 4 ◆ 65 CALORIES PER 1-CUP SERVING ◆ COOKING TIME: 12 TO 18 MINUTES

1 teaspoon full-flavored olive oil
1 garlic clove, minced
3 cups chicken broth
½ cup orange juice
1 tablespoon dry vermouth or sherry
2 cups thinly sliced romaine lettuce

1 small zucchini, cut into long thin strips
¼ cup chopped fresh parsley
2 green onions, thinly sliced
⅛ teaspoon cayenne pepper
4 thin lemon slices

Combine the oil and garlic in a 3-quart casserole. Cook on HIGH for 35 seconds, or until the garlic is tender. Pour in the broth. Cover tightly and cook on HIGH for 7 to 10 minutes, or until boiling.

Add the remaining ingredients, except the lemon slices. Cover again and cook on HIGH for 5 to 8 minutes, or

until the vegetables are tender-crisp. Serve each bowl with a lemon slice.

◆ *For 1 Serving:* Combine ¼ teaspoon oil and 1 small minced garlic clove in a 1-quart casserole. Cook on HIGH for 30 seconds. Stir in ¾ cup broth, 1 tablespoon orange juice, 1 teaspoon vermouth, ½ cup thinly sliced romaine lettuce, ¼ cup thinly sliced zucchini, 1 tablespoon chopped parsley, ½ thinly sliced green onion, and a pinch cayenne pepper. Cover tightly and cook on HIGH for 3 to 6 minutes, or until the broth is hot and the vegetables are tender-crisp. Garnish with 1 thin lemon slice.

For the single eater, the single servings of many of these recipes call for just part of a zucchini. Two medium zucchini can be stored for 2 weeks or so, so that one purchase can take you through a number of summer menus.

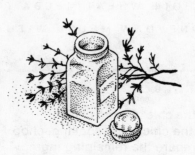

Creamy Chicken Salad with Grapes

SERVINGS: 4 ◆ 190 CALORIES PER 1-CUP SERVING ◆ COOKING TIME: 5 TO 7 MINUTES

2 whole skinless, boneless chicken breasts (about 1 pound), split in half
1 tablespoon lemon juice
2 cups seedless grapes
1 cup thinly sliced celery

¼ cup thinly sliced green onions
½ cup low-fat plain yogurt
1 head red-tipped or other lettuce

Place the chicken in a 9-inch pie plate with the thicker sections of the meat to the outside. Sprinkle with the lemon juice. Cover with wax paper and cook on HIGH for 3 minutes. Turn the chicken over, placing the less-cooked sections to the outside. Cover again and cook on HIGH for 2 to 4 minutes more, or until the chicken is cooked through and tender. Cool the chicken, covered, in the refrigerator or speed chill it for 15 minutes in the freezer, turning the chicken over occasionally. Cut the cooled chicken into ½-inch cubes.

Combine the remaining ingredients, except the lettuce, in a large bowl. Fold in the chicken. Refrigerate until the chicken is chilled.

To serve: Line 4 dinner plates with lettuce and top each plate with a generous cup of chicken salad. Serve each with the 4 melba toasts.

◆ *For 2 Servings:* Place 1 boneless chicken breast (½ pound) on a microwaveproof plate. Sprinkle with 1 teaspoon lemon juice. Cover with wax paper and cook on HIGH for 3 to 5 minutes, turning over once. Let it cool, covered, in the freezer for 10 minutes or so. Cube the chicken and combine it with 1 cup seedless grapes, ½ cup thinly sliced celery, 1 tablespoon thinly sliced green onion, and 2 table-spoons yogurt. Chill and serve on let-tuce.

Variation:

Curried Chicken Salad with Grapes: Add 1 teaspoon curry powder with the yogurt. 2 calories.

Honeydew Melon with Lime and Raspberries

SERVINGS: 4 ◆ 84 CALORIES PER SERVING

The other half of the honeydew melon will be nice for a breakfast or lunch the next day.

**½ large honeydew melon, quartered and
    seeded**
2 cups raspberries
1 lime, quartered

Place the melons on 4 serving plates. Fill the crescent with berries and serve with the juice of a lime quarter squeezed on top.

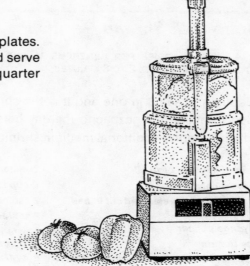

Menu

7

362 calories
per serving

GAZPACHO WITH SHRIMP GARNISH

BREADSTICKS

SUMMER SCROD BAKE

HERBED GREEN BEANS

NECTARINE PINWHEELS WITH LEMON CREAM

Plan of action

30 MINUTES BEFORE SERVING

1. Prepare the gazpacho and speed chill it in the freezer until serving time.
2. Prepare and cook the fish.
3. While the fish is cooking, prepare the green beans for cooking.
4. Cook the beans. Meanwhile, prepare the dessert, or do that immediately before serving.
5. Serve the gazpacho.

Gazpacho with Shrimp Garnish

SERVINGS: 4 ◆ 173 CALORIES PER GENEROUS ½ CUP SERVING, PLUS 46 CALORIES PER 2 BREADSTICKS ◆ COOKING TIME: 2 TO 3 MINUTES

This is a soup and salad in one and it is the shrimp garnish that adds a unique flavor. Plan to make this gazpacho the day before the shrimp salad, Menu #8, and purchase 1 pound additional medium shrimp at the same time.

1 teaspoon full-flavored olive oil

1 garlic clove, minced

4 medium raw shrimp, peeled and cut in half lengthwise
 Dash cayenne pepper

1 large ripe tomato

½ green pepper, seeded and cut into quarters

2 green onions, cut into 1-inch pieces

1 pimento, rinsed and quartered

1 cup tomato juice

2 tablespoons wine vinegar

2 tablespoons chopped fresh basil

1 small cucumber, peeled and cut into ¼-inch cubes

8 4½"- × -½" breadsticks

Combine the olive oil and garlic in a small dish or ramekin. Cook on HIGH for 35 seconds, or until the garlic is tender. Stir in the shrimp. Sprinkle on the cayenne pepper. Cover tightly and cook on HIGH for 35 to 45 seconds, or until the shrimp are pink and cooked through. Set aside.

Pierce the tomato once with a small knife. Place it in the microwave oven and cook it on HIGH for 30 seconds, to heat and loosen the skin. Peel and quarter the tomato. Combine the tomato, green pepper, green onions, pimento, tomato juice, wine vinegar, and basil into the bowl of a food processor or blender. Puree until smooth.

Remove the shrimp from the oil mixture and set them aside. Add the garlic and oil from the shrimp to the processor bowl. Puree the mixture until well blended and chill until serving time, or speed chill in the freezer for 15 minutes.

To serve: Pour the soup into bowls and top each bowl with ¼ cup cucumber cubes and 2 shrimp halves. Serve with 2 breadsticks.

♦ *For Fewer Servings:* Rather than cutting this recipe in half, it makes more sense to cook the entire thing and refrigerate the remaining servings for the next day. Even if you eat a double portion today, you still won't be in bad shape.

OLIVE OIL

Olive oil is a monosaturate which nutrition experts now consider to be beneficial because it lowers the body's harmful blood cholesterol, but leaves the beneficial cholesterol intact.

Olive oil still has 119 calories per tablespoon (or 40 per teaspoon), so if you are watching your weight why not get the most for your calories and buy a flavorful olive oil.

Good extra-virgin olive oil is very savory and doesn't have to cost an arm and a leg.

According to United States standards, a virgin oil means an unrefined oil from the first pressing. Look for a deep green-golden color, which means that it will be fuller in flavor.

Olive oil should be consumed rather quickly or, if purchased in larger containers, it should be decanted into smaller bottles for less exposure to the air, since air spoils its flavor. It is best to store these bottles away from the light.

Summer Scrod Bake

SERVINGS: 4 ◆ 126 CALORIES PER SERVING ◆ COOKING TIME: 6 TO 9 MINUTES

It is best to cook this thicker fillet on MEDIUM power for more tender results. The slower cooking also helps to develop more flavor.

4 4-ounce scrod fillets
4 green onions, thinly sliced
1 teaspoon minced ginger

2 cups sliced mushrooms (¼ pound)
4 teaspoons lemon juice
 Freshly ground black pepper

Arrange the fish with the thicker sections to the outside of a 9-inch pie plate. Top each piece with 1 sliced green onion, ¼ teaspoon minced ginger, ¼ cup sliced mushrooms, 1 teaspoon lemon juice, and a little freshly ground pepper. Cover with a paper towel and cook on MEDIUM for 6 to 9 minutes, or until the fish flakes under the pressure of a fork. Set the fish aside, covered.

To serve: Place each fillet on a serving dish and top it with onions and mushrooms. Spoon the juices over the fish and serve with the green beans.

◆ *For 1 Serving:* Place one 4-ounce fillet in an 8-ounce oval ramekin. Top the fish with one-quarter of the basic recipe ingredients. Cover with a paper towel and cook on HIGH for 2 to 4 minutes, or until cooked through.

Herbed Green Beans

SERVINGS: 4 ◆ 40 CALORIES PER 1-CUP SERVING ◆ COOKING TIME: 4 TO 10 MINUTES

1 pound green beans, trimmed
¼ cup water
1 tablespoon chopped fresh basil

1 tablespoon chopped fresh parsley
 Lemon wedges

Combine the beans and water in a 2-quart casserole. Cover tightly and cook on HIGH for 4 to 10 minutes, or until the desired doneness is reached, stirring twice. Sprinkle with the herbs and serve with a lemon wedge.

◆ *For 1 Serving:* Cook ¼ pound trimmed green beans with 1 tablespoon water in a 1-quart casserole or 8-ounce oval ramekin. Cover tightly and cook on HIGH for 1½ to 3 minutes, or until the desired doneness is reached, stirring once. Sprinkle with 1 teaspoon each freshly chopped basil and parsley. Serve with a lemon wedge.

Nectarine Pinwheels with Lemon Cream

SERVINGS: 4 ◆ 77 CALORIES PER SERVING

1 pound ripe nectarines, pitted and cut into ¼-inch slices
½ cup low-fat plain yogurt

2 teaspoons sugar
1 teaspoon grated lemon peel

Arrange one-quarter of the nectarines on each plate, fanning them out in a pinwheel.

Combine the remaining ingredients together in a small bowl. Blend well. Spoon 2 tablespoons of the cream into the center of each pinwheel. Chill or serve immediately.

This entire meal is served chilled, so we suggest that you prepare it early in the day or, better yet, make it the night before.

CHILLED MINTED TOMATO SOUP

SHRIMP AND PINEAPPLE SALAD

WHOLE WHEAT MELBA TOASTS (4, 64 CALORIES)

RASPBERRY SORBET WITH FRESH BERRIES
OR FRESH RASPBERRIES (1 CUP, 70 CALORIES)

Menu

8

374 calories
per serving

Plan of action

30 MINUTES BEFORE SERVING IF SPEED CHILLING

1. Cook the shrimp and chill it.
2. Prepare the sorbet and freeze it.

3. Prepare the soup and chill it.
4. Put the salad together.

Chilled Minted Tomato Soup

SERVINGS: 4 ◆ 51 CALORIES PER 1-CUP SERVING

Mint gives a surprising fresh taste to this tomato soup and with no cooking at all.

4 cups tomato juice
2 teaspoons lemon juice
  Few dashes hot pepper sauce

4 thin lemon slices
4 teaspoons chopped fresh mint

Combine the tomato juice, lemon juice, and hot pepper sauce in a small pitcher and chill until serving time.

To serve: Divide between 4 soup bowls. Place a lemon slice in the center of each bowl and sprinkle each with 1 teaspoon chopped mint on top.

Shrimp and Pineapple Salad

SERVINGS: 4 ◆ 170 CALORIES PER 1-CUP SERVING ◆ COOKING TIME: 3 TO 5 MINUTES

1 pound medium shrimp
1 tablespoon lemon juice
2 cups fresh pineapple chunks, or 1 20-ounce can pineapple chunks in their own unsweetened juices, drained
½ cup Mock Sour Cream (page 289)

2 tablespoons chopped chives or green onion tops
1 teaspoon grated lemon peel
4 cups washed and dried lettuce leaves (red leaf or oakleaf is nice)

Place the shrimp around the outer rim of a 9-inch pie plate. Sprinkle with lemon juice. Cover tightly and cook on HIGH for 3 to 5 minutes, or until the shrimp are pink and cooked through, but still tender. Chill for at least 1 hour or speed chill in the freezer for 20 to 30 minutes.

Peel the chilled shrimp and slice them into ½-inch pieces. Toss with the pineapple, sour cream, chives or green onion, and lemon peel.

To serve: Arrange the lettuce leaves on a dinner plate and mound 1 cup shrimp salad in the center of each plate. Serve each portion with 4 whole wheat melba toasts.

Variation:

Shrimp Salad in Cantaloupe: Substitute 2 small chilled cantaloupes, cut in half and seeded, for the lettuce, spooning 1 cup of the shrimp salad into each melon half. Add 50 calories per serving.

◆ *Tip:* Save the reserved pineapple juice and freeze for ice cubes for a Hawaiian Bubbler summer drink (page 87).

Raspberry Sorbet with Fresh Berries

MAKES: 2 CUPS ◆ 70 CALORIES PER 2-SCOOP SERVING (½ CUP), PLUS 19 CALORIES FOR ¼ CUP FRESH RASPBERRIES (OPTIONAL) ◆ COOKING TIME: 1 MINUTE

1 12-ounce bag frozen unsweetened raspberries
1 tablespoon sugar
¼ cup low-fat plain yogurt

1 tablespoon Triple Sec or concentrated orange juice
1 cup fresh raspberries (optional)

Defrost the berries on HIGH for 35 seconds to 1 minute, or until the berries will separate easily. Pour the berries into the bowl of a food processor or blender and cut into very small chunks. Add the sugar, yogurt, and Triple Sec or juice. Process until smooth. Serve as is, or freeze until solid.

Garnish each ½-cup serving with ¼ cup fresh berries.

◆ *Tip:* If the puree is too solid after being frozen, heat it in the microwave on LOW for 1 to 2 minutes.

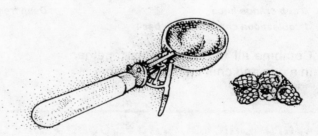

Menu

9

*458 calories
per serving*

When you are in a real hurry, this is an extremely simple menu to prepare.

TOMATO-ORANGE SOUP

WARM CHICKEN WITH AVOCADO AND CANTALOUPE SALAD

FROZEN STRAWBERRY DELIGHT (PAGE 47) OR
SLICED STRAWBERRIES WITH CARDAMOM (PAGE 107)

Plan of action

20 MINUTES BEFORE SERVING

1. Cook the chicken.
2. Mix up the soup and chill it.
3. Assemble the salad.

4. Serve the soup and then the salad.
5. Prepare the dessert right before serving.

Tomato-Orange Soup

SERVINGS: 1 ◆ 68 CALORIES PER 1-CUP SERVING

A soup that is full of vitamin C, this recipe represents a 1-cup serving. Simply repeat the procedure for each additional cup.

¾ cup tomato juice
¼ cup orange juice
1 tablespoon chopped fresh basil

Dash cayenne pepper
Dash freshly ground black pepper

Combine all the ingredients together
in a cup and chill until serving time.

Warm Chicken with Avocado and Cantaloupe Salad

SERVINGS: 4 ◆ 367 CALORIES PER SERVING ◆ COOKING TIME: 5 TO 8 MINUTES

This is a unique chicken salad that combines a sweet cantaloupe, a creamy avocado, a sprinkling of salty capers, and the slight tartness of lime. Walnuts give the whole mixture a crunch.

106

2 **whole chicken breasts (about 1 pound),**
   split in half
5 **tablespoons lime juice**
1 **cantaloupe**
1 **avocado (about 1 pound)**

1 **bunch watercress**
¼ **cup capers**
¼ **cup chopped walnuts**
   Freshly ground black pepper

Place the chicken in a 9-inch pie plate, with the thicker sections to the outside. Sprinkle with 1 tablespoon lime juice. Cover with wax paper and cook on HIGH for 3 minutes. Turn over, placing less-cooked sections to the outside. Cover again and cook on HIGH for 2 to 4 minutes more, or until cooked through and tender. Let stand, covered, for 10 minutes. (As the chicken cools it will be easier to slice.)

While the chicken is standing, quarter the cantaloupe and remove the seeds and rind. Cut each quarter into 6 long pieces. Do the same with the avocado.

After the chicken has stood for 10 minutes, slice each breast in half, lengthwise, and then thinly slice each quarter into 6 strips.

To serve: Divide the watercress between 4 plates, then arrange alternate slices of melon, chicken, and avocado in a circle on top around the outside of the plate. Sprinkle the 4 plates evenly with the capers, walnuts, and the remaining 4 tablespoons lime juice. Sprinkle with pepper.

Sliced Strawberries with Cardamom

SERVINGS: 4 ◆ 23 CALORIES PER ½-CUP SERVING

This dessert may be served in place of Frozen Strawberry Delight to save time and a few calories.

2 **cups sliced strawberries**
   Dash ground cardamom

Sprinkle each serving of strawberries with a little cardamom.

Menu

10

*363 calories
per serving*

CHILLED MUSHROOM SOUP

CLAMS IN TOMATO SAUCE WITH ''ZUCCHINI PASTA''

ITALIAN BREAD (1 SLICE, 75 CALORIES)

INDIVIDUAL CHERRY ''CLAFOUTI''

Plan of action

1. Make the soup and chill it.
2. While the soup is cooking, prepare the dessert for cooking.
3. Cook the dessert. Meanwhile, prepare the first step of the tomato sauce. Speed chill the soup.

25 TO 30 MINUTES BEFORE SERVING

4. Cook the tomato sauce and clams. Meanwhile, cut up the zucchini.
5. Cook the zucchini during the standing time of the tomatoes and clams.
6. Serve the soup.

Chilled Mushroom Soup

SERVINGS: 4 ◆ 47 CALORIES PER ¾-CUP SERVING ◆ COOKING TIME: 4 TO 5 MINUTES

1 **medium onion, chopped**
6 **ounces sliced mushrooms (2 cups)**
1½ **cups chicken broth**
½ **cup low-fat plain yogurt**

1 **tablespoon chopped fresh tarragon, or 1 teaspoon dried**
Dash freshly ground black pepper
Pinch cayenne pepper

Place the onion in a 1-quart casserole. Cover tightly and cook on HIGH for 1 minute, or until tender. Stir in the mushrooms. Cook, uncovered, on HIGH for 3 to 4 minutes, or until the mushrooms are steamed. Spoon the mushrooms and onions into a blender or processor and puree until very fine.

Stir in the yogurt and mix well. Stir in the remaining ingredients and speed chill for 20 to 30 minutes in the freezer until serving time.

◆ *For 1 Serving:* Place 1 tablespoon chopped onion in a 1-quart casserole. Cook on HIGH for 30 seconds. Stir in ½ cup chopped mushrooms. Cook on HIGH for 1 to 1½ minutes. Pour into the food processor with ⅓ cup broth and 2 tablespoons low-fat yogurt. Stir in 1 teaspoon chopped tarragon and black and red pepper to taste.

"Speed chilling" is the process of chilling something in a hurry, and that can come in handy for summer menus. Speed chilling only works, though, if you have a space ready in your freezer, or if you have something, like coffee, that can be moved out for a time, without any harm coming to it. Here are some suggested speed-chilling methods for various foods:

▲▲▲▲▲▲▲▲▲▲▲▲

- ◆ **Speed chill soups in the original cooking dish for 20 to 30 minutes, stirring them once.**
- ◆ **Speed chill cooked chicken and fish for 15 minutes before making into salads, spreading them out and turning them over once.**
- ◆ **Speed chill shrimp or scallops for salads for 30 minutes, spreading them out and stirring them once.**

▼▼▼▼▼▼▼▼▼▼▼▼

Clams in Tomato Sauce with "Zucchini Pasta"

SERVINGS: 4 ◆ 173 CALORIES PER 6 CLAMS, 1 CUP ZUCCHINI PASTA, AND ¾ CUP SAUCE
◆ COOKING TIME: 14 TO 19 MINUTES

1 teaspoon full-flavored olive oil
1 garlic clove, minced
2 tablespoons chopped onion
2 cups chopped, peeled, and seeded fresh or canned plum tomatoes, undrained
2 tablespoons tomato paste

½ cup chopped fresh basil
¼ teaspoon red pepper flakes
24 littleneck clams, scrubbed
4 small (¼-pound) zucchini
¼ cup grated Parmesan cheese

Combine the oil, garlic, and onion in a 3-quart casserole. Cover tightly and cook on HIGH for 1 minute. Add the tomatoes, tomato paste, ¼ cup basil, and pepper flakes. Cover again and cook on HIGH for 3 minutes; stir.

Add the clams. Cover again and cook on HIGH for 7 to 11 minutes, or until the clams have opened, stirring after 4 minutes. Let stand, covered, for 4 minutes. Discard any unopened clams.

While the clams are cooking, thinly slice the zucchini lengthwise with a grater or mandolin, to resemble spaghetti. Put the zucchini around the outer rim of a 10-inch pie plate, leaving the center open. Cover with wax paper. Cook on HIGH for 3 to 4 minutes, or until tender-crisp.

To serve: Divide the cooked zucchini between 4 large soup bowls. Sprinkle the zucchini with 1 tablespoon grated Parmesan cheese. Arrange 6 clams on top of each bowl of zucchini, and spoon the sauce over all. Sprinkle with the remaining ¼ cup basil.

◆ *For 1 Serving:* Place ¼ teaspoon olive oil, ¼ teaspoon minced garlic and 2 teaspoons chopped onion in a 1-quart casserole. Cook on HIGH for 35 seconds. Stir in ½ cup chopped peeled tomatoes, 2 teaspoons tomato paste, 2 tablespoons chopped fresh basil, and a pinch red pepper flakes. Cover tightly and cook on HIGH for 2 minutes; stir. Add 6 clams. Cover tightly and cook on HIGH for 2 to 4 minutes, or until the clams are opened.

Place 1 zucchini, sliced lengthwise, in a soup bowl, leaving the center open. Cover with wax paper and cook on HIGH for 1 to 2 minutes. Sprinkle with 1 tablespoon Parmesan cheese. Spoon the clams, tomato sauce, and 1 tablespoon chopped basil on top. For 2 servings, double the 1-serving ingredients and cooking times.

A mandolin is not a musical instrument (in this case) but a kitchen tool which somewhat resembles one. It is a long, flat grater that can be purchased for about $12 and which makes longer, thinner strips out of vegetables than any food processor or grater is able to. The advantage is that as the long strips pile up on your plate, the amount of food seems to quadruple. For dieters, we think it is worth the investment.

Individual Cherry "Clafouti"

SERVINGS: 4 ◆ 68 CALORIES PER 1-CUP SERVING ◆ COOKING TIME: 7 TO 9 MINUTES

"Clafouti" is traditionally a French dessert where a pancake-type batter of milk, eggs, sugar, and flour is poured over cherries before baking. In this version, we pare down the ingredients to make it more custardy and light.

½ pound sweet cherries, washed and pitted
1 egg, beaten
1 tablespoon sugar
¼ cup low-fat plain yogurt
1 tablespoon Kirsch or ½ teaspoon vanilla extract

Divide the cherries between four 6- or 7-ounce custard cups. Cook on HIGH for 1 minute.

Combine the remaining ingredients together in a small bowl, mixing well. Spoon equal amounts over the cherries, about 2 tablespoons for each. Place the custard cups in a circle in the microwave, leaving at least a 1-inch space between them. Cover the tops with wax paper. Cook on MEDIUM for 6 to 8 minutes, or until set, repositioning after 3 minutes. Serve warm or chilled.

◆ *For Fewer Servings:* This recipe doesn't divide easily, so make the whole thing and serve the remainder chilled for breakfast with a piece of whole wheat toast, or as another dinner dessert.

CHILLED STRAWBERRY SOUP

GRILLED CORNISH HENS WITH
APRICOT-RASPBERRY SAUCE

SEASONAL VEGETABLE PLATTER

MELON BALLS WITH FRESH MINT

Menu

11

*358 calories
per serving*

Plan of action

1. Prepare and chill the soup.
2. Cook the apricots. Meanwhile, prepare the hens for cooking.
3. Place the hens in the microwave and preheat the grill.
4. While the hens are cooking, make the fruit sauce and prepare the vegetable platter.

40 MINUTES BEFORE SERVING

5. While the hens are grilling, cook the vegetable platter and prepare the melons. Cover the hens with foil.
6. Serve the soup.

Chilled Strawberry Soup

SERVINGS: 4 ◆ 79 CALORIES PER ½-CUP SERVING

1 pint strawberries, trimmed and cut in half;
   plus 4 nice large berries for garnish, sliced
1 cup low-fat plain yogurt
2 tablespoons dry white wine

1 tablespoon sugar
Dash freshly grated nutmeg
Mint sprigs

Place the strawberries, yogurt, wine, and sugar in the bowl of a blender or food processor. Puree until smooth. Chill until serving time.

   To serve: Pour ½ cup soup into glass bowls or stemmed ice glasses and top with the reserved strawberries, the nutmeg, and mint.

◆ *For 1 Serving:* Combine ¼ pint (about ½ cup) halved strawberries, ¼ cup yogurt, 2 teaspoons white wine, and 1 teaspoon sugar in a food processor. Puree and chill. Serve, topped with 1 sliced strawberry, nutmeg, and a mint sprig.

111

Grilled Cornish Hens with Apricot-Raspberry Sauce

SERVINGS: 4 ◆ 166 CALORIES PER ½ HEN WITH 2 TABLESPOONS SAUCE AND ¼ CUP BERRIES
◆ COOKING TIME: 18 TO 20 MINUTES MICROWAVE, PLUS 8 TO 10 MINUTES GRILLING.

2 1½-pound Cornish hens, split in half
  lengthwise
  Freshly ground black pepper
½ pound ripe apricots, pitted and halved

1 tablespoon raspberry vinegar
1 cup raspberries or blackberries

Preheat the barbecue grill.

Place the hens, skin side down, in a 2-quart rectangular dish, with the thicker portions to the outside. Cover with wax paper. Cook on HIGH for 16 minutes, or until just about done, turning the hens over and placing the less-cooked areas to the outside after 8 minutes.

Sprinkle the chicken with pepper and grill for 4 to 5 minutes per side, or until the outside reaches the desired crispness.

Place the apricots in a 1-quart casserole. Cover tightly. Cook on HIGH for 2 to 4 minutes, or until tender. Spoon them into the bowl of a blender or processor. Add the raspberry vinegar and puree.

To serve: Place half a hen in the center of each plate. Spoon 2 tablespoons sauce around the outside of the hen and sprinkle ¼ cup berries onto the sauce.

◆ *For 2 Servings:* Split one 1½-pound Cornish hen. Place it skin side down in a pie or cake plate. Cover with wax paper and cook on HIGH for 6 to 8 minutes, turning it over after 3 minutes. Grill for 4 to 5 minutes on each side.

Variation:

Grilled Cornish Hens with Blueberries: Substitute 1 cup blueberries for the raspberries, and 1 tablespoon blueberry vinegar for the raspberry vinegar to make Apricot-Blueberry Sauce. 5 calories.

Seasonal Vegetable Platter

SERVINGS: 4 ◆ 58 CALORIES PER SERVING ◆ COOKING TIME: 5 TO 7 MINUTES

2 large carrots, cut into ¼-inch slices
1 cup green beans, trimmed and broken in half
1 small yellow summer squash, cut into ¼-inch slices
1 small zucchini, cut into ¼-inch slices

1 large tomato, quartered
2 tablespoons water
1 tablespoon chopped fresh parsley
1 tablespoon chopped fresh basil or chives
4 lemon wedges

Arrange the carrots in a circle around the outer rim of a 10- to 12-inch round microwaveproof platter, overlapping them slightly. Make an inner circle of green beans, then another circle inside that of alternating green and yellow squash. Place the tomato in the center.

Sprinkle with the water. Cover tightly and cook on HIGH for 5 to 7 minutes, or until the desired doneness is reached, rotating once. Let stand, covered, for 2 minutes. Sprinkle with the fresh herbs and serve with lemon wedges.

◆ *For 1 Serving:* Reduce the vegetable amounts to one-quarter and arrange them as described in the basic recipe on a 6- or 8-inch microwaveproof plate. Add 1 teaspoon water. Cover tightly and cook on HIGH for 2 to 3 minutes. Sprinkle with 2 teaspoons chopped parsley, basil, or a combination. Serve with a lemon wedge.

◆ *Tip:* If only one person is dieting, it is best to buy your vegetable combinations at a salad bar. This will keep your refrigerator inventory down and allows for more variety.

Variation:

Chilled Vegetable Platter with Mustard Vinaigrette: Pour ¼ cup Mustard Vinaigrette (page 288) over the vegetable platter after cooking. Cover again and chill for 30 minutes, or until ready to serve. Add 17 calories per serving.

Melon Balls with Fresh Mint

SERVINGS: 4 ◆ 55 CALORIES PER 1-CUP SERVING

4 cups plain or mixed melon balls
  Mint leaves

Serve in a bowl with mint.

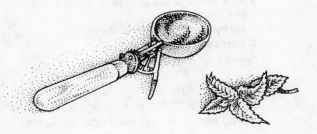

Menu

12

440 calories
per serving

CHILLED CURRIED SUMMER SQUASH SOUP

TUNA PROVENÇALE

MIXED GREENS WITH MUSTARD VINAIGRETTE

VERY BERRY ROLL

Plan of action

25 TO 30 MINUTES BEFORE SERVING

1. Mix the berries with the liqueur to marinate them.
2. Prepare and cook the soup.
3. While the soup is cooking, start the preparations for the fish. Chill the soup.
4. Prepare and cook the fish.
5. While the fish is cooking, prepare the salad.
6. Serve the soup, then the fish and salad.
7. Cook the dessert roll right before serving.

Chilled Curried Summer Squash Soup

SERVINGS: 4 ◆ 35 CALORIES PER 1-CUP SERVING ◆ COOKING TIME: 3 TO 5 MINUTES

2 cups sliced yellow squash or zucchini or a combination
1 teaspoon chopped fresh thyme
2 cups chicken broth
½ cup skim milk

1 teaspoon curry powder
1 tablespoon lemon juice
4 thyme sprigs or squash blossoms

Combine the squash and chopped thyme in a 2-quart casserole. Cover tightly and cook on HIGH for 3 to 5 minutes, or until tender. Pour into the bowl of a food processor or blender and puree until smooth. Add the remaining ingredients and blend. Chill until serving time.

To serve: Garnish each bowl with a thyme sprig or squash blossom.

◆ *For 1 Serving:* Combine ½ cup sliced yellow squash or zucchini with ¼ teaspoon chopped fresh thyme in a 1-quart casserole. Cover tightly and cook on HIGH for 2 to 3 minutes, or until tender. Puree in a food processor or blender. Add ¼ cup chicken broth, 2 tablespoons skim milk, ¼ teaspoon curry powder, and 1 teaspoon lemon juice; blend. Chill before serving.

Tuna Provençale

SERVINGS: 4 ◆ 244 CALORIES PER SERVING ◆ COOKING TIME: 14 TO 16 MINUTES

This dish is equally good served warm or cold. We have taken it on a picnic and served it tucked into a pita bread and the results were marvelous and virtually mess-free.

1 tablespoon full-flavored olive oil
2 garlic cloves, minced
2 green onions, thinly sliced
1 cup peeled, seeded, and chopped fresh or canned plum tomatoes, undrained
2 tablespoons lemon juice
1 pimento, rinsed and finely chopped
2 tablespoons chopped fresh parsley

Dash freshly ground black pepper
¼ cup chopped fresh basil
1 pound tuna, swordfish, or shark steak, trimmed and cut into 4-ounce pieces
1 green or red bell pepper, seeded and cut lengthwise into ¼-inch-thick strips
1 yellow bell pepper, seeded and cut lengthwise into ¼-inch-thick strips

Combine the oil, garlic, and green onions in a 9-inch pie plate. Cook on HIGH for 1 minute. Stir in the tomatoes, lemon juice, pimento, parsley, black pepper, and 2 tablespoons basil. Cook on HIGH for 3 minutes. Stir well and place the fish steaks on top of the sauce around the outer rim of the plate, with the thicker areas to the outside.

Cover with wax paper and cook on MEDIUM for 5 minutes; turn over and place the lesser cooked areas to the outside. Cover again and cook on HIGH for 5 to 7 minutes, or until the fish flakes under the pressure of a fork. Let stand, covered, for 5 minutes.

To serve: Place 1 steak on each plate and spoon ¼ of the sauce on top. Divide the remaining 2 tablespoons chopped basil between the fish and arrange one-quarter of the pepper strips on each plate.

◆ *For 1 Serving:* Combine 1 teaspoon olive oil, 1 small minced garlic clove, and ½ chopped green onion in an 8-ounce oval ramekin. Cook on HIGH for 30 seconds. Stir in ¼ cup chopped peeled tomatoes, ½ chopped pimento, 1½ teaspoons each lemon juice, parsley, and basil, and a pinch black pepper. Cook on HIGH for 1 to 2 minutes. Place a 4-ounce fish steak on top. Cover with wax paper and cook on MEDIUM for 3 to 5 minutes, or until done. Arrange one-quarter sliced red, green, or yellow pepper on top.

Mixed Greens with Mustard Vinaigrette

SERVINGS: 4 ◆ 44 CALORIES PER 1-CUP SERVING

4 cups mixed salad greens
½ cup Mustard Vinaigrette (page 288)

Combine all the ingredients in a medium bowl. Toss and serve.

A salad dressing will stretch farther if you toss it with the greens in a large bowl, rather than serving it in dollops on top of individual plates of greens.

Just make sure that the greens are well dried before preparing the salad; a lettuce spinner is great for this. If water remains on the leaves, it will repel the oil, and the dressing will end up on the bottom of the bowl.

Very Berry Roll

SERVINGS: 4 ◆ 116 CALORIES PER SERVING ◆ COOKING TIME: 1 TO 3 MINUTES

1 cup blueberries
1 cup raspberries
2 tablespoons raspberry or blackberry brandy
2 eggs, separated
¼ teaspoon cream of tartar
1 tablespoon sugar
1 tablespoon water
1 teaspoon grated orange peel

Combine the berries and liqueur in a medium bowl. Toss well and set aside.

In another medium mixing bowl combine the egg whites and cream of tartar. Beat until stiff but not dry. Combine the yolks, sugar, water, and orange peel in a small bowl, beating together well. Gently fold the yolk mixture into the whites.

Pour into a 9-inch pie plate and spread to smooth the top. Cook on HIGH for 1½ to 2½ minutes, or until set.

To serve: Spoon 1 cup of the liqueured berries down the center, in a 3-inch row. Fold each side of the egg soufflé over the berries in envelope fashion. Cut into 4 serving pieces and, using a spatula, lift the pieces onto individual serving plates. Divide the remaining 1 cup berries between the 4 plates.

◆ For Fewer Servings: This is a difficult recipe to cut in half, so if you've been good this week, indulge in a second piece and save the rest for tomorrow. Even chilled, it is delicious.

WATERMELON CRUSH

WARM SEAFOOD, VEGETABLE, AND RICE SALAD

ALMOND AMARETTO–STUFFED PEACHES

Plan of action

30 MINUTES BEFORE SERVING

1. Cook the rice.
2. While the rice is cooking, chop and prepare the additions and make and chill the soup.
3. Prepare and cook the peaches.
4. Serve the soup, during the standing time of the rice.

Watermelon Crush

SERVINGS: 4 ◆ 43 CALORIES PER ½-CUP SERVING

This is an icy pink mixture that is sipped like a soup. A grinding of black pepper is the perfect flavor and color accent.

1 2-pound watermelon
2 tablespoons fresh lime juice
 Dash freshly ground black pepper
4 thin lime slices

Remove the rind from the melon. Cut the melon into 1- or 2-inch cubes, removing the seeds as you go. Combine the watermelon cubes and lime juice in the bowl of a food processor or blender and puree until finely chopped but not pureed. Chill until serving time.

To serve: Pour into large goblets or soup bowls and top with black pepper and lime slices.

Warm Seafood, Vegetable, and Rice Salad

SERVINGS: 4 ◆ 305 CALORIES PER 2-CUP SERVING ◆ COOKING TIME: 11 TO 15 MINUTES

This is wonderful to pack for a meal at the beach or an evening summer concert because the salad is tasty cold or warm. It is visually beautiful, too, with the pink sea legs and red and green vegetables against a background of white rice.

1 tablespoon full-flavored olive oil
2 tablespoons finely chopped onion
¾ cup long-grain rice
1½ cups chicken broth
¼ pound snow peas, trimmed and cut into 1½-inch pieces

2 green onions, thinly sliced
1 cup thinly sliced red radishes
1 medium cucumber, peeled and thinly sliced
2 tablespoons chopped fresh parsley
1 pound sea legs, cut into 1-inch pieces

Combine the oil and onion in a 3-quart casserole. Cook on HIGH for 35 seconds to 1 minute, or until the onion is tender. Add the rice and stir well to coat with oil. Pour in the broth. Cover tightly and cook on HIGH for 5 to 7 minutes, or until boiling, then on MEDIUM for 6 to 8 minutes, until rice is tender and most of the liquid is absorbed.

Stir in the remaining ingredients. Cover again and let stand for 5 minutes. (During this time the vegetables are steamed to tender-crisp and the seafood warms through.)

Serve warm.

◆ For 2 Servings: If you only need a single serving, make 2 and serve the remainder the next day for lunch.

Combine 1 teaspoon oil and 1 tablespoon chopped onion in a 2-quart casserole on HIGH for 30 seconds. Stir in ⅓ cup and 2 tablespoons rice to coat with oil. Stir in ¾ cup chicken broth. Cook on HIGH for 2 to 3 minutes to boil and then on MEDIUM for 4 to 6 minutes, or until the rice is tender and most of the liquid is absorbed. Stir in 2 ounces snow peas, cut into pieces; 1 thinly sliced green onion; ½ cup thinly sliced radishes; ½ medium cucumber, peeled and thinly sliced; 1 tablespoon chopped fresh parsley, and ½ pound sea leg pieces. Let stand, covered, for 5 minutes.

Variation:

Chilled Seafood, Vegetable, and Rice Salad: Combine 2 tablespoons fresh lemon juice and 2 teaspoons Dijon-type mustard and fold into the warm rice salad. Chill the salad for 1 hour or more. Serve on greens. 4 calories.

Almond Amaretto–Stuffed Peaches

SERVINGS: 4 ◆ 117 CALORIES PER SERVING ◆ COOKING TIME: 3 TO 5 MINUTES

2 large ripe peaches, halved and pitted
4 amaretti or almond macaroons, crushed
1 tablespoon sugar
1 tablespoon chopped almonds

1 tablespoon amaretto, or ½ teaspoon almond extract
1 teaspoon grated lemon peel

Spoon out 1 tablespoon pulp from each peach half. Finely chop the peach pulp. Combine the pulp with the remaining ingredients in a small bowl.

Spoon the peach mixture into the peach halves and place the halves around the outer rim of a 9-inch pie plate or microwaveproof serving plate. Cover with wax paper and cook on HIGH for 3 to 5 minutes, until the peaches are fork tender, repositioning the peaches and rotating the dish halfway through cooking. Serve at room temperature.

◆ *For 2 Servings:* Cut 1 large peach in half, pit it and remove and chop 2 tablespoons pulp from it. Combine the peach pulp with 1½ teaspoons each crushed amaretti, sugar, chopped almonds, and amaretto; and ½ teaspoon grated lemon peel. Spoon the filling into the peach halves and place them on 2 microwaveproof plates. Place them in the microwave, leaving at least a 1-inch space between them. Cover with wax paper and cook on HIGH for 1½ to 2½ minutes.

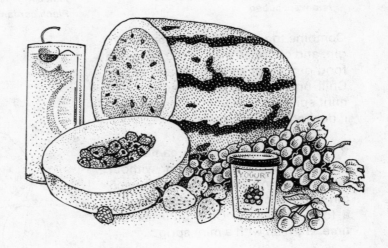

SPIKED MINTED MELON SOUP

VEAL-STUFFED EGGPLANT

1 SLICE ITALIAN BREAD OR 2 BREADSTICKS
(75 CALORIES)

PEACHES WITH SPICED CREAM

Plan of action

1. Prepare and cook the eggplant.
2. While the eggplant is cooking, make the soup and dessert and

30 MINUTES BEFORE SERVING

chill them until serving time.
3. Serve the soup during the standing time of the eggplant.

Spiked Minted Melon Soup

SERVINGS: 4 ◆ 62 CALORIES PER GENEROUS ½-CUP SERVING

½ *cantaloupe, rind and seeds removed,*
cubed
1 *pound watermelon, rind and seeds*
removed, cubed

2 *tablespoons gin*
2 *tablespoons chopped fresh mint, plus 4*
mint sprigs for garnish
Pinch cardamom (optional)

Combine the cantaloupe, watermelon, gin, and chopped mint in the bowl of a food processor or blender and puree. Chill until serving time. Garnish with mint sprigs and a pinch of cardamom, if desired.

◆ *For 1 Serving:* Cube ¼ cantaloupe and ¼ pound watermelon without seeds and rind, and 1 teaspoon each gin and chopped fresh mint. Puree in a food processor. Chill until serving time. Garnish with a mint sprig.

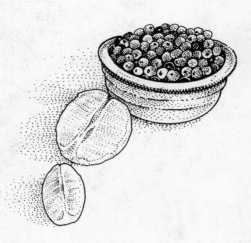

Veal-Stuffed Eggplant

SERVINGS: 4 ◆ 250 CALORIES PER ½ EGGPLANT WITH 1 CUP STUFFING ◆ COOKING TIME: 22 TO 23 MINUTES

If you don't wish to stuff the eggplant shells, serve the stuffing alongside, warm or chilled.

2 medium (1-pound) eggplants, cut in half lengthwise
1 tablespoon lemon juice
2 garlic cloves, minced
2 tablespoons chopped onion
1 green pepper, coarsely chopped
1 pound ground veal (see Note)

½ cup chopped fresh basil
1 pound ripe or canned tomatoes, seeded and cut into 1-inch cubes, undrained
1 tablespoon grated Parmesan cheese
½ teaspoon grated nutmeg
½ teaspoon paprika
¼ teaspoon black pepper

Using a grapefruit knife, scoop out the flesh from the eggplant halves, leaving a ¼-inch shell. Rub the shells with lemon juice, to keep them from discoloring, and set them aside. Chop the eggplant flesh into ½-inch pieces; set aside.

Combine the garlic, onion, and green pepper in a 2-quart casserole. Cover with wax paper and cook on HIGH for 2 to 3 minutes. Stir in the ground veal. Cook, uncovered, on HIGH for 5 minutes, stirring after 3 minutes.

Stir in the cubed eggplant, ¼ cup basil, the tomatoes, Parmesan, nutmeg, paprika, and black pepper. Stir well to blend. Cover with wax paper and cook on HIGH for 10 minutes, stirring after 5 minutes, or until well blended and the flavors have developed. Add more nutmeg or paprika to taste, if desired.

Divide the cooked mixture between the 4 eggplant shells. Position the shells around the outer rim of a 12-inch round microwaveproof dish, leaving the center open. Sprinkle the remaining ¼ cup basil on top. Cover with wax paper and cook on HIGH for 5 minutes. Let them stand, covered, for 5 minutes.

◆ For 2 Servings: Cut 1 medium eggplant in half, and scoop it out, leaving a ¼-inch shell. Rub the shell with 1 teaspoon lemon juice to keep it from discoloring. Cube the flesh and set it aside.

Combine 1 small minced garlic clove, 1 tablespoon chopped onion, and ½ coarsely chopped green pepper in a 1-quart casserole. Cover with wax paper and cook on HIGH for 1 to 2 minutes. Stir in ½ pound ground veal. Cook, uncovered, on HIGH for 2½ minutes, stirring after 1 minute.

Stir in the cubed eggplant, 2 table-

121

spoons chopped basil, ½ pound seeded and cubed tomatoes, 1½ teaspoons Parmesan, ¼ to ⅛ teaspoon nutmeg, ¼ teaspoon paprika, and a dash black pepper. Cover with wax paper and cook on HIGH for 5 minutes, stirring after 5 minutes, or until the flavors have developed. Add more seasonings to taste, if desired.

Divide the mixture between the eggplant shells and place the shells on a microwaveproof plate. Sprinkle the remaining 2 tablespoons chopped basil on top. Cover with wax paper and cook on HIGH for 2½ minutes. Let stand, covered, for a few minutes.

Note: You can substitute ground turkey for the veal.

Some experts say that a diet that revolves around high-fiber foods such as fruits, vegetables, and whole grains is more satisfying than one that relies heavily on dairy products and desserts. This is because high-fiber foods take longer to eat and take up more space in your stomach and small intestine so that you consume less. This can be a boon to weight loss. When you crave that gooey, sticky dessert, reach for a juicy ripe nectarine or peach instead. Your body will feel satisfied for longer and with fewer calories.

Peaches with Spiced Cream

SERVINGS: 4 ◆ 73 CALORIES PER SERVING

½ cup low-fat cottage cheese
1 tablespoon sugar
½ teaspoon vanilla extract
¼ teaspoon ground ginger

¼ teaspoon grated nutmeg
1 pound peaches, pitted and cut into ¼-inch slices

Combine all the ingredients, except the peaches, in a small bowl. Place a dollop of the cream in the center of each of 4 dessert dishes. Arrange the peaches in spoke fashion around the cream.

This is delicious on a cool summer evening. Cooking unpeeled shrimp in the broth not only increases the flavor of the broth, but will slow you down at the dinner table. Place an extra bowl on the table to collect the shrimp peelings.

SHRIMP IN SUMMER HERB BROTH

ITALIAN BREAD (1 SLICE, 75 CALORIES)

CRISPY CUCUMBER SALAD

PLUM ''ICE CREAM'' WITH BERRIES

Menu

15

350 calories
per serving

Plan of action

10 MINUTES THE NIGHT BEFORE
20 MINUTES BEFORE SERVING

1. Make the dessert the night before and freeze it.
2. On the serving day, make the salad and chill it.

3. Cook shrimp in broth and serve it.
4. Serve the salad.

Shrimp in Summer Herb Broth

SERVINGS: 4 ◆ 135 CALORIES PER 10 SHRIMP AND ⅓ TO ½ CUP BROTH ◆ COOKING TIME: 9 TO 11 MINUTES

This is the soup and main course, all in one.

1 cup chicken broth or light clam broth
3 ounces dry white wine
2 garlic cloves, minced
2 tablespoons chopped fresh parsley
2 tablespoons fresh lemon juice
1 teaspoon chopped fresh ginger

½ teaspoon paprika
¼ teaspoon cayenne pepper (optional)
4 sprigs fresh basil, or ¼ teaspoon dried
4 sprigs fresh thyme, or ¼ teaspoon dried
1 pound medium raw shrimp (about 40)

Combine all the ingredients, except the shrimp, in a 2-quart casserole. Cover tightly and cook on HIGH for 3 minutes, or until boiling. Stir in the shrimp. Cover again and cook on HIGH for 4 minutes; stir to move the shrimp from the outside to the inside. Cover again and cook on HIGH for 2 to 4 minutes more, or until the shrimp are pink.

To serve: Place about 10 shrimp in each soup bowl and pour ⅓ to ½ cup broth on top. Peel the shrimp, dipping them into the broth before eating.

◆ *For 2 Servings:* Even if you only want 1 serving, it is best to make 2 servings and chill the rest for lunch the next day with the Balsamic Peppercorn Sauce (see Sidebar).

Cut the ingredients in half. Combine all but the shrimp in a 1-quart casse-role. Cover tightly and cook on HIGH for 2 minutes, or until boiling. Stir in the shrimp. Cover again and cook on HIGH for 3 to 5 minutes, stirring after 2 minutes.

For 8 servings, double the basic recipe ingredients. Cover and cook the broth for 5 minutes, or until boiling. Stir in the shrimp and cover again, cooking on HIGH for 9 to 12 minutes, stirring after 5 minutes.

BALSAMIC PEPPERCORN SAUCE

MAKES: ¾ CUP ◆ 7 CALORIES PER TABLESPOON

Serve this chilled sauce with any poached chilled shrimp or fish.

¼ cup chopped chives or thinly sliced green onion tops
2 tablespoons chopped fresh parsley
1 tablespoon ground black peppercorns

¼ cup balsamic vinegar or herb vinegar
¼ cup dry white wine

Combine all the ingredients in a small bowl.
Chill until serving time.

BALSAMIC VINEGAR

Balsamic vinegar is not just any wine vinegar. During the cooking of the grapes, the fruit's sugar carmelizes, creating a unique sable color and deep, rich flavor. The liquid is then aged in wooden barrels, where it mellows and becomes more concentrated.

In Italy, when *aceto balsamico* is aged long enough and well enough, it is even served as an after-dinner liqueur. The product sold in this country is more often added in dashes to sauces, salads, and marinades. In these instances, it will add a flurry of vibrant flavor and may eliminate the need for salt.

HERB VINEGAR

MAKES: 4 CUPS ◆ 2 CALORIES PER TABLESPOON

Fresh herbs contain more oils than dried ones and thus are better for flavoring these luscious vinegars. Not only are they tasty, but they make nice gifts because the whole herbs look so attractive in glass jars sealed with corks.

The ratio of herbs to vinegar is about 1 to 4, so that you can make any quantity you want. They are best stored in a warm environment . . . your summer kitchen.

1 cup fresh whole tarragon, fennel, sage, rosemary, chives (when measuring, bend but don't break the herb stems), or 2 garlic cloves

1 quart good-quality cider, red or white wine vinegar

Wash and dry the herbs, or peel the garlic cloves. Divide the herbs equally among glass bottles and then pour in the vinegar. Store at room temperature for 2 to 4 weeks.

Crispy Cucumber Salad

SERVINGS: 4 ◆ 51 CALORIES PER 1-CUP SERVING

1 pound young thin-skinned cucumbers, washed and thinly sliced
1 red bell pepper, diced
1 green bell pepper, diced
¼ cup chopped fresh parsley
1 tablespoon chopped fresh mint (optional)

½ cup low-fat plain yogurt
1 tablespoon lemon juice
½ teaspoon sugar
  Dash cayenne pepper
  Dash freshly ground black pepper

Combine the cucumbers, bell peppers, parsley, and mint, if desired, in a medium bowl. Combine the remaining ingredients in a 1-cup measure and spoon over the cucumbers. Toss the cucumber slices until well coated. Chill until serving time.

Plum "Ice Cream" with Berries

SERVINGS: 4 ◆ 78 CALORIES PER ¼-CUP SERVING, PLUS 11 CALORIES PER ¼ CUP BERRIES ◆ COOKING TIME: 3 TO 4 MINUTES

Here's another one of those fruit "ice creams" that tastes sinfully delicious but is not loaded with calories. We like to make this dessert in the morning or evening before it is to be served, and freeze it for later.

1 pound ripe sweet damson plums
2 tablespoons low-fat plain yogurt
1 tablespoon sugar

½ teaspoon vanilla extract
1 cup blueberries, strawberries, or raspberries

Place the plums in a 1-quart casserole. (The skins give the ice cream its color.) Cover tightly and cook on HIGH for 2½ to 4 minutes, or until tender, stirring after 2 minutes. Place the plums in the bowl of a food processor or blender. Add the yogurt, sugar, and vanilla and puree until smooth.

Spoon the mixture into an ice cube container, with the sections removed. Freeze for 3 to 4 hours. If too hard to serve at this point, spoon the mixture into the processor and whir it quickly to break up the ice crystals.

To serve: Spoon ¼ cup "ice cream" into each of 4 dessert bowls or goblets. Spoon ¼ cup berries on top of each.

This menu is well suited to entertaining since all but the soup can be prepared in advance and chilled.

To entertain 8 people, you will need to double the soup, sauce, and ice cream recipes. Allow yourself about 30 minutes the night before to cook the fish, make the sauces and the ice cream. Allow about 20 minutes to make the soup on the day that you are entertaining.

The fish can be brought out whole, on a platter surrounded by dill or watercress. Or remove the skin and slice the fish into 16 pieces and serve 2 slices on each plate with the sauces spooned on the side or dribbled down the center of the slices.

Add a basket of melba toasts and baguettes to the menu: 1 slice bread or 3 melba toasts will add 65 to 70 calories to your total count.

CORN CHOWDER WITH CHILES

STEAMED WHOLE FISH WITH TWO SAUCES

SUMMER SQUASH SALAD WITH MUSTARD VINAIGRETTE

PEACH "ICE CREAM" OR SUNDAES

Plan of action

30 MINUTES THE NIGHT BEFORE
30 TO 35 MINUTES BEFORE SERVING

1. Early in the day or on the night before, cook the fish and chill it and freeze the peaches if making "Ice Cream."
2. Make the vegetable platter and chill it.
3. Prepare the soup.
4. Cook the soup. Meanwhile, prepare the sauces for the fish.
5. Serve the soup, then the fish.
6. If you haven't made the ice cream, make it now and serve it softer than when frozen.

127

Corn Chowder with Chiles

SERVINGS: 4 ◆ 67 CALORIES PER ¾-CUP SERVING ◆ COOKING TIME: 6 TO 10 MINUTES

1 teaspoon full-flavored olive oil
1 garlic clove, minced
2 tablespoons chopped onion
1 cup fresh or frozen corn

½ jalapeño pepper, seeded and thinly sliced
1 red bell pepper, coarsely chopped
2 cups chicken broth

Combine the oil, garlic, and onion in a 2-quart casserole. Cook on HIGH for 1 minute. Stir in the corn and peppers. Cover tightly and cook on HIGH for 3 to 5 minutes, or until the vegetables are tender-crisp. Pour in the broth. Cover again and cook on HIGH for 3 to 5 minutes, or until heated through.

◆ For 1 Serving: Combine ¼ teaspoon olive oil, 1 small minced garlic clove and 2 teaspoons chopped onion in a 1-quart casserole. Cook on HIGH for 30 seconds. Stir in ¼ cup corn, ¼ jalapeño pepper, chopped, and ¼ red bell pepper, chopped. Cover tightly and cook on HIGH for 1½ to 2 minutes or until cooked through. Stir in ½ cup broth. Cover tightly and cook on HIGH for 1 minute or until heated through.

For 8 servings, double the basic recipe ingredient amounts and cooking times.

Variation:

For extra zip, add 1 tablespoon Fresh Tomato Salsa (page 43) to each serving. Add 4 calories.

Steamed Whole Fish with Two Sauces

SERVINGS: 8 ◆ 149 CALORIES PER 4-OUNCE SERVING OF FISH AND ¼ CUP (2 TABLESPOONS EACH) SAUCES ◆ COOKING TIME: 20 TO 25 MINUTES

One recipe is enough for dinner tonight and the fish salad the next night. You can make just one of the sauces for serving 4, or both if you want a variety, saving the remainder for a later meal.

1 3-pound bluefish, tuna, mullet, or salmon, cleaned
2 tablespoons dry white wine
2 tablespoons lemon juice
4 whole green onions, trimmed

2 bunches fresh dill or watercress
1 cup Salsa with Cilantro (page 44) and 1 cup Dill Cucumber Sauce (see below), or double the amount of just one sauce

Place the fish on a large microwave-proof platter or 3-quart (13"-×-9") dish. Sprinkle the cavity with white wine and lemon juice and insert the green onions.

Cover the eye with a strip of aluminum foil. Cover tightly and cook on MEDIUM for 20 to 25 minutes, or until the fish flakes in the thickest part under the pressure of a fork.

To serve: Remove the foil and present the fish whole, warm or chilled, on a platter (if the cooking platter is suitable all the better). Tuck in fresh dill or watercress around the outer rim and serve with the chilled sauces.

◆ *For 4 Servings:* Place a 1-pound thick fillet in a 2-quart dish. Sprinkle with 1 tablespoon each lemon juice and wine. Cover tightly and cook on MEDIUM for 9 to 11 minutes.

Dilled Cucumber Sauce

MAKES: 1 CUP ◆ 28 CALORIES PER ¼ CUP

½ cup low-fat plain yogurt
½ cup peeled and chopped cucumber
2 tablespoons chopped fresh chives
2 tablespoons chopped fresh parsley

2 tablespoons chopped fresh dill
1 tablespoon lemon juice
  Dash cayenne pepper

Combine all the ingredients together in a bowl and chill.

Summer Squash Salad with Mustard Vinaigrette

SERVINGS: 4 ◆ 22 CALORIES PER 1-CUP SERVING PLUS 1 TABLESPOON DRESSING (17 CALORIES)

1 pound mixed baby summer squash or small
  squash, sliced ¼-inch thick
1 teaspoon lemon juice
¼ cup Mustard Vinaigrette (page 288)

Place the squash in a 2-quart casserole. Sprinkle with lemon juice. Cover tightly and cook on HIGH for 2 to 3 minutes, until tender-crisp, stirring once.

Plunge into cold water to stop cooking. Drain and toss with dressing. Chill until serving time.

Peach "Ice Cream"

MAKES: 3 CUPS ◆ 61 CALORIES PER ½-CUP SERVING ◆ COOKING TIME: 1 MINUTE

This is delicious in its creamy state, as it comes from the food processor. It may also be served frozen in an ice cream—like consistency. If you use fresh peaches, leave the peels on, because they will naturally add color to the ice cream.

1 16-ounce bag frozen peach slices; or 1 pound fresh peaches, pitted and sliced
2 tablespoons sugar

½ cup low-fat plain yogurt
1 tablespoon amaretto

Place the frozen peaches still in the bag in the microwave. Heat on DE- FROST for 1 minute to defrost slightly; break the pieces apart. Pour the de- frosted or fresh peach slices into the bowl of a food processor and chop them into small pieces. Add the re- maining ingredients and puree until smooth. Serve immediately or freeze until later.

Variation:

Peach Sundaes: Spoon ½ cup ice cream into a dessert bowl and top with ½ thinly sliced fresh peach. Add 19 calories.

◆ *Tip:* For 6 cups, double recipe but make it in two batches.

Make this menu with the chilled, leftover Steamed Whole Fish from Menu #16. If you haven't any leftovers, cook a 1-pound fillet according to the 4-servings method under that recipe.

CREAMY POTATO-ZUCCHINI SOUP

FISH SALAD WITH APRICOTS

GREEN BEAN AND TOMATO SALAD

CHERRIES ON THE STEM (SOME WITH CHOCOLATE COATING)

Plan of action

35 MINUTES BEFORE SERVING

1. Coat the cherries with chocolate and refrigerate.
2. Cook the green beans.
3. Prepare the green bean and fish salads and chill them.
4. Prepare and cook the soup.
5. Serve the soup.

Creamy Potato-Zucchini Soup

SERVINGS: 4 ◆ 88 CALORIES PER 1-CUP SERVING ◆ COOKING TIME: 8 TO 13 MINUTES

1 onion, chopped
1 medium potato, washed and quartered
1 pound zucchini, washed and sliced
1½ cups chicken broth
½ cup low-fat plain yogurt

¼ cup chopped fresh parsley
2 tablespoons lemon juice
  Freshly ground black pepper
¼ cup chopped fresh chives

Combine the onion, potato, zucchini, and ½ cup broth in a 2-quart casserole. Cover tightly and cook on HIGH for 6 to 8 minutes, or until the vegetables are tender, stirring once. Pour into the bowl of a food processor or blender and puree.

Return the mixture to the casserole and stir in the remaining 1 cup broth and other ingredients, except the

131

chives. Cover again and cook on HIGH for 2 to 5 minutes, or until heated through. Spoon the soup into the bowls and sprinkle each with 1 tablespoon chives.

◆ *For 2 Servings:* It is more practical to make 2 servings and save or freeze the remaining 1 serving.

Combine 2 tablespoons chopped onion, 1 small quartered potato, ½ pound sliced zucchini, and ¼ cup broth in a 1-quart casserole. Cover tightly and cook on HIGH for 4 to 5 minutes. Puree in a food processor or blender and return to the casserole. Stir in ½ cup broth, ¼ cup yogurt, 2 tablespoons chopped parsley, 1 tablespoon lemon juice, and a pinch pepper. Cover again and heat on HIGH for 2 to 3 minutes. Garnish with 2 tablespoons chopped chives.

Fish Salad with Apricots

SERVINGS: 4 ◆ 247 CALORIES PER 1-CUP SERVING

1 **pound cooked and chilled fish, leftover from Steamed Whole Fish (page 128)**
½ **pound fresh apricots, cut into ¼-inch cubes (1 cup)**
1 **cup thinly sliced celery**
2 **green onions, thinly sliced**
¼ **cup chopped fresh parsley**

½ **cup low-fat plain yogurt**
1 **tablespoon Dijon mustard with seeds**
1 **tablespoon lemon juice**
  Pinch freshly ground black pepper
4 **cups torn lettuce leaves**
  Chive or nasturtium blossoms

Combine the fish, apricots, celery, green onions, and parsley in a medium bowl. In a small bowl combine the yogurt, mustard, lemon juice, and pepper. Fold the sauce into the fish mixture until it is well blended. Chill until serving time.

To serve: Arrange the lettuce on a serving plate. Top with 1 cup salad and garnish with the edible flowers.

Variation:

Fish Salad with Apples: Substitute ½ pound cubed tart apples for the apricots. 179 calories per 1-cup serving.

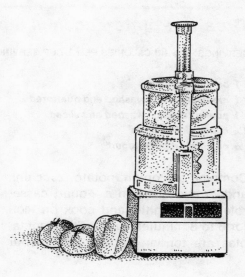

Green Bean and Tomato Salad

SERVINGS: 4 ◆ 64 CALORIES PER 1-CUP SERVING ◆ COOKING TIME: 5 TO 7 MINUTES

1 pound fresh green beans, trimmed and cut
   into 2-inch pieces
¼ cup water
2 ripe tomatoes, cut into eighths
2 green onions, thinly sliced

1 tablespoon chopped fresh basil
¼ cup Mustard Vinaigrette (page 288)
   Dash freshly ground black pepper

Combine the green beans and water in a 2-quart casserole. Cover tightly and cook on HIGH for 4 minutes; stir. Cover again and cook on HIGH for 1 to 3 minutes more, or until tender-crisp. Rinse under cold water to stop the cooking. Cool the green beans and drain them.

Stir in the remaining ingredients; chill. Stir just before serving time.

◆ *For 1 Serving:* Combine ¼ pound green beans and 1 tablespoon water in a 1-quart casserole. Cover tightly and cook on HIGH for 2 to 3 minutes, or until tender-crisp. Drain the green beans and run them under cold water. In a medium bowl combine the drained green beans; 1 small tomato, cut into eighths; ½ sliced green onion; 1 teaspoon chopped basil; 1 tablespoon Mustard Vinaigrette; and a pinch pepper. Stir well, then chill.

Cherries on the Stem (Some with Chocolate Coating)

SERVINGS: 4 ◆ 52 CALORIES PER ½ CUP FRESH CHERRIES, 69 CALORIES PER 3 CHOCOLATE-COATED CHERRIES ◆ COOKING TIME: 2 TO 3 MINUTES

During cherry season you should take full advantage of all their natural sweetness. Serve each person a plate with fresh and chocolate cherries, or eliminate the chocolate cherries. (At 30 calories per chocolate cherry you may want to.) At any rate, you can save the remaining 12 chocolate cherries for snacks or garnish. Store in the refrigerator for up to 4 days.

But whether you're eating the uncoated or coated cherries, take your time and savor each juicy berry from stem to stone.

3 ounces semisweet chocolate pieces
1 pound cherries washed and dried

Arrange the chocolate pieces around the outer rim in a paper or microwave-proof cereal bowl, leaving the center open. Cook on MEDIUM for 2 minutes; stir. Cook on MEDIUM for 30 seconds to 1 minute, or until melted and smooth, stirring every 30 seconds.

One at a time, take 24 cherries and hold them by the stems. Dip each one into the chocolate, twirling to cover half the cherry. Place the cherries on a wax paper—lined dish and refrigerate for 30 minutes to set.

To serve: Arrange the plain cherries in a double circle, place the chocolate-covered cherries in the center.

Variation:

Chocolate-Covered Strawberries: Substitute 1 cup whole strawberries with hulls, washed and dried, for cherries. Follow basic recipe. Makes 12 at 41 calories per strawberry.

◆ *Tip:* A paper bowl is suggested for melting the chocolate, but it is not necessary. The advantage is that cleanup is but a toss away, and the temptation to lick the bowl is virtually eliminated.

Menu

18

Summer Brunch

404 calories per serving

Indulge yourself with champagne? Why not? You deserve it. It could be that you got through a particularly hectic week, or you reached your weight goal. Whatever the reason, celebrate and enjoy!

CHAMPAGNE COCKTAIL

EGG CUSTARD IN PEPPER SHELLS

WARM HERBED PITA ROUNDS

FRESH FRUIT CUP

Plan of action

25 TO 30 MINUTES BEFORE SERVING

1. Prepare the fruit cup and chill it.
2. Prepare the pepper cups and cook them.
3. While the pepper cups are cooking, prepare the pitas.
4. During the standing time of the pepper cups, cook the pita.
5. Prepare and serve the cocktails.

Champagne Cocktail

SERVINGS: 1 ◆ 74 CALORIES PER 4 OUNCES

2 ounces Blanc de Blanc champagne (lowest in calories)
¼ cup fresh orange juice

1 fresh whole strawberry
1 mint sprig

Chill the champagne and orange juice. Combine the two in a fluted champagne glass. Garnish with the strawberry and mint.

Good news! A glass of white wine or champagne taken occasionally with your meals can boost the absorption of vitamins and minerals from vegetables and grain products. But beware: Alcohol in large amounts can prevent the absorption of thiamine, calcium, vitamins D and B_{12}.

Egg Custard in Pepper Shells

SERVINGS: 4 ◆ 148 CALORIES PER PEPPER CUP ◆ COOKING TIME: 15 TO 20 MINUTES

4 medium green bell peppers, with flat bottoms (see Note)
2 tablespoons water
1 red bell pepper, rib and seeds removed, coarsely chopped
¼ cup thinly sliced green onions

4 eggs, beaten
¾ cup low-fat cottage cheese
2 tablespoons chopped fresh parsley
⅛ teaspoon cayenne pepper

Remove the stem and ½ inch of the top from the green peppers. Set the tops aside. Remove the ribs and seeds from the peppers. Place the pepper shells, cut side down, in a 10-inch pie plate. Pour in the water. Cover with plastic wrap and cook on HIGH for 2 to 3 minutes, or until tender-crisp, rotating once. Let the peppers stand, covered, for 2 minutes. Remove the peppers from the dish and drain them.

Meanwhile, remove the stems from the tops that were set aside, and coarsely chop the green tops. Combine this with the red pepper in a small bowl and set it aside. In the same 10-inch pie plate, combine the chopped pepper and green onions. Cover tightly and cook on HIGH for 2 to 3 minutes, or until tender-crisp.

Combine the cooked pepper and onions with the eggs, cheese, parsley, and cayenne pepper in a medium microwaveproof bowl. Cook on HIGH for 2 minutes, stirring after 1 minute. Stir again.

Place the pepper cups, cut side up, around the outer rim of the 10-inch pie plate. Pour the egg mixture into the 4 pepper cups, dividing it evenly. Cover with wax paper. Cook on MEDIUM for 9 to 12 minutes, or until the egg mixture is firm and a knife inserted close to the center comes out clean; rotate the cups after 5 minutes. Let stand, covered, for 5 minutes.

◆ *For 1 Serving:* Remove the top from 1 green pepper and set it aside. Seed and remove the ribs from the pepper and place it cut side down, in a 6- or 7-ounce custard cup. Cover tightly and cook on HIGH for 1 minute. Let it stand a minute, then drain.

Eliminate the red pepper. Chop the green pepper top and combine it in another custard cup with 1 tablespoon chopped green onion. Cover tightly and cook on HIGH for 1 minute. Combine ¼ cup low-fat cottage cheese, 1 beaten egg, 1 tablespoon parsley, and a dash cayenne in a 2-cup glass measure or bowl; mix well with a fork. Cook on HIGH for 1 minute, stirring after 30 seconds; stir again.

Place the pepper cup upright in the custard cup, and spoon the egg filling into it. Cover with wax paper and cook on MEDIUM for 3 to 5 minutes, or until the filling is set. For 2 servings, double the ingredients and cooking times for 1 serving. Cook the final filled peppers on MEDIUM for 4 to 7 minutes, or until set.

◆ *Note:* It is important to choose peppers with flat bottoms, so they will stand upright when filled with the egg mixture. If you need to trim the peppers to even up the bottoms, make sure not to cut into the cavity. Also, the pepper cups should have no slits where the liquid may escape. To determine this, fill the seeded peppers with water and see if there are any leaks.

Warmed Herbed Pita Rounds

SERVINGS: 4 ◆ 117 CALORIES PER 2 HALVES ◆ COOKING TIME: 2 TO 3 MINUTES

4 1-ounce whole wheat pitas
1 teaspoon full-flavored olive oil

1 tablespoon water
¼ teaspoon hot pepper sauce

1 tablespoon grated Parmesan cheese
1 tablespoon chopped fresh parsley
1 tablespoon chopped fresh basil

*1 tablespoon chopped fresh chives or green
    onion tops*
1 teaspoon paprika

Split each pita in half, lengthwise, making each into 2 thin rounds. Place the pita rounds, cut side up, on a 12-inch round serving platter lined with a paper towel. If you do not have a 12-inch platter, place the pitas on the paper towel and put this directly into the microwave.

Combine the oil, water, and hot pepper sauce in a custard cup. Brush each pita with this mixture. Sprinkle evenly with the remaining ingredients. Cook on HIGH for 2 to 3 minutes, or until heated through.

Fresh Fruit Cup

SERVINGS: 4 ◆ 65 CALORIES PER 1-CUP SERVING

While you are cutting up the fruit for this dish, you may want to double these ingredients and save the rest for meals over the next few days.

1 cup sliced strawberries
1 cup fresh pineapple cubes
1 cup blueberries
1 cup cubed cantaloupe

Combine all the fruit in a large bowl. Chill.

Lunch Suggestions

Here are some lunch suggestions that round out to about 200 calories each. Many of them will help you make use of your leftovers from the summer entrées.

Cheese-Vegetable Pita

½ cup low-fat cottage cheese mixed with	82 calories
2 tablespoons low-fat plain yogurt	18 calories
1 green onion, chopped	5 calories
2 teaspoons chopped fresh dill	3 calories
1-ounce whole wheat pita bread, topped with	95 calories
1 small tomato, sliced	22 calories
Seltzer or mineral water	
	TOTAL 225 calories

Chilled Grilled Hen and Berries

¼ Grilled Cornish Hen, chilled (page 112), without sauce	63 calories
½ cup raspberries or strawberries	31 calories
2 melba toasts	30 calories
½ cup skim milk	44 calories
	TOTAL 168 calories

Steak and Pepper Sandwich

2 ounces Fajita steak, sliced (page 87)	109 calories
½ green or red bell pepper, sliced	10 calories
1-ounce whole wheat pita	95 calories
1 medium peach	38 calories
Seltzer or mineral water	
	TOTAL 252 calories

Shrimp and Cucumber Salad in Pita

5 cooked shrimp, sliced lengthwise (page 123)	130 calories
¼ cup Crispy Cucumber Salad (page 126)	7 calories
1-ounce whole wheat pita	95 calories
1 large peach, plum, or orange	73 calories
Seltzer or mineral water	
	TOTAL 305 calories

Chilled Zucchini Boat and Salsa

1 Mexican Stuffed Zucchini Boat (page 95)	106 calories
2 tablespoons Fresh Tomato Salsa (page 43)	8 calories
2 melba toasts	30 calories
1 large peach, plum, or nectarine	71 calories
Seltzer or mineral water	
	TOTAL 215 calories

Chicken and Cantaloupe with Sprouts in Pita

2 ounces cooked chicken, thinly sliced (page 146)	108 calories
Bean sprouts and ¼ cantaloupe, thinly sliced	55 calories
1-ounce pita bread	95 calories
½ cup skim milk	44 calories
	TOTAL 302 calories

Chicken and Grapes on Melon Crescent

½ cup Creamy Chicken Salad with Grapes (page 98)	95 calories
¼ melon, seeded	47 calories
4 melba toasts	60 calories
½ cup skim milk	44 calories
	TOTAL 246 calories

Chilled Seafood, Vegetable, and Rice Salad

1 cup Seafood, Vegetable, and Rice Salad (page 118), chilled and stirred with 1½ teaspoons fresh lemon juice and ½ teaspoon Dijon mustard	157 calories
1 medium peach	38 calories
½ cup skim milk	44 calories
TOTAL	239 calories

Scallop Salad and Melon Slices

½ cup Scallop and Avocado Salad (page 90)	155 calories
¼ melon, seeded, peeled, and thinly sliced, arranged around the salad	47 calories
2 melba toasts	30 calories
½ cup skim milk	44 calories
TOTAL	276 calories

FALL MENUS

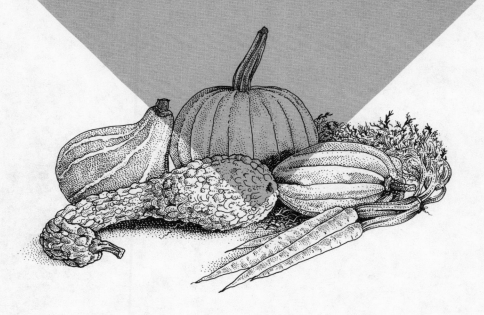

At the end of the summer we like to take advantage of the abundance of seasonal produce that we find in gardens and grocery stores. In the weeks to come, all of it will vanish, so it's worth taking a little extra time to preserve any extra you may not use in everyday cooking.

For example, Chunky Apple and Pear Sauce (page 165) can be made and frozen for a dessert throughout the fall. Apricots and plums can be put up in small amounts as indicated below.

Low-Calorie Poached Apricots or Plums

SERVINGS: 4 ◆ 54 CALORIES PER SERVING

**1 pound ripe apricots or plums (about 4),
    pitted and quartered**
1 teaspoon vanilla extract

Combine the fruit and vanilla in a casserole. Cover tightly and cook on HIGH for 3 to 4 minutes, or until tender. Chill, covered, and serve later with poached chicken or as a dessert.

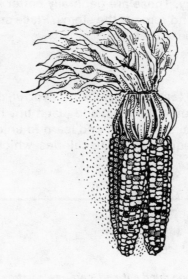

Variations:

Substitute 1 tablespoon sugar for vanilla extract for 62 calories per serving, or 1 tablespoon apple juice for 52 calories per serving.

We hate to part with herbs from our garden, so we dry them to achieve more flavor than their commercial counterparts. The best way to dry large amounts of herbs is on a window screen so that air can reach them from all sides. When dried, remove from stems and crumble the herbs, then pack in airtight containers to use in cooking. Small amounts of herbs can be dried in the microwave oven.

Microwave Dried Herbs

MAKES: ½ CUP OR A FEW SPRIGS SAGE, ROSEMARY, BAY LEAVES, THYME, MARJORAM, OR OREGANO

Place herbs between nonrecycled paper towels in the microwave. Heat on HIGH for 2 to 3 minutes until dry and crumbly. Pack in airtight containers.

Some herbs, such as parsley, chives, tarragon, and basil, freeze better than they dry. These are generally better for cooking than for steeping. Wash and dry them and remove the stems. Place small quantities in sandwich bags, label them, and freeze them.

Herb teas are terrifically flavorful, calorie-free decaffeinated drinks. If you need to sweeten the teas, add just a tiny bit of sugar, rather than a whole package of artificial sweetener, and learn to enjoy the full taste of the herbs. (One teaspoon sugar equals about 16 calories, which is nothing when you think about it. . . .)

Herb Teas

MAKES: 1 CUP

1 teaspoon dried aniseed, caraway, comfrey chamomile, mint, peppermint, and sage

Combine the herbs and water and let steep 3 minutes.

To make a pot of tea, triple or qua-druple ingredients but add 1 teaspoon dried herbs extra for the pot.

SPINACH RIBBON SOUP
WHOLE WHEAT MELBA TOASTS (2, 32 CALORIES)
ORANGE CHICKEN WITH LEMON PEPPER
BANANA CHEESECAKES GARNISHED WITH GRAPES

Menu

1

*356 calories
per serving*

Plan of action

35 MINUTES BEFORE SERVING

1. Prepare and cook the cheesecakes. Speed chill or refrigerate them.
2. While the cheesecakes are chilling, prepare the soup and chicken for cooking.
3. Cook the soup and serve it with the melba toasts.
4. Cook and serve the chicken.

Spinach Ribbon Soup

SERVINGS: 4 ◆ 35 CALORIES PER GENEROUS ½-CUP SERVING ◆ COOKING TIME: 5 TO 7 MINUTES

½ *pound spinach, washed, trimmed, and cut into ¼-inch strips*
2 *cups chicken broth*
1 *teaspoon lemon juice*
½ *teaspoon grated nutmeg*
4 *lemon slices*

Place the spinach into a 2-quart casserole. Cover tightly and cook on HIGH for 2 to 3 minutes, or until partially tender. Add the remaining ingredients except for the lemon slices. Cover again and cook on HIGH for 3 to 4 minutes, or until heated through. Serve each bowl with a thin lemon slice.

◆ *For 1 Serving:* Cut 4 spinach leaves into thin strips and place them in a microwaveproof bowl. Add ½ cup broth, ¼ teaspoon lemon juice, and a pinch nutmeg. Cover tightly and cook on HIGH for 1½ to 2½ minutes, or until heated through.

Orange Chicken with Lemon Pepper

SERVINGS: 4 ◆ 187 CALORIES PER 1 CHICKEN BREAST WITH A MEDIUM ORANGE ◆ COOKING TIME:
6 TO 10 MINUTES

4 3- to 4-ounce skinless, boneless chicken breast halves
1 tablespoon grated Parmesan cheese
1 tablespoon chopped fresh parsley
2 teaspoons grated orange peel
¼ cup orange juice

1 tablespoon dry white wine
1 teaspoon lemon juice
4 medium oranges, peeled and segmented
2 teaspoons Lemon Pepper (see sidebar)

Place the chicken breasts around the outer rim of a 9-inch pie plate. Sprinkle the cheese, parsley, orange peel, orange juice, white wine, and lemon juice over the chicken. Cover tightly and cook on HIGH for 4 minutes. Turn the breasts over and add the orange segments to the center of the dish. Cover again and cook on HIGH for 2 to 6 minutes, or until the chicken tests done. Let it stand for 3 minutes.

To serve: Slice each chicken breast across into 4 pieces, and divide the pieces among 4 dinner plates. Surround the chicken with the orange segments. Divide the cooking juices (2 to 4 tablespoons) among the chicken pieces, spooning them on top. Sprinkle each breast with ½ teaspoon

lemon pepper. Place the rest of the lemon pepper on the table to pass.

◆ *For 1 Serving.* Place 1 breast in an 8-ounce ramekin. Sprinkle with 1 teaspoon grated Parmesan cheese, 1 teaspoon chopped fresh parsley, ½ teaspoon grated orange rind, 1½ tablespoons orange juice, 1 teaspoon white wine, and ½ teaspoon lemon juice. Cover tightly and cook on HIGH for 2 minutes. Place the orange segments from 1 orange on top of the chicken, around the outer rim of the ramekin. Cook on HIGH for 30 seconds to 1 minute more, or until cooked through. Sprinkle with ½ teaspoon lemon pepper.

146

LEMON PEPPER

This is one of those condiments that you should keep on the table in a little container along with multicolored peppercorns in a clear pepper grinder. Both will add zest to mealtime. 3 calories per teaspoon.

2 tablespoons grated lemon peel
1 tablespoon coarsely ground black pepper

Spread the lemon peel out on an unrecycled paper towel or a paper plate. Heat on HIGH for 2 to 3 minutes, or until dried but not dark, rotating the plate after 2 minutes. Combine the lemon peel with the pepper and mix well.

Cheeseless Banana Cheesecakes Garnished with Grapes

SERVINGS: 4 ◆ 102 CALORIES PER CHEESECAKE, PLUS 32 CALORIES FOR 10 SEEDLESS GRAPES ◆ COOKING TIME: 6 TO 8 MINUTES

You may want to cook and chill these cheesecakes the night before. If there are just one or two of you at home, make this dessert anyway and serve the leftovers for breakfast the next morning. They are delicious!

2 medium bananas
1 egg
1 tablespoon sugar
1 tablespoon Triple Sec
1 teaspoon vanilla extract
1 teaspoon grated lemon peel
40 seedless grapes

Combine all the ingredients, except the grapes, in the bowl of a food processor or blender. Puree until blended. Spoon ⅓ cup into each of 4 custard cups. Place the cups in the microwave with at least a 1-inch space between them. Cook on MEDIUM for 6 to 8 minutes, or until the puddings are set and don't jiggle when shaken, but are still moist on the top.

Speed chill in the freezer for 30 minutes, or chill in the refrigerator for 2 hours before serving.

To serve: Invert each cheesecake onto a serving plate and surround with 9 grapes, cutting the last grape in half to garnish the top.

◆ *Tip:* If you put the custard cups on an 8- to 10-inch glass tray or plate before cooking, they will be easier to rotate and remove from the oven.

147

Menu

2

396 calories
per serving

CITRUS BEET SOUP

SCALLOPS PROVENÇALE

MIXED GREENS WITH MUSTARD VINAIGRETTE

CINNAMON APPLE CUSTARDS

VANILLA WAFERS

Plan of action

30 MINUTES BEFORE SERVING

1. Prepare the soup.
2. While the soup is cooking, prepare the scallops for cooking, and prepare the salad.
3. Serve the soup.
4. Cook the scallops.
5. While the scallops are cooking, prepare to cook the dessert.

6. Serve the scallops and salad. Cook the dessert while clearing the table. (If you want the dessert chilled, cook it before preparing the soup or make it the night before.)

Citrus Beet Soup

SERVINGS: 4 ♦ 60 CALORIES PER 1-CUP SERVING ♦ COOKING TIME: 11 TO 17 MINUTES

2 tablespoons chopped onion
¾ pound beets, peeled and grated (2 cups)
¼ cup orange juice
1 tablespoon lemon juice
2 cups chicken broth

1 cup grated cucumber (peeled only if waxy)
Dash freshly ground black pepper
4 tablespoons low-fat plain yogurt
Chives

Combine the onions, beets, and orange juice in a 2-quart casserole. Cover tightly and cook on HIGH for 8 to 12 minutes, or until the beets are tender, stirring once or twice. Add the lemon juice, broth, cucumber, and pepper. Cover again and cook on HIGH

for 3 to 5 minutes, or until heated through, but not boiling.

To serve: Spoon the soup into bowls and top with 1 tablespoon yogurt and some chives. Pass the pepper grinder.

◆ *For 2 Servings:* Reduce the quantities and cooking times by half. Cook the soup in a 1-quart casserole. This soup is also good chilled, so you might want to make the whole recipe, and serve the rest another time as a chilled soup.

Scallops Provençale

SERVINGS: 4 ◆ 199 CALORIES PER 1 CUP SCALLOPS WITH BROTH ◆
COOKING TIME: 5 TO 7 MINUTES

This dish incorporates the fresh flavors and aromas of Provence. A spoon is best for eating this so that you can scoop up both scallops and broth.

1 tablespoon full-flavored olive oil
1 garlic clove, minced
½ cup thinly sliced green onions
1 pound bay or sea scallops
2 large ripe tomatoes, peeled and coarsely chopped
½ pound mushrooms, thinly sliced
2 tablespoons chopped fresh parsley
2 ounces ripe black olives, coarsely chopped
Dash freshly ground black pepper
¼ cup chopped fresh basil

Combine the oil, garlic, and onions in a 2-quart casserole. Cook on HIGH for 30 seconds. If using the sea scallops, quarter them. Add the scallops to the garlic and stir to coat. Stir in the remaining ingredients, using only 2 tablespoons basil. Cover with wax paper and cook on HIGH for 3 minutes; stir. Cover again and cook on HIGH for 2 to 4 minutes, or until the scallops are opaque and cooked through.

To serve: Spoon into individual serving bowls and sprinkle with the remaining 2 tablespoons basil.

◆ *For 1 Serving:* Combine ½ teaspoon oil, 1 small minced garlic clove, and 2 tablespoons sliced green onion in a microwaveproof soup bowl. Cook on HIGH for 15 seconds. Stir in ¼ pound scallops (quarter the sea scallops), 1 small peeled and chopped tomato, 2 ounces thinly sliced mushrooms, ½ teaspoon chopped fresh parsley, 3 chopped olives, a pinch pepper, and 2 teaspoons chopped fresh basil. Cover with wax paper and cook on HIGH for 1½ to 3 minutes, stirring once. Sprinkle with ½ teaspoon basil and serve.

Mixed Greens with Mustard Vinaigrette

SERVINGS: 4 ◆ 44 CALORIES PER 1-CUP SERVING

4 cups mixed salad greens (romaine, Bibb,
   and arugula)
½ cup Mustard Vinaigrette (page 288)

Toss the greens and dressing in a
salad bowl just before serving.

Cinnamon Apple Custards

SERVINGS: 4 ◆ 76 CALORIES FOR EACH TART, PLUS 17 CALORIES FOR 1 VANILLA WAFER ◆ COOK-
ING TIME: 7 TO 10 MINUTES

1 ½-pound tart Granny Smith apple, peeled
   and coarsely chopped
1 egg, beaten
¼ cup low-fat plain yogurt
1 tablespoon sugar

½ teaspoon vanilla extract
   Dash ground cinnamon
4 vanilla wafers

Divide the apples between four 6- or 7-
ounce custard cups. Place the cups in
a circle in the microwave, with at least
a 1-inch space between them. Cover
them loosely with a large piece of wax
paper. Cook on HIGH for 2 minutes.

Meanwhile, combine the egg, yogurt, sugar, and vanilla in a small
bowl. Spoon 2 tablespoons of this
mixture over each dish of apples.
Cover again and cook on MEDIUM for 5
to 8 minutes, or until set, repositioning after 3 minutes. Serve warm or
chilled.

To serve: Turn each custard cup out
onto a dessert plate and sprinkle with
cinnamon. Serve with a vanilla wafer.

This menu was conceived when cleaning the squash and tomatoes out of the garden in mid-fall. We feel healthy just thinking about it. Pears can be cooked and chilled the night before or served warm as in Plan of action.

SEA LEG SOUP

SPAGHETTI SQUASH WITH
FRESH TOMATO SAUCE AND RICOTTA

CAULIFLOWER SALAD

PEARS IN RED WINE

Menu

3

*474 calories
per serving,
549 calories
with 1 piece
whole wheat
Italian bread*

Plan of action

1. Cook the pears.
2. Meanwhile, prepare the soup for cooking.
3. Cook the spaghetti squash.
4. While the squash is cooking, prepare the sauce for cooking.
5. Cook the soup. Meanwhile, prepare the salad.

40 MINUTES BEFORE SERVING

6. Serve the soup and put the spaghetti squash sauce in to cook.
7. While eating the soup, allow the sauce to cook.
8. Serve squash and sauce.

Sea Leg Soup

SERVINGS: 4 ◆ 48 CALORIES PER ⅔-CUP SERVING ◆ COOKING TIME: 4 TO 6 MINUTES

2 cups clam broth
¼ pound sea legs, flaked
2 green onions, thinly sliced
2 tablespoons chopped fresh parsley

1 tablespoon lemon juice
1 sprig thyme, or ⅛ teaspoon dried
   Dash cayenne pepper
4 thin lemon slices

Combine all the ingredients, except the lemon slices, in a 1-quart casserole. Cover tightly and cook on HIGH for 4 to 6 minutes, or until heated through. Garnish each bowl with a lemon slice.

◆ *For 1 Serving:* Place ½ cup clam broth, 1 ounce flaked sea leg, ½ sliced green onion, 1 teaspoon chopped parsley, 1 teaspoon lemon juice, and a pinch cayenne pepper in a microwaveproof soup bowl. Cover tightly and cook on HIGH for 1 to 2 minutes. Garnish with a lemon slice.

Spaghetti Squash with Fresh Tomato Sauce and Ricotta

SERVINGS: 4 ◆ 227 CALORIES PER 1 CUP SQUASH STRANDS, ½ CUP SAUCE, 2 OUNCES RICOTTA, AND 1 TABLESPOON GRATED PARMESAN CHEESE, 180 CALORIES PER SERVING WITH TOFU ◆ COOKING TIME: 18 TO 23 MINUTES

1 1½- to 2-pound spaghetti squash
1 tablespoon full-flavored olive oil
2 garlic cloves, minced
2 pounds ripe tomatoes, preferably plum, peeled, seeded, and chopped, or 2 cups canned, undrained
½ cup finely chopped fresh basil leaves

Dash freshly ground black pepper
⅛ teaspoon red pepper flakes (optional)
8 ounces low-fat ricotta, or 6 ounces cubed tofu
¼ cup grated Parmesan cheese

Pierce the skin of a squash in 4 places. Place on a paper towel in the microwave oven and cook on HIGH for 12 to 16 minutes, or until fork tender. Set aside while making the sauce.

Combine the oil and garlic in a 2-quart casserole. Cook on HIGH for 45 seconds to 1 minute. Add the tomatoes, basil, and peppers. Cover with wax paper and cook on HIGH for 5 to 6 minutes, stirring once.

Cut the cooled squash in half. Remove the seeds. With a fork remove the strands of squash from the shell. Place 1 cup strands into each of 4 large soup or pasta bowls. Mix each bowl of spaghetti squash strands with 2 ounces ricotta or 1½ ounces tofu. Spoon ½ cup sauce over each bowl and sprinkle each with 1 tablespoon grated Parmesan cheese.

◆ For 1 Serving: Cut a 1-pound spaghetti squash in half and cover the cut end of it with plastic wrap. Place this in the microwave and cook on HIGH for 4 to 8 minutes. Combine 1 teaspoon olive oil and 1 small minced garlic clove in a 1-quart casserole. Cook on HIGH for 20 seconds. Add ½ cup peeled, seeded, and chopped tomatoes, 2 tablespoons chopped basil, a pinch each black pepper and red pepper flakes. Cook on HIGH for 1 to 3 minutes, or until heated through. Remove the seeds from the cooled squash and pull out all the strands, placing them in a soup or pasta bowl. Toss them with 2 ounces ricotta cheese or 1½ ounces cubed tofu. Pour the tomato sauce on top and sprinkle with 1 tablespoon grated Parmesan cheese.

Cauliflower Salad

SERVINGS: 4 ◆ 46 CALORIERS PER 1-CUP SERVING

2 cups salad greens
1 cup thinly sliced raw cauliflower
½ cup thinly sliced radishes

10 black olives, chopped
¼ cup Mustard Vinaigrette (page 288)

Line each of four salad plates with ½ cup salad greens, topped with ¼ cup cauliflower and 2 tablespoons rad-ishes. Sprinkle each with 1 teaspoon chopped olives and 1 tablespoon dressing.

Pears in Red Wine

SERVINGS: 4 ◆ 153 CALORIES PER SERVING ◆ COOKING TIME: 10 TO 12 MINUTES

These pears are delicious warm or chilled. If you want to serve them chilled, put them in the freezer for 30 minutes.

4 firm ripe pears (about 1¼ pounds)
1 lemon, quartered
2 tablespoons sugar

1 bay leaf
4 peppercorns
½ cup dry red wine

Keeping the stems intact, core the pears from the base with a grapefruit knife. Peel the pears and rub each with a cut lemon to prevent discoloration.

Combine the remaining ingredients in a 2-quart casserole. Place the pears on their sides, positioning the thicker ends toward the outside of the casserole. Cover tightly and cook on HIGH for 6 minutes; or turn the pears over and baste. Cover again and cook on HIGH for 4 to 6 minutes, or until the pears are tender when pierced with a knife. Serve them warm or chilled. The pears may be kept in the refrigerator for 2 to 3 days.

To serve: Place each pear, standing upright, in a goblet. Spoon about 2 tablespoons cooking juices over each pear.

◆ For 1 Serving: Keeping the stem intact, peel and core a pear and rub it with cut lemon quarter. Place the pear upright in a small microwaveproof bowl. Add the ¼ lemon, 2 tablespoons red wine, 2 teaspoons sugar, ¼ bay leaf, and 1 peppercorn. Cover tightly and cook on HIGH for 2 to 4 minutes, or until tender when pierced with a knife. Serve warm or chilled.

153

Menu

4

*403 calories
per serving*

BROCCOLI SOUP WITH GINGER

FISH STEAKS AU POIVRE WITH
HERB-CROWNED TOMATOES

FALL FRUIT CHANTILLY

Plan of action

25 TO 30 MINUTES BEFORE SERVING

1. Prepare and chill the fruit.
2. Prepare and cook the broccoli soup.
3. While the soup is cooking, prepare

the fish and tomatoes for cooking.
4. Serve the soup, while the fish is cooking.

Broccoli Soup with Ginger

SERVINGS: 4 ◆ 41 CALORIES PER 1-CUP SERVING ◆ COOKING TIME: 8 TO 15 MINUTES

Buy 1 pound broccoli and save the rest for the Pasta with Vegetables and Sunflower Seeds in Menu #6.

2 tablespoons chopped onion
½ pound broccoli, trimmed and chopped (2 cups)
2 cups chicken broth
½ teaspoon grated fresh ginger
⅛ teaspoon cayenne pepper
½ cup low-fat plain yogurt

Combine the onion, broccoli, and ½ cup broth in a 2-quart casserole. Cover tightly and cook on HIGH for 6 to 9 minutes, or until the broccoli is tender, stirring once. Pour the mixture into the bowl of a food processor or blender and finely chop. Return the mixture to the casserole.

Stir in the remaining ingredients.

Cover and cook on HIGH for 2 to 6 minutes, or until just heated through, but not boiling.

◆ For 2 Servings: Reduce the ingredient amounts and cooking times by half. Cook the soup in a 1-quart casserole.

Fish Steaks au Poivre with Herb-Crowned Tomatoes

SERVINGS: 4 ◆ 197 CALORIES PER 4-OUNCE SERVING OF FISH AND 1 TOMATO ◆ COOKING TIME: 10 TO 12 MINUTES

1 pound swordfish, mako, or salmon steaks, cut ¾-inch thick
2 teaspoons coarsely ground black peppercorns
1 teaspoon grated lemon peel
4 medium-size tomatoes
1 slice fresh bread with crust, processed into fine crumbs

1 clove garlic, minced
1 green onion, thinly sliced
1 tablespoon chopped fresh basil
1 tablespoon chopped fresh parsley
Dash freshly ground black pepper
Lemon wedges

Cut the fish steaks into four 4-ounce servings. Place the steaks around the outer rim of a 10-inch pie plate or serving dish. Sprinkle the top of each steak with ½ teaspoon coarse pepper and ¼ teaspoon lemon peel, pressing the pepper and lemon into the surface of the fish with the heel of your hand.

Remove the stems from the tomatoes, and cut a ¼-inch slice from the top; set the tops aside. Place the tomato halves, cut side up, in the center of the fish dish.

Coarsely chop the tomato tops and combine them in a small bowl with the remaining ingredients, except the lemon wedges. Spoon the tomato-herb mixture on top of the tomatoes. Cover the dish with wax paper and cook on MEDIUM for 10 to 12 minutes, or until the fish is opaque and flakes under the pressure of a fork, and the tomatoes are heated through.

Serve with the lemon wedges.

◆ *For 1 Serving:* Place a 4-ounce fish steak on a dinner-size microwave serving plate. Press ½ teaspoon coarse black pepper and ¼ teaspoon grated lemon peel into the top of the fish steak. Remove the stem and slice ¼ inch from the top of 1 tomato. Finely chop the top. Combine it in a custard cup with 1 tablespoon fine fresh bread crumbs, 1 small minced garlic clove, 1 teaspoon each chopped fresh basil and parsley, and a pinch pepper. Place the tomato next to the fish and sprinkle the tomato-herb mixture on top of the tomato. Cover the plate with wax paper and cook on MEDIUM for 3 to 5 minutes, or until the fish is opaque and flakes under the pressure of a fork.

Keep a clear plastic pepper grinder filled with red, green, black, white, and burnt orange Szechuan peppercorns, the latter found in specialty and Oriental grocery stores. Each pepper adds its own unique flavor to the blend and it is better to reach for this attractive container than for the salt.

Fall Fruit Chantilly

SERVINGS: 4 ◆ 165 CALORIES PER 1-CUP SERVING

You may wish to double this recipe and serve the remainder for breakfast along with a piece of whole wheat toast or a bowl of warm cereal.

2 *large oranges, peeled and cut into segments (1 cup)*
1 *large grapefruit, peeled and cut into segments (1 cup)*
2 *large apples, cubed (2 cups)*

Juice from ½ lemon
1 *cup low-fat plain yogurt*
2 *tablespoons brown sugar*
½ *teaspoon vanilla extract*

Combine the fruit in a medium bowl; reserve the rinds. Squeeze the lemon juice and juice from the other rinds over the fruit. Stir to mix.

Combine the yogurt, brown sugar, and vanilla in a small bowl. Pour over the fruit and stir to coat. Chill until serving time.

◆ *For 2 Servings:* This recipe can be cut in half by just reducing the ingredient amounts by half. Save the leftover ½ grapefruit for breakfast.

156

SHERRIED MUSHROOM SOUP
VEAL AND VEGETABLE LOAVES
ORANGE-JICAMA SALAD
SPICED STEAMED PEARS

Menu

5

439 calories
per serving

Plan of action

1. Prepare and cook the pears. (This can be done the night before.)
2. While the pears are cooking, prepare the soup and meat loaves for cooking and set them aside.

25 TO 30 MINUTES BEFORE SERVING

3. Prepare the salad.
4. Cook the soup.
5. Serve the soup, and meanwhile cook the meat loaves.

Sherried Mushroom Soup

SERVINGS: 4 ◆ 26 CALORIES PER GENEROUS ½-CUP SERVING ◆ COOKING TIME: 2 TO 4 MINUTES

2 cups chicken broth
1 cup thinly sliced mushrooms
2 green onions, thinly sliced

1 tablespoon dry sherry
1 tablespoon low-sodium soy sauce
4 thin lemon slices

Combine all the ingredients, except the lemon slices, in a 1-quart casserole. Cover tightly and cook on HIGH for 2 to 4 minutes, until hot but not boiling.

To serve: Pour the soup into 4 serving bowls and top each with a lemon slice.

◆ *For 1 Serving:* Combine ½ cup broth, ¼ cup sliced mushrooms, 1 tablespoon chopped green onion, 1 teaspoon sherry, and ¾ teaspoon soy sauce in a microwaveproof soup bowl. Cover tightly and cook on HIGH for 1 to 2 minutes. Top with a lemon slice to serve.

Veal and Vegetable Loaves

SERVINGS: 4 ◆ 245 CALORIES PER 4-OUNCE SERVING ◆ COOKING TIME: 8 TO 12 MINUTES

This recipe makes very tasty loaves that are as good cold, served with horse-radish or mustard, as they are hot. Even if there are just one or two in your household, you may want to make the whole amount and save it for dinner the next day, or for lunch.

1 pound ground veal
1 slice whole wheat bread, crumbled
8 ounces alfalfa sprouts
½ cup chopped green pepper
2 tablespoons chopped onion
1 egg, beaten

1 tablespoon Dijon mustard
½ teaspoon dried thyme leaves
¼ teaspoon Worcestershire sauce
   Dash cayenne pepper
   Paprika

Combine all the ingredients, except the paprika, in a large mixing bowl. Mix together well. Form four round 3½-inch-diameter loaves, using about 1 cup of the mixture for each.

Place the loaves around the outer rim of a 10- to 12-inch serving plate, leaving at least a 1-inch space between the loaves. Sprinkle the tops lightly with a little paprika. Cover with wax paper and cook on HIGH for 8 to 12 minutes, rotating the dish after 5 minutes. Cook until the centers are al-most firm. Let them stand for 5 or more minutes.

◆ For 2 Servings: Combine ½ pound ground veal, ½ slice crumbled whole wheat bread, 4 ounces alfalfa sprouts, ¼ cup chopped green pepper, 1 table-spoon chopped onion, 1 beaten egg, ½ tablespoon Dijon mustard, ¼ tea-spoon dried thyme, a dash Worcester-shire sauce, and a pinch cayenne pepper in a small mixing bowl. Form into 2 round loaves and place them in a 9-inch pie plate, with at least a 1-inch space between them. Sprinkle the tops with paprika. Cover with wax paper and cook on HIGH for 4 to 6 min-utes. Let them stand for 5 minutes. Add 10 calories to each serving, be-cause you are using more egg per serving.

Orange-Jicama Salad

SERVINGS: 4 ◆ 50 CALORIES PER SERVING

A wonderfully flavorful salad.

12 small romaine leaves
1 cup orange segments
1 cup jicama strips
2 green onions, thinly sliced
    Dash freshly ground black pepper

2 tablespoons orange juice
1 teaspoon raspberry or cider vinegar
1 teaspoon full-flavored olive oil
1 tablespoon finely chopped fresh cilantro

Arrange about 3 lettuce leaves on each of 4 salad plates. Arrange ¼ cup orange segments and ¼ cup jicama on top of each plate of lettuce. Sprinkle with green onions and black pepper.

Combine the orange juice, vinegar, and olive oil in a custard cup and beat it with a fork to blend. Spoon about 2 teaspoons over each salad and sprinkle with cilantro. Chill until serving time.

◆ For 1 Serving: Arrange lettuce, orange segments, and jicama as described in basic recipe. Sprinkle ½ sliced green onion and black pepper on top. Combine 1½ teaspoons orange juice, ¼ teaspoon each vinegar and olive oil in a custard cup. Spoon on salad and garnish with about 1 teaspoon chopped cilantro.

Spiced Steamed Pears

SERVINGS: 4 ◆ 118 CALORIES PER SERVING ◆ COOKING TIME: 10 TO 12 MINUTES

These are delicious warm or chilled, so you may want to save time by making them the night before.

4 firm ripe pears (about 1¼ pound)
1 lemon, quartered
¼ cup dry vermouth
1 teaspoon vanilla extract

½ teaspoon ground cinnamon
¼ teaspoon ground ginger
    Grated nutmeg (optional)

Keeping the stems in place, core the pears from the base with a grapefruit knife so that they retain their shape. Peel the pears and rub each with a quarter of a lemon to prevent discoloration. Save the lemons.

Combine the vermouth, vanilla, cinnamon, and ginger in a 1½-quart casserole. Place the pears on their sides, positioning the thicker ends toward the outside of the casserole. Add the lemon quarters. Cover tightly and cook on HIGH for 6 minutes. Turn the pears over and baste. Cover again and continue to cook on HIGH for 4 to 6 minutes, or until the pears are tender. Let the pears cool in their liquid, turning them over occasionally. The pears

may be kept in the refrigerator for 2 to 3 days.

To serve: Place each pear standing upright in a dessert dish. Spoon about 1 tablespoon cooking liquid over each pear. Sprinkle with nutmeg, if desired.

◆ *For 1 Serving:* Keeping the stem in place, peel and core 1 pear and rub it with ¼ lemon. Place the pear upright in a small microwaveproof bowl. Add 1 tablespoon vermouth, the ¼ lemon, a dash cinnamon, and a pinch ginger. Cover tightly and cook on HIGH for 2½ to 4 minutes. Let the pear cool and, if desired, serve it with a sprinkling of nutmeg.

Menu

6

406 calories per serving

JAPANESE SNOW PEA SOUP

PASTA WITH VEGETABLES AND SUNFLOWER SEEDS

RED AND GREEN SEEDLESS GRAPES WITH
BROWN SUGAR CREAM

Plan of action

20 MINUTES BEFORE SERVING

1. Prepare and cook the soup.
2. While the soup is cooking, prepare the ingredients for the vegetable pasta sauce and boil the water for the pasta.

3. Serve the soup, and meanwhile cook the vegetable pasta sauce and the pasta.
4. While the pasta is cooking, prepare the dessert and chill it.

Japanese Snow Pea Soup

SERVINGS: 4 ◆ 26 CALORIES PER GENEROUS ½-CUP SERVING ◆ COOKING TIME: 4 TO 6 MINUTES

2 **cups chicken, fish, or seaweed broth**
2 **slices fresh ginger, peeled**
¼ **pound snow peas, trimmed and cut into ½-inch pieces**

1 **tablespoon dry sherry**
1 **teaspoon white vinegar**
   Dash cayenne pepper

Combine all the ingredients in a 2-quart casserole. Cover tightly and cook on HIGH for 4 to 6 minutes, or until just heated through.

◆ *For 1 Serving:* Combine ½ cup broth, 1 slice peeled ginger, 1 ounce trimmed snow peas, 1 teaspoon sherry, a few drops of white vinegar, and a dash cayenne in a microwave-proof soup bowl. Cover tightly and cook on HIGH for 1 to 2 minutes.

Pasta with Vegetables and Sunflower Seeds

SERVINGS: 4 ◆ 278 CALORIES PER SERVING ◆ COOKING TIME: 5 TO 8 MINUTES

This collection of vegetables over pasta in a light creamy sauce makes a delicious vegetarian meal.

2 **quarts water**
4 **ounces dry thin spaghetti**
1 **tablespoon full-flavored olive oil**
2 **garlic cloves, minced**
2 **tablespoons chopped fresh parsley**
1 **tablespoon chopped fresh basil**
1 **tablespoon chopped fresh oregano, or 1 teaspoon dried**
2 **cups spinach leaves, cut into 1-inch strips**

½ **pound broccoli, sliced ¼-inch thick (2 cups)**
1 **cup carrots, cut into ¼-inch slices**
2 **green onions, thinly sliced**
¼ **cup water**
¼ **cup sunflower seeds**
½ **cup low-fat ricotta cheese**
¼ **cup grated Parmesan cheese**
   Dash freshly ground black pepper (optional)

Bring the 2 quarts water to a boil on top of a conventional stove and cook the spaghetti until it is al dente, or still firm to the bite.

Meanwhile, combine the oil and garlic in a 2-quart casserole. Cook on HIGH for 35 seconds. Stir in the herbs, vegetables, and water. Cover tightly and cook on HIGH for 5 to 8 minutes, or until the carrots and broccoli are tender-crisp, stirring after 3 minutes. Stir in the sunflower seeds, ricotta and Parmesan cheese.

To serve: Drain the pasta and place ½ cup into each of 4 pasta bowls and top with 1 cup vegetables. Toss to combine. Sprinkle with pepper, if desired.

◆ *For 1 Serving:* Cook 1 ounce spaghetti on top of the conventional stove. Meanwhile, combine 1½ teaspoons oil and 1 small minced garlic clove in a microwaveproof pasta or cereal bowl. Add 2 teaspoons chopped parsley, 1 teaspoon each chopped fresh basil and oregano, ¼ cup strips of spinach leaves, ½ cup sliced broccoli, ¼ cup sliced carrots, ½ sliced green onion, and 1 tablespoon water. Cover tightly and cook on HIGH for 2 to 4 minutes, or until the carrots and broccoli are tender-crisp, stirring after 1 minute. Stir in 1 tablespoon sunflower seeds, 2 tablespoons low-fat ricotta and 1 tablespoon grated Parmesan cheese. Toss with the drained pasta and serve.

Red and Green Seedless Grapes with Brown Sugar Cream

SERVINGS: 1 ◆ 102 CALORIES

Here is one serving of this arranged dessert. It can be easily quadrupled for 4.

10 each red and green grapes
2 tablespoons low-fat plain yogurt

1 teaspoon brown sugar
¼ teaspoon vanilla extract

Place the grapes on a dessert plate. Combine the yogurt, sugar, and vanilla in a small bowl. Spoon the mixture on one side of the dish. Dip the grapes into the cream and enjoy this simple but seductive treat.

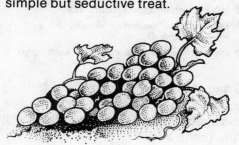

162

CREAM OF CAULIFLOWER SOUP WITH SUNFLOWER SEEDS

ORIENTAL CHICKEN BREASTS WITH VEGETABLES
AND SOBA NOODLES

CHUNKY APPLE AND PEAR SAUCE

Plan of action

30 MINUTES BEFORE SERVING

1. Make the apple and pear sauce and set it aside.
2. While that sauce is cooking, prepare the ingredients for the soup and chicken. Put the water on to boil for the soba.

3. Cook the soup.
4. Place the chicken in the oven to cook, and cook the noodles. Meanwhile, serve the soup.

Cream of Cauliflower Soup with Sunflower Seeds

SERVINGS: 4 ◆ 58 CALORIES PER 1-CUP SERVING ◆ COOKING TIME: 6 TO 10 MINUTES

Lemon Pepper (page 147) is a tangy addition to this soup.

½ medium cauliflower, trimmed
2 cups chicken broth
1 garlic clove, minced
  Dash cayenne pepper

1 tablespoon grated Parmesan cheese
¼ cup low-fat plain yogurt
4 teaspoons toasted sunflower seeds

Wrap the cauliflower in plastic wrap and place it in the microwave. Cook it on HIGH for 4 to 6 minutes, or until tender.

Unwrap the cauliflower, place it in the bowl of a food processor and finely chop it. Pour the broth, garlic, and pepper into a 2-quart casserole. Add the chopped cauliflower. Cover

tightly and cook on HIGH for 2 to 4 minutes, or until hot. Stir in the grated Parmesan cheese and yogurt.

To serve: Pour the soup into 4 bowls and sprinkle each with 1 teaspoon sunflower seeds.

◆ *For 2 Servings:* Cut the ingredient amounts and cooking times in half.

Oriental Chicken Breasts with Vegetables and Soba Noodles

SERVINGS: 4 ◆ 139 CALORIES PER SERVING, PLUS 100 FOR ½ CUP SOBA NOODLES ◆ COOKING TIME: 6 TO 8 MINUTES

These chicken breasts cook best in individual ramekins because they can be surrounded with cooking juices. Purchase the soba noodles in a specialty or Oriental grocery store—the most nutritious and delicious noodles are the ones made with buckwheat.

2 quarts water

4 ounces soba noodles (wheat or buckwheat), or other whole wheat pasta

4 3- to 4-ounce boneless, skinless chicken breasts

5 tablespoons Ginger Oriental Dressing (page 287)

8 large red radishes, thinly sliced

8 large mushrooms, thinly sliced

4 green onions, thinly sliced

1 medium green pepper, thinly sliced

Bring the water to boil on top of the conventional range. Cook the soba until tender.

Place each chicken breast in an 8-ounce oval ramekin. Divide the Oriental dressing among them by spooning it on top. Divide the vegetables among the 4 dishes, placing them on top of the chicken. Cover tightly, making sure not to cover the handles, or they will get hot from the steam. Place the ramekins in a circle in the microwave oven with a 1-inch space between them. Cook on HIGH for 6 to 8 minutes, or until the chicken is cooked through and the vegetables are tender-crisp.

To serve: Drain the soba and place on 4 dinner plates, spooning a portion of the vegetables and chicken next to it.

◆ For 1 Serving: Cook 1 ounce soba noodles until tender in 1 quart boiling water on top of the conventional stove. Place one 3- to 4-ounce boneless, skinless chicken breast in an 8-ounce ramekin. Spoon 1 tablespoon plus 1 teaspoon Ginger Oriental Dressing on top. Place 2 large thinly sliced radishes, 2 large thinly sliced mushrooms, 1 thinly sliced green onion, and ¼ thinly sliced medium green pepper on top. Cover tightly and cook on HIGH for 2½ to 3½ minutes, or until the chicken is cooked through. Let stand for 2 minutes. Drain the soba and serve with the vegetables and chicken.

Chunky Apple and Pear Sauce

SERVINGS: 4 ◆ 138 CALORIES PER ½-CUP SERVING ◆ COOKING TIME: 10 TO 14 MINUTES

This recipe is a double-duty dessert. Serve it warm one night, with a dollop of yogurt or sprinkling of cinnamon or nutmeg, then mix the remainder with yogurt and freeze it for dessert another time.

1 pound ripe pears, peeled, cored, and thinly sliced

1 pound MacIntosh apples, peeled, cored, and thinly sliced

¼ cup water

1 tablespoon sugar

1 teaspoon ground cinnamon

1 teaspoon vanilla extract

Combine the pears, apples, and water in a 2-quart casserole. Cover tightly and cook on HIGH for 10 to 14 minutes, or until the fruit is tender. Stir in the remaining ingredients. Let the sauce stand at room temperature and serve it warm.

Variation:

Frozen Apple-Pear Cream: Combine ½ cup low-fat plain yogurt and 1 cup Apple and Pear Sauce in the bowl of a food processor or blender. Puree until smooth. Pour into four 3-ounce dishes or paper cups and freeze for 2 hours or overnight. Each 3-ounce (¾ cup) serving is 87 calories.

NOUVELLE SEAFOOD GUMBO WITH RICE

LETTUCE AND TOMATO SALAD

PEACH OR ORANGE FAN WITH GRAND MARNIER CREAM

Plan of action

30 MINUTES BEFORE SERVING

1. Cook the rice (page 294). Meanwhile, prepare the gumbo.
2. While the rice is standing, cook the gumbo.
3. While the gumbo is cooking, prepare the salad and dessert; chill them until serving time.
4. Serve the gumbo, followed by the salad and dessert.

Nouvelle Seafood Gumbo with Rice

SERVINGS: 4 ◆ 170 CALORIES PER SERVING, PLUS 134 FOR ½ CUP RICE ◆ COOKING TIME: 12 TO 16 MINUTES

This is a soup and main course all in one. All the flavors of this wonderful Cajun-inspired dish remain—only the calories have been cut out.

1 teaspoon full-flavored olive oil
2 garlic cloves, minced
1 medium onion, chopped
1 bell pepper, coarsely chopped
1 large celery rib, coarsely chopped
¼ teaspoon cayenne pepper
¼ teaspoon freshly ground black pepper
¼ teaspoon dried thyme leaves
¼ teaspoon dried oregano leaves
½ pound scrod or cod fillets, cut into 1-inch chunks

¼ pound peeled small shrimp
¼ pound sea legs, cut into ½-inch chunks or ¼ pound crabmeat
¼ pound okra, sliced into ¼-inch pieces
3 cups bottled clam juice
1 bay leaf
1 recipe cooked Basic Rice (page 294)
¼ cup chopped fresh parsley
Hot pepper sauce (optional)

Combine the oil, garlic, onion, pepper, and celery in a 3-quart casserole. Cover tightly and cook on HIGH for 2 minutes. Stir in the cayenne and black peppers, thyme, and oregano. Cover again and cook on HIGH for 2 minutes.

Stir in the fillets, shrimp, sea legs, okra, clam juice, and bay leaf. Cover again and cook on HIGH for 8 to 12 minutes, or until the soup is heated through and the fish is cooked.

To serve: Place ½ cup cooked rice in 4 large soup bowls and spoon 1½ cups gumbo over each portion. Sprinkle with the fresh parsley and pass some hot pepper sauce, if desired.

◆ *For 2 Servings:* This recipe is too difficult to cut down to 1 serving, so make a double amount and freeze the rest. Just cut the ingredient amounts and cooking times in half. Cook the gumbo in a 2-quart casserole.

Lettuce and Tomato Salad

SERVINGS: 4 ◆ 34 CALORIES PER 1 CUP LETTUCE, 1 TOMATO, AND 1 TABLESPOON DRESSING

4 cups lettuce leaves, torn into pieces
4 tablespoons Creamy Mustard Dressing
  (page 290)
4 tomatoes, sliced

Combine the lettuce and 3 tablespoons dressing in a salad bowl and toss. Serve the greens on 4 salad plates and top each with a sliced to-mato. Divide the remaining 1 tablespoon dressing between the salads, spooning it on top of the tomato.

In this menu and the next we call for grated orange peel. While you are at it, you might grate a number of oranges and lemons and store them, separately, in plastic bags to be frozen. That way you will have grated peel ready on a moment's notice.

Peach or Orange Fan with Grand Marnier Cream

SERVINGS: 4 ◆ 81 CALORIES PER 1 PEACH WITH 2 TABLESPOONS CREAM, 86 CALORIES PER 1 ORANGE WITH 2 TABLESPOONS CREAM

½ cup low-fat plain yogurt

1 tablespoon orange-flavored liqueur or orange juice

1 tablespoon sugar

1 teaspoon grated orange peel

½ teaspoon vanilla extract

4 peaches (1 pound), cut into 16 slices each, or 4 small oranges, peeled and segmented

Combine all the ingredients, except the peaches or oranges, in a small mixing bowl.

To serve: Fan out the fruit on 4 plates and spoon 2 tablespoons cream at the base of each fan.

Menu

9

281 calories per serving

This is a unique menu that yields one meal for today and one for later in the week. The Boiled Beef takes slightly longer to cook and delays the serving time a bit because the Vegetable Beef Soup is made with the cooking juices. As this is the case, choose this as a dinner for an evening when you want to relax with a refreshing drink and the newspaper, or do a chore before dinner. Just put the meat on to cook and turn it over once.

VEGETABLE-BEEF SOUP

BOILED BEEF AND POTATO WITH
HORSERADISH AND MUSTARD

½ PINK GRAPEFRUIT (49 CALORIES)

Plan of action

1. Start cooking the beef.
2. Prepare the vegetables and add them to the beef.
3. Wash the potatoes and place them in the cooking dish.
4. Cut the grapefruit. Loosen the sec-

45 MINUTES TO 1 HOUR BEFORE SERVING

tions with a grapefruit knife and chill them.
5. Prepare the soup and serve.
6. Slice the beef and serve it with the potatoes.

168

Vegetable-Beef Soup

SERVINGS: 4 ◆ 26 CALORIES PER ½-CUP SERVING ◆ COOKING TIME: SAME AS BOILED BEEF (BELOW)

Cooking liquid and vegetables remaining from Boiled Beef (below)

Freshly grated nutmeg

Remove 2 cups combined vegetables and broth and divide them evenly between 4 bowls. Top each bowl of soup with fresh nutmeg. (Refrigerate the remaining broth for another meal.)

Boiled Beef and Potato with Horseradish and Mustard

SERVINGS: 8 ◆ 206 CALORIES PER SERVING ◆ COOKING TIME: 43 TO 64 MINUTES

1 2-pound bottom round steak, trimmed
2¼ cups water
1 garlic clove, minced
1 medium onion, coarsely chopped
2 carrots, cut into ¼-inch slices
1 celery rib, thinly sliced
3 whole cloves
4 peppercorns
2 sprigs parsley
1 sprig thyme, or ¼ teaspoon dried
4 medium boiling potatoes, washed but unpeeled
Horseradish
Mustard

Combine the meat and 2 cups water in a 2- to 3-quart casserole. Cover tightly and begin to cook on HIGH for about 10 to 12 minutes. As soon as you have chopped up the garlic, onion, carrots, and celery, add them to the meat, along with the cloves, peppercorns, parsley, and thyme. Cover again and continue to cook on HIGH until boiling (10 to 12 minutes altogether as described above).

Turn the meat over. Cover again and cook on MEDIUM for 25 to 40 minutes, or until the meat is tender. Let it stand, covered, for 5 to 10 minutes.

Meanwhile, combine the potatoes with the remaining ¼ cup water in a 1-quart casserole. Cover tightly and cook on HIGH for 8 to 12 minutes, until tender. Let stand, covered, until serving time.

Remove the beef and potatoes from the casserole, and reserve the cooking liquid and remaining vegetables for Vegetable Beef Soup. Keep it warm until after you have served the soup.

To serve: Thinly slice the beef across the grain and serve 3 ounces of meat with each potato, along with horseradish and mustard on the side.

◆ *For 2 Servings:* Before doing this, you may want to consider making the entire recipe and serving the leftover beef in sandwiches. Or, you can keep the cooked meat and broth for about a week in the refrigerator.

Combine 1 pound bottom round steak, trimmed, with 1 cup water in a 1½-quart casserole. Add 1 small minced garlic clove, 1 small coarsely chopped onion, 1 sliced carrot, ½ celery rib, sliced, 2 whole cloves, 2 peppercorns, 1 parsley sprig, and ⅛ teaspoon dried thyme. Cover tightly and cook on HIGH for 5 to 6 minutes, or until boiling. Turn the meat over. Cover again and cook on MEDIUM for 12 to 20 minutes, or until the meat is tender. Let it stand, covered, for 5 to 10 minutes.

Meanwhile, combine 2 medium boiling potatoes, unpeeled, with 2 tablespoons water in a 1-quart casserole. Cover tightly and cook on HIGH for 4 to 6 minutes, or until tender. Let stand, covered, until serving time.

Remove the beef and potatoes from the cooking liquid. Cover and keep warm until you have served the soup. Spoon 1 cup remaining vegetables and broth into 2 soup bowls and serve hot as a first course soup. Then, thinly slice the beef and serve 3 ounces of meat with each potato, along with horseradish and mustard.

Is meat always bad for you? Well, too much meat and too much of the wrong kind (hot dogs, bacon, and sausages) certainly is not good for you, but to eliminate meat entirely is to shortchange yourself of one of the best sources of iron available.

In fact, what most people don't realize is that certain cuts of meat may have no more cholesterol than an equal serving of poultry. The key is to choose the right cut. That is, one that is lean (with very little fat marbled through the grain). Stay away from rib-eye, T-bones and club steaks and choose instead round, chuck steak, flank steak, and sirloin. They all have between 156 and 171 calories per 3-ounce serving with 24 grams of protein and 3 milligrams of iron. You'd have to eat about 1 pound of fish to receive the same amount of iron.

QUICK GINGERED TOMATO AND ORANGE SOUP
WITH BREAD STICK

FISH STEAKS WITH HORSERADISH CREAM

PARMESAN SPINACH OR SWISS CHARD

FROZEN APPLE-PEAR CREAM WITH RASPBERRY SAUCE

Menu

10

433 calories
per serving

Plan of action

10 MINUTES THE NIGHT BEFORE
15 MINUTES BEFORE SERVING

1. The night before, prepare the Frozen Apple-Pear Cream, and make the Raspberry Sauce.
2. On the serving day, make the Horseradish Cream and then prepare the fish for cooking.

3. Make the soup and serve it.
4. Cook the fish steaks.
5. While the steaks are cooking, wash and cut up the spinach.
6. Cook the spinach during the standing time for the fish.

Quick Gingered Tomato and Orange Soup

SERVINGS: 4 ◆ 74 CALORIES PER 1-CUP SERVING, PLUS 23 CALORIES PER BREADSTICK
◆ COOKING TIME: 8 TO 10 MINUTES

3 cups tomato juice

1 cup orange juice

1 teaspoon lemon juice

¼ to ½ teaspoon ground ginger or more, to taste

4 orange slices

4 4½"-x-½" breadsticks

Combine the juices and ginger in a 2-quart casserole. Cover tightly and cook on HIGH for 8 to 10 minutes, or until the soup is heated through but not boiling.

To serve: Ladle 1 cup into each of 4 bowls and place an orange slice on top and a breadstick on the side.

◆ *For 1 Serving:* Combine ¾ cup tomato juice, ¼ cup orange juice, ¼ teaspoon lemon juice, and a pinch ginger in a microwaveproof bowl. Cover tightly and cook on HIGH for 2 to 3 minutes, or until heated through. Serve with an orange slice and breadstick.

Fish Steaks with Horseradish Cream

SERVINGS: 4 ◆ 178 CALORIES PER 4-OUNCE SERVING OF FISH AND ¼ CUP CREAM ◆ COOKING TIME: 7 TO 9 MINUTES

Horseradish Cream:

1 cup low-fat plain yogurt
2 tablespoons prepared horseradish
1 teaspoon lemon juice

Dash freshly ground black pepper
Pinch cayenne pepper (optional)

1 pound swordfish, mako, or salmon steaks, ½ to ¾ inch thick
Chopped fresh parsley

4 lemon wedges

Combine all the cream ingredients in a small bowl; set aside.

Cut the steaks into 4-ounce serving pieces and arrange them around the outer edge of a 9-inch pie plate with the thicker sections to the outside, leaving the center open. Cover with wax paper and cook on MEDIUM for 7 to 9 minutes, or just until the fish flakes under the pressure of a fork. Let the steaks stand for 5 minutes.

To serve: Place each piece of fish on a serving plate and divide the horseradish cream between the fish. Garnish with chopped parsley and a lemon wedge.

◆ For 1 Serving: Place 4 ounces of fish on an individual serving plate. Cover with wax paper and cook on HIGH for 3 to 5 minutes, or until the fish flakes under the pressure of a fork. Let the fish stand for 2 to 3 minutes. Top with ¼ cup horseradish cream.

Recent medical research indicates that low calcium intake may be a more important link to the causes of high blood pressure than high sodium intake. To combat low calcium intake, make sure that you are getting enough calcium through milk and dairy products such as yogurt.

Other sources of calcium are some of the less expensive leafy vegetables: Kale, collard greens, bok choy and mustard or turnip greens are good. Although spinach is a good source of vitamin A and iron, certain oxalic acids in spinach link up with calcium to prevent its absorption by the body.

Parmesan Spinach or Swiss Chard

SERVINGS: 4 ◆ 51 CALORIES PER ½- TO ¾-CUP SERVING ◆ COOKING TIME: 5 TO 9 MINUTES

If you are concerned about your calcium intake and want to substitute 2 pounds trimmed collards, kale, or mustard greens for spinach, follow the basic recipe, but double the cooking time.

2 pounds spinach or chard leaves, trimmed
2 tablespoons chopped fresh basil

2 tablespoons grated Parmesan cheese
1 tablespoon lemon juice

Wash the spinach and cut it into ½-inch strips, while it is still wet. *Do not drain* or pat dry. Place the spinach into a 3-quart casserole. Cover tightly and cook on HIGH for 5 to 9 minutes, or until tender, stirring once. Stir in the basil, cheese, and lemon juice. Serve with the fish.

◆ *For 1 Serving:* Wash ½ pound spinach and cut it into ½-inch strips while it is still wet. Place the wet spinach into a 1-quart casserole. Cover tightly and cook on HIGH for 1 to 2 minutes, or until tender, stirring once. Stir in 1 tablespoon each chopped basil and grated Parmesan, and 1 teaspoon lemon juice.

Frozen Apple-Pear Cream with Raspberry Sauce

SERVINGS: 4 ◆ 87 CALORIES PER 3-OUNCE SERVING OF CREAM, PLUS 30 CALORIES PER 2 TABLESPOONS SAUCE

1 recipe Frozen Apple-Pear Cream (page 165)
½ cup Raspberry Sauce (page 199)

Drizzle 2 tablespoons of raspberry sauce over the top of each serving of apple-pear cream.

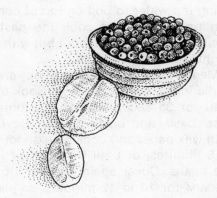

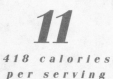

Menu

11

418 calories
per serving

This is a meatless meal that incorporates soup and main dish in one.

PASTA E FAGIOLI
MIXED GREENS WITH MUSTARD VINAIGRETTE
PEAR SLICES WITH GORGONZOLA CHEESE

Plan of action

30 MINUTES BEFORE SERVING

1. Cook the soup.
2. While the soup is cooking, prepare the salad and dessert.
3. Serve the soup and salad.

Pasta e Fagioli (Pasta and Bean Soup)

SERVINGS: 4 ◆ 287 CALORIES PER 1½-CUP SERVING ◆ COOKING TIME: 15 TO 20 MINUTES

2 *quarts water*
4 *ounces ditalini or other small tube-shaped*
  macaroni
1 *tablespoon full-flavored olive oil*
1 *garlic clove, minced*
2 *cups coarsely chopped canned plum*
  tomatoes, undrained
2 *tablespoons chopped fresh basil*

Freshly ground black pepper
2 *cups canned cannellini beans with juices*
  (see Note)
¼ *cup chopped fresh parsley*
4 *teaspoons grated Parmesan cheese*
Red pepper flakes (optional)

Bring the water to boil on top of conventional stove and cook the pasta until it is al dente, or tender but with a slight bite.

Meanwhile, combine the oil and garlic in a 2-quart casserole. Cook on HIGH for 35 seconds. Add the tomatoes, basil, and black pepper. Cover with wax paper and cook on HIGH for 5 to 8 minutes, or until boiling. Stir in the beans. Cover again and cook on MEDIUM for 10 to 12 minutes, or just until heated through.

To serve: Drain the pasta and place ½ cup into each of 4 large soup plates. Top each with 1 cup of tomato-bean mixture. Sprinkle each bowl with 1 tablespoon parsley and 1 teaspoon cheese. Pass the red pepper flakes at the table.

Note: To make home-cooked beans, see Soaking and Cooking Dry Beans, page 293.

Mixed Greens with Mustard Vinaigrette

SERVINGS: 4 ◆ 44 CALORIES PER 1-CUP SERVING

4 cups mixed salad greens
½ cup Mustard Vinaigrette (page 288)

Toss the salad greens and dressing in
a salad bowl, right before serving.

Pear Slices with Gorgonzola Cheese

SERVINGS: 4 ◆ 104 CALORIES PER SERVING

There is nothing like the sweet, winelike flavor of pears complemented by a
creamy, blue-veined cheese.

2 Bosc pears (¾ pound), cored and thinly
*   sliced*

2 ounces Gorgonzola or blue cheese, cut into
*   4 cubes*

Fan out the pear slices on each dessert plate. Place 1 cube of cheese at
the base of the fan. Serve, eating a bit
of cheese with each pear.

◆ *For 1 Serving:* Fan out ½ pear,
sliced onto a dessert plate. Add ½
ounce cube of cheese to the plate and
serve.

MEXICAN LIME SOUP
TEQUILA SHRIMP WITH PEPPERS
MEXICAN RICE
CARDAMOM-LACED HONEYDEW

Plan of action

25 MINUTES BEFORE SERVING

1. Cook the rice and let it stand.
2. While the rice is cooking, chop the tomatoes and onions. Prepare the soup.
3. While the soup is cooking, prepare the shrimp.

4. Serve the soup.
5. Cook the shrimp. Serve the shrimp with the rice.

Mexican Lime Soup

SERVINGS: 4 ◆ 120 CALORIES PER 1-CUP SERVING ◆ COOKING TIME: 8 TO 10 MINUTES

1 garlic clove, minced
2 green onions, thinly sliced
3 cups chicken broth
1 ripe avocado, cut into ¼-inch chunks

2 tablespoons chopped fresh cilantro leaves
2 thyme sprigs, or ½ teaspoon dried
   Pinch cayenne pepper (optional)
2 limes

Combine the garlic and green onions in a 2-quart casserole. Cook on HIGH for 35 seconds. Stir in the broth, avocado, cilantro, thyme, pepper, and the juice of 1 lime. Cover tightly and cook on HIGH for 8 to 10 minutes, or until the soup is heated through, but not boiling.

To serve: Quarter the remaining lime and serve a wedge with each bowl of soup.

◆ *For 1 Serving:* Combine 1 small minced garlic clove; ½ thinly sliced green onion; ¾ cup broth; ¼ avocado, cut into chunks; ½ tablespoon chopped cilantro; a dash thyme leaves; and a pinch cayenne pepper, if desired, in a microwaveproof soup bowl. Cover tightly and cook on HIGH for 2 to 4 minutes, or until the soup is hot, but not boiling.

Tequila Shrimp with Peppers

SERVINGS: 4 ◆ 131 CALORIES PER 1-CUP SERVING ◆ COOKING TIME: 4 TO 6 MINUTES

1 teaspoon full-flavored olive oil
1 garlic clove, minced
1 pound peeled shrimp
½ teaspoon red pepper flakes

1 tablespoon lemon juice
1 tablespoon tequila or brandy
2 large green or red bell peppers, seeded and cut into ½-inch cubes

Combine the oil and garlic in a 10-inch pie plate. Cook on HIGH for 30 seconds. Add the shrimp, pepper flakes, lemon juice, and tequila or brandy, stirring to coat the shrimp. Push the shrimp to the outer rim of the dish. Place the bell pepper cubes in the center. Cover with wax paper and cook on HIGH for 3 minutes. Stir the shrimp and peppers together, making sure that any shrimp that haven't yet turned pink are moved near the outside of the dish. Cover again and cook on HIGH for 1 to 3 minutes more, or until all the shrimp are cooked and the peppers are heated through. Stir well and serve with Mexican Rice.

◆ For 1 Serving: Combine 1 small minced garlic clove, ¼ pound peeled shrimp, 1 teaspoon each lemon juice and tequila, and a dash red pepper flakes in a microwaveproof soup bowl or 8-ounce oval ramekin. Push the shrimp to the outer rim. Place the cubes from ½ bell pepper in the center. Cover with wax paper and cook on HIGH for 1½ to 3 minutes, stirring after 1 minute.

Mexican Rice

SERVINGS: 4 ◆ 145 CALORIES PER AN APPROXIMATE ¾-CUP SERVING ◆ COOKING TIME: 12 TO 15 MINUTES

Adding the vegetables at the end of cooking time will nicely warm them through without making them soggy.

1 recipe Basic Rice (page 294)
1 cup coarsely chopped ripe tomatoes
2 green onions, thinly sliced

Cook the rice. Add the tomatoes and onions at end of the cooking time, before the standing time. Let the rice stand, covered, for 5 minutes.

◆ *For 1 Serving:* Add ¼ cup coarsely chopped tomatoes and ½ sliced green onion to ½ cup cooked rice in a 1½-cup microwaveproof serving dish.

Cover with wax paper and cook on HIGH for 1 to 2 minutes. Stir and serve. See page 294 for ½ cup cooked rice.

A SNACK SUGGESTION FROM MEXICAN VENDORS:

Peel and cube cucumbers or jicama and sprinkle them with chili powder for a low-calorie snack that your taste buds will remember.

Cardamom-Laced Honeydew

SERVINGS: 4 ◆ 19 CALORIES PER WEDGE

Buy a 2-pound melon and save half for the Fresh Melon Granita in Menu #15.

1 1-pound (or half a 2-pound) honeydew
  melon, cut into 4 2"- × -7" wedges
  Ground cardamom or cumin

Sprinkle each melon wedge with cardamom or cumin and serve.

178

BEEF BROTH WITH PASTINA

SLICED COLD BEEF WITH HORSERADISH CREAM

ORIENTAL BROCCOLI AND RED PEPPER SALAD

BAKED APPLES

Menu

13

433 calories
per serving

Plan of action

1. Cook the broccoli and assemble the salad.
2. Bake the apples and let them stand at room temperature until serving time.

20 MINUTES BEFORE SERVING

3. While the apples are cooking, slice the beef and make the Horseradish Cream.
4. Cook the soup and serve it.

Beef Broth with Pastina

SERVINGS: 4 ◆ 64 CALORIES PER ½-CUP SERVING ◆ COOKING TIME: 5 TO 8 MINUTES

2 cups beef broth
2 ounces dry pastina

Combine the broth and pastina in a 1½-quart casserole. Cover tightly and cook on HIGH for 5 to 8 minutes, or until boiling. Let the soup stand, covered, for 3 minutes.

◆ *For 1 Serving:* Combine ½ cup beef broth and ½ ounce dry pastina in a serving bowl. Cover tightly and cook on HIGH for 1 to 3 minutes, or until boiling. Let it stand for 2 minutes.

Sliced Cold Beef with Horseradish Cream

SERVINGS: 4 ◆ 192 CALORIES PER 3-OUNCE SERVING OF BEEF WITH ¼ CUP HORSERADISH CREAM

12 ounces boiled beef (page 169), thinly sliced
1 cup Horseradish Cream (page 172)

179

Thinly slice the beef across the grain. Slightly overlap the slices on each of 4 plates. Place ¼ cup Horseradish Cream on each plate.

Oriental Broccoli and Red Pepper Salad

SERVINGS: 4 ◆ 36 CALORIES PER 1-CUP SERVING ◆ COOKING TIME: 2 TO 3 MINUTES

4 cups 1½-inch broccoli flowerets (reserve the stalks for broccoli soup)
2 tablespoons water
1 red bell pepper, cut into ¼-inch slices
2 tablespoons finely chopped green onions
¼ cup Ginger Oriental Dressing (page 287)

Arrange the broccoli around the outer rim of a 9-inch pie plate, with the stems facing the outside rim. Add the water. Cover tightly with plastic wrap and cook on HIGH for 2 to 3 minutes, or until tender-crisp. Rinse the broccoli in a colander under cold water to arrest the cooking, then drain.

Meanwhile, combine the remaining ingredients in a bowl and add the broccoli and toss. Let the salad marinate until serving time.

◆ For 1 Serving: Place 1 cup broccoli flowerets on a small microwaveproof plate with the stems toward the outer rim. Add 1 teaspoon water. Cover tightly and cook on HIGH for 45 seconds to 1 minute. Rinse under cold water and drain. Combine the broccoli with ¼ cut-up bell pepper, 1 teaspoon chopped green onion, and 1 tablespoon Ginger Oriental Dressing.

Baked Apples

SERVINGS: 4 ◆ 141 CALORIES PER APPLE ◆ COOKING TIME: 6 TO 7 MINUTES

4 medium tart baking apples
4 tablespoons raisins
4 teaspoons brown sugar

¼ cup orange juice
½ teaspoon ground cinnamon

Core the apples from the top, but not all the way to the bottom. Peel a 1-inch strip around the top of the apple. Halfway down the apple, cut a ¼-inch-deep slit in the skin all the way round the center circumference (this will let steam escape and keep the skin from splitting).

Place the apples in four individual 10-ounce microwaveproof dishes or around the outside of a 9-inch pie plate, leaving the center open. Spoon 1 tablespoon raisins, 1 teaspoon brown sugar, and 1 tablespoon orange juice into the center of each apple. Sprinkle with cinnamon. Cover tightly and cook on HIGH for 6 to 7 minutes, repositioning or rotating them once. If using individual dishes, leave a 1-inch space between them in the microwave oven.

◆ *For 1 Serving:* Core and peel a strip from the top of one apple as described above, and halfway down the side, make a slit all the way around. Place the apple in a 10-inch microwaveproof dish and spoon 1 tablespoon raisins, 1 teaspoon brown sugar, and 1 table-spoon orange juice into the center. Cover tightly and cook on HIGH for 2 to 4 minutes.

◆ *For 2 Servings:* Follow the instructions above, but prepare 2 apples. Cover tightly and cook on HIGH for 3 to 6 minutes.

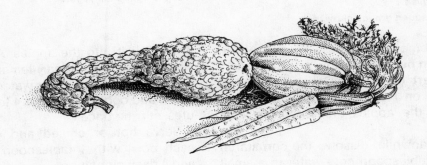

APPLE WINE SOUP

FISH FILLETS ROJO

BRUSSELS SPROUTS AND POTATOES

MELON BALLS WITH RASPBERRY SAUCE

Plan of action

25 TO 30 MINUTES BEFORE SERVING

1. Prepare and cook the soup.
2. While the soup is cooking, prepare the fish recipe and vegetables for cooking.
3. Cook the vegetables; while they are cooking, serve the soup.
4. During the standing time of the vegetables, cook the fish.
5. During the standing time of the fish, prepare the dessert.
6. Serve the fish.

Apple Wine Soup

SERVINGS: 4 ◆ 88 CALORIES PER ¾-CUP SERVING ◆ COOKING TIME: 8 TO 12 MINUTES

½ *pound tart apples, peeled, cored, and thinly sliced*
1 *cup plus 1 tablespoon water*
1 *tablespoon grated lemon peel*
½ *teaspoon ground cinnamon, plus extra for garnish*
⅛ *teaspoon ground cloves*

1 *tablespoon cornstarch*
½ *cup dry white wine*
2 *tablespoons sugar*
1 *tablespoon lemon juice*
¼ *cup low-fat plain yogurt*

Combine the apples, ½ cup water, lemon peel, cinnamon, and cloves in a 2-quart casserole. Cover tightly and cook on HIGH for 4 to 6 minutes, or until the apples are tender, stirring once.

Meanwhile, dissolve the cornstarch in 1 tablespoon cold water in a small bowl. Stir it into the apples. Add the wine, cornstarch, sugar, lemon juice, and the remaining ½ cup water. Cover again and cook on HIGH for 4 to 6 minutes, stirring once.

Serve hot or chilled and garnish each bowl with 1 tablespoon yogurt and a dash cinnamon.

◆ *For 2 Servings:* Combine ¼ pound peeled, cored, and thinly sliced tart apples, 1½ teaspoons grated lemon peel, ¼ teaspoon cinnamon, ¼ cup water, and ⅛ teaspoon ground cloves in a 1-quart casserole. Cover tightly and cook on HIGH for 2 to 3 minutes, or until the apples are tender; stir.

Meanwhile, dissolve ½ tablespoon cornstarch and ½ tablespoon water in a small bowl. Stir it into the apples. Add ¼ cup each white wine and water, 1 tablespoon sugar, and ½ tablespoon lemon juice. Cover again and cook on HIGH for 2 to 3 minutes, stirring once. Garnish each serving with 1 tablespoon low-fat plain yogurt and a dash cinnamon.

Can you find an interesting place to walk to that is thirty minutes from your home? A novel card store (where you won't be tempted to spend too much money), an art gallery, or even a cozy coffee shop are good destinations. You'll have walked an hour, total!

Fish Fillets Rojo

SERVINGS: 4 ◆ 133 CALORIES PER 4-OUNCE SERVING OF FISH AND 2 TABLESPOONS VEGETABLES AND SAUCE, COMBINED ◆ COOKING TIME: 8 TO 12 MINUTES

1 tablespoon full-flavored olive oil
1 garlic clove, minced
½ cup coarsely chopped carrots
½ cup thinly sliced celery
2 green onions, thinly sliced

½ cup dry red wine
    Dash freshly ground black pepper
4 4-ounce thin lean fish fillets (flounder, sole, or whiting)

Combine the oil and garlic in a 9- or 10-inch pie plate. Cook on HIGH for 35 seconds. Add the carrots, celery, green onions, wine, and pepper. Cover with wax paper and cook on HIGH for 4 to 6 minutes, or until the vegetables are tender-crisp and some of the wine has evaporated; stir.

Tuck the thinner ends of each fish fillet under the thicker center, in three-fold letter fashion. Place the fillets seam side down around the outer edge of the dish, leaving the center open. Cover again and cook on HIGH for 3½ to 6 minutes, or until the fish flakes when pressed with a fork. Let it stand, covered, for 2 minutes.

To serve: Divide vegetables and sauce between each fillet, spooning them over the top.

◆ *For 1 Serving:* Combine 1 teaspoon olive oil, 1 small minced garlic clove, and 2 tablespoons each chopped carrots and sliced celery, ½ sliced green onion, 2 tablespoons dry red wine, and a pinch pepper in an 8-ounce ramekin. Cover with wax paper and cook on HIGH for 1 to 2 minutes. Add the 4-ounce fish fillet with the thin ends folded under the thicker center. Cover again and cook on HIGH for 1 to 3 minutes, until the fish flakes when pressed with a fork.

Brussels Sprouts and Potatoes

SERVINGS: 4 ◆ 69 CALORIES PER 3 BRUSSELS SPROUTS AND 1 POTATO ◆ COOKING TIME: 7 TO 10 MINUTES

½ pound small red potatoes (2 ounces each), washed and quartered
½ pound Brussels sprouts (about 12), trimmed with an X cut into the base
½ cup chicken broth or water
Dash freshly ground black pepper

2 tablespoons chopped fresh parsley
2 tablespoons chopped fresh chives or green onion tops
4 lime wedges

Combine the potatoes, Brussels sprouts, and broth or water in a 2-quart casserole. Cover tightly and cook on HIGH for 4 minutes; stir. Cover again and cook on HIGH for 3 to 6 minutes, or until the vegetables are tender. Let them stand, covered, for 5 minutes.

To serve: Sprinkle the vegetables with pepper and herbs and serve with a lime wedge on the plate with the fish.

◆ *For 1 Serving:* Combine 1 quartered potato, 3 trimmed Brussels sprouts with X's cut into the bottom, and 2 tablespoons water or broth in an 8-ounce ramekin or cereal bowl. Cover tightly and cook on HIGH for 3 to 5 minutes, or until tender, stirring once. Let them stand, covered, for 2 minutes. Sprinkle with pepper, and 2 teaspoons each parsley and chives; serve with a lime wedge.

Melon Balls with Raspberry Sauce

SERVINGS: 4 ◆ 58 CALORIES PER SERVING

2 cups fresh melon balls
½ cup Raspberry Sauce (page 199)
4 mint sprigs

Place ½ cup melon balls in each of 4 goblets and spoon 2 tablespoons sauce over each. Garnish with mint.

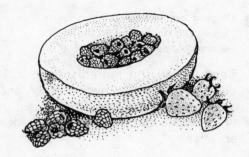

TOMATO-BASIL SOUP WITH CELERY STICKS

RISOTTO WITH MUSHROOMS AND CHICKEN LIVERS

MIXED GREENS WITH CREAMY MUSTARD DRESSING

FRESH MELON GRANITA

Menu

15

392 calories
per serving

Plan of action

5 MINUTES THE NIGHT BEFORE
40 MINUTES BEFORE SERVING

1. If you haven't done this from Menu #12, cube, process, and freeze the melon for the granita the night before.
2. Cook the chicken livers for the risotto. Meanwhile, combine the remaining ingredients for the risotto.
3. Cook the risotto. Meanwhile, combine the ingredients for the soup and make the salad dressing.
4. Heat the soup. Meanwhile, wash and dry the lettuce for the salad.
5. Serve the soup.
6. Toss the salad and serve it with the risotto.

Tomato-Basil Soup

SERVINGS: 4 ◆ 25 CALORIES PER ½-CUP SERVING ◆ COOKING TIME: 8 TO 10 MINUTES

1½ *cups tomato juice*
½ *cup chicken or beef broth*
¼ *cup chopped fresh basil*

1 *teaspoon lemon juice*
  Dash cayenne pepper
  Dash freshly ground black pepper

Combine all the ingredients in a 2-quart casserole. Cover tightly and cook on HIGH for 8 to 10 minutes, or until heated through. Serve with celery sticks.

◆ *For 1 Serving:* Combine ⅔ cup tomato juice, ⅓ cup chicken or beef broth, 1 tablespoon chopped basil, ½ teaspoon lemon juice, and a pinch each cayenne and black pepper in a microwaveproof soup bowl. Cook on HIGH for 2 to 3 minutes, until heated through.

Risotto with Mushrooms and Chicken Livers

SERVINGS: 4 ◆ 314 CALORIES PER 1-CUP SERVING ◆ COOKING TIME: 15 TO 23 MINUTES

¾ *pound chicken livers, washed and diced*
1 *sage leaf, chopped, or ¼ teaspoon dried*
1 *tablespoon full-flavored olive oil*
1 *medium onion, coarsely chopped*
¾ *cup Arborio or long-grain rice*

1½ *cups chicken broth*
2 *tablespoons dry white wine*
2 *tablespoons grated Parmesan cheese*
1 *cup sliced mushrooms*
¼ *cup chopped fresh parsley*

Place the chicken livers around the outer rim of a 9-inch pie plate, leaving the center open. Sprinkle with sage. Cover with wax paper and cook on MEDIUM for 4 to 6 minutes, or until the livers have just lost their pink color, stirring after 3 minutes. Set aside.

Combine the oil and onion in a 3-quart casserole. Cook on HIGH for 1 minute. Stir in the rice, broth, and wine. Cover tightly and cook on HIGH for 4 to 8 minutes, or until the broth boils; then cook on MEDIUM for 6 to 8 minutes, or until most of the liquid is absorbed and the rice is al dente. Stir in the cheese and mushrooms. Drain the livers and stir them into the rice. Let the rice stand, covered, until serving time. Sprinkle with parsley before serving.

◆ *For 2 Servings:* Place 6 ounces washed and chopped chicken livers in an 8-ounce ramekin. Sprinkle with 1 small chopped sage leaf. Cover with wax paper and cook on MEDIUM for 2 to 4 minutes, or until the livers have just lost their pink color. Set aside.

Combine 1 teaspoon olive oil and 1 small chopped onion in a 1-quart casserole and cook on HIGH for 35 seconds. Add ¾ cup broth, 1 tablespoon white wine, and ⅓ cup plus 2 tablespoons rice. Cover tightly and cook on HIGH for 2 to 4 minutes, or until boiling, then on MEDIUM for 4 to 6 minutes, or until the liquid has been absorbed. Stir in 1 tablespoon grated Parmesan cheese and ½ cup sliced mushrooms. Drain the livers and stir them into the rice. Let the rice stand, covered, until serving time. Sprinkle with 1 tablespoon chopped parsley before serving.

Mixed Greens with Creamy Mustard Dressing

SERVINGS: 4 ◆ 32 CALORIES PER 1-CUP SERVING

4 cups mixed salad greens
½ cup Creamy Mustard Dressing (page 290)

Combine the salad greens and dressing in a salad bowl and toss immediately before serving.

Fresh Melon Granita

SERVINGS: 4 ◆ 21 CALORIES PER SERVING

Granita is a frozen grainy fruit dessert. Since no sugar is added, the riper and sweeter the melon, the more delicious the granita will be. It is a good idea to make this the day you make the Cardamom-Laced Honeydew from Menu #12, utilizing the leftover melon, so that it will be ready for this menu.

½ pound sweet, ripe honeydew melon, cubed
1 tablespoon melon-flavored liqueur
   Freshly grated nutmeg or mint leaf

Place the cubed melon in the bowl of a food processor or blender. Process the melon until mushy. Pour the mixture into an ice-cube tray with sections. Return to the freezer for 2 to 6 hours, or until frozen. Put the frozen cubes back in the processor with the liqueur and puree again until smooth. Spoon the granita into 4 dessert glasses and serve immediately, or freeze again to serve later. Garnish the top with nutmeg or mint.

Menu

16

379 calories
per serving

Because of the frozen sorbet, this menu will take 5 minutes of your time the night before (or in the morning) and an hour or so before serving to properly freeze it. But it is all worth it to produce this luscious dessert.

PARSNIPS IN BROTH

FALL VEGETABLE, TOFU, AND CHEESE MÉLANGE

MIXED GREENS WITH DRESSING

BANANA SORBET

Plan of action

5 MINUTES THE NIGHT BEFORE
1 HOUR BEFORE SERVING

1. Slice and freeze the bananas the night before, for making the sorbet the next day. You forgot? Then serve a fresh whole fruit, or half a banana, for dessert.
2. Make the sorbet and put it in the freezer until serving time.
3. Prepare and cook the vegetable

mélange up to the point where the cheese is added.
4. While the vegetables are cooking, prepare the salad, then the soup for cooking.
5. Cook the soup.
6. Serve the soup and finish heating the vegetables.

Parsnips in Broth

SERVINGS: 4 ◆ 51 CALORIES PER ¾-CUP SERVING ◆ COOKING TIME: 6 TO 9 MINUTES

½ pound parsnips, grated (about 1 cup)
1 garlic clove, minced
2 cups chicken broth
2 tablespoons chopped fresh cilantro
   or parsley

Dash cayenne pepper
Dash freshly ground black pepper

Combine the parsnips, garlic, and ¼ cup broth in a 1-quart casserole. Cover tightly and cook on HIGH for 2 to 3 minutes, or until the parsnips are slightly tender. Stir in the remaining

1¾ cups broth, cilantro or parsley, cayenne, and black pepper. Cover again and cook on HIGH for 4 to 6 minutes, or until heated through.

188

◆ *For 1 Serving:* Combine ¼ cup (2 ounces) grated parsnips, ¼ teaspoon minced garlic, and 1 tablespoon chicken broth in a microwaveproof soup bowl. Cover tightly and cook on HIGH for 1 to 2 minutes. Stir in another ½ cup broth, 1 teaspoon chopped cilantro or parsley, and a pinch cayenne and black pepper. Cover tightly and cook on HIGH for 1 to 2 minutes.

Fall Vegetable, Tofu, and Cheese Mélange

SERVINGS: 4 ◆ 242 CALORIES PER 1½-CUP SERVING ◆ COOKING TIME: 12 TO 17 MINUTES

1 **tablespoon full-flavored olive oil**
1 **garlic clove, minced**
1 **onion, chopped**
1 **green pepper, cut into ½-inch squares**
1 **medium eggplant (1 pound), cut into ½-inch cubes**
4 **medium tomatoes, peeled and cut into 1-inch cubes**
2 **tablespoons chopped fresh basil**
¼ **teaspoon freshly ground black pepper**
8 **ounces skim-milk mozzarella, grated**
4 **ounces tofu, cut into ½-inch cubes**

Combine the oil, garlic, onion, pepper, and eggplant in a 2-quart casserole. Cover tightly and cook on HIGH for 5 minutes; stir. Cover again and cook on HIGH for 2 to 4 minutes, or until the eggplant is tender.

Stir in the tomatoes, basil, and black pepper. Cover and cook on HIGH for 4 to 6 minutes, or until the tomatoes are heated through, stirring once. Stir in the cheese and tofu. Cover and cook on MEDIUM for 1 to 2 minutes, or until the cheese is melted.

◆ *For 1 Serving:* Combine 1 teaspoon olive oil, ¼ teaspoon minced garlic, 1 sliced green onion, ¼ cubed green pepper, and 1 small cubed eggplant (¼ pound) in a 2-cup casserole. Cover tightly and cook on HIGH for 2 minutes. Add 1 peeled and cubed tomato, 1 tablespoon chopped basil, and a pinch freshly grated black pepper. Cover and cook on HIGH for 2 to 3 minutes. Stir in 2 ounces grated skim-milk mozzarella and 1 ounce cubed tofu. Cover tightly and cook on MEDIUM for 1 to 1½ minutes, or until the cheese is melted.

Mixed Greens with Dressing

SERVINGS: 4 ◆ 23 CALORIES PER 1-CUP SERVING

4 cups mixed salad greens
¼ cup salad dressing of your choice
  (pages 287–91)

Toss the salad greens with dressing in
a bowl, right before serving.

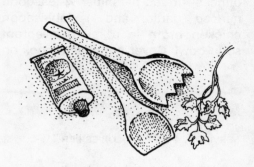

Banana Sorbet

SERVINGS: 4 ◆ 64 CALORIES PER ½-CUP SERVING

If you love bananas you will enjoy this dessert. Remember that the riper the
bananas, the sweeter the sorbet will be. When you are making this, you may wish
to double the recipe so that you have it on hand for other meals.

2 medium ripe bananas, peeled and sliced
  into ½-inch pieces

1 tablespoon orange-flavored liqueur or
  orange juice concentrate

Place the sliced bananas on a pie dish
or other flat dish and freeze them
overnight.

The next day, place the plate of frozen banana pieces in the microwave
and heat on HIGH for 30 seconds, to
defrost slightly. Combine the banana
and liqueur in the bowl of a food processor or blender. Process until
smooth. Freeze the mixture for 1 to 2
hours, to form a soft custard consistency.

Thanksgiving should be bountiful—but in a low-calorie way. This menu takes a little longer to prepare, but, considering that it is our holiday menu, 40 minutes isn't so bad!

CUMIN-SCENTED CORN CHOWDER

CORNISH GAME HENS IN A GRAND MANNER

ORANGE-AND-SUNFLOWER RICE STUFFING

HARVEST VEGETABLE PLATTER

NOUVELLE WALDORF SALAD
(SALAD OR DESSERT)

Plan of action

40 MINUTES BEFORE SERVING

1. Cook the rice for the stuffing.
2. While the rice is cooking, chop the remaining stuffing ingredients, then cut the hens in half, and mix the basting sauce.
3. Cook the Cornish hens. Mean-while, prepare the soup, vegetable platter, and salad.
4. While the hens are standing, cook and serve the soup.
5. Cook the vegetables while serving the soup.

Cumin-Scented Corn Chowder

SERVINGS: 4 ◆ 53 CALORIES PER ¾-CUP SERVING ◆ COOKING TIME: 6 TO 8 MINUTES

1 green pepper, coarsely chopped
2 green onions, thinly sliced
1 cup cooked corn kernels
2 cups chicken broth

1 teaspoon lemon juice
⅛ teaspoon ground cumin
Dash cayenne pepper

Combine the green pepper, green onions, and corn in a 1½-quart casserole. Add 2 tablespoons broth. Cover tightly and cook on HIGH for 2 minutes, or until the pepper is tender-crisp.

Add the remaining 1⅞ cup chicken broth, the lemon juice, cumin, and cayenne pepper. Cover again and cook on HIGH for 4 to 6 minutes, or until heated through.

191

◆ *For 1 Serving:* Combine ¼ coarsely chopped green pepper and ½ chopped green onion in a microwave-proof soup bowl. Cover tightly and cook on HIGH for 30 seconds to 1 min-

ute. Add ¼ cup corn, ½ cup chicken broth, ¼ teaspoon lemon juice, and a dash each cayenne and cumin. Cover again and cook on HIGH for 1 to 2 minutes, or until hot.

Since Thanksgiving can be a heavy meal, you may wish to have a light appetizer beforehand. One suggestion is to make the Creamy Herb Dressing II (page 288), and serve it as a dip with celery and cucumber sticks. The dressing will be 12 calories per tablespoon. One cup celery sticks adds up to 18 calories, but they are so fibrous that you burn up more calories than that by chewing them. One cup of unpeeled cucumber sticks is 16 calories.

Cornish Game Hens in a Grand Manner

SERVINGS: 4 ◆ 257 CALORIES FOR ½ HEN WITHOUT SKIN (314 CALORIES WITH SKIN)
◆ COOKING TIME: 14 TO 20 MINUTES

The hens will become golden brown after cooking, but if you want the skin to be crisp, follow the tip at the end of the recipe.

3 cups Orange-and-Sunflower Rice Stuffing (see below)
2 1½-pound Cornish hens, cut in half

1 tablespoon orange juice concentrate
1 teaspoon low-sodium soy sauce

Place 4 mounds of rice stuffing (¾ cup each) in a 2-quart oval or rectangular dish, leaving the center open. Place one-half a hen, skin side up, over each rice mound. Combine the orange juice and soy in a small dish. Brush the hens with the mixture. Cover them with wax paper and cook on HIGH for

14 to 20 minutes, or until the juices run clear, rotating the dish once if necessary. Let them stand for 5 to 10 minutes.

◆ *For 2 Servings:* Place 2 mounds of rice in a 10-inch pie plate. Place one-half of a whole Cornish hen, skin side

192

up, over each mound. Combine 1½ teaspoons orange juice concentrate and ½ teaspoon low-sodium soy sauce in a small dish. Baste the hens with this mixture. Cover them with wax paper and cook on HIGH for 8 to 10 minutes, or until the juices run clear in the thickest part of the thigh, rotating the dish once if necessary.

◆ *Tip:* To crisp the skins on the hens, preheat the conventional oven to 500°F at the same time you begin to cook the hens in the microwave oven. (Make sure that the dish is glass or heatproof plastic.) After cooking the hens in the microwave, transfer them in their dish to the oven and crisp them for 5 minutes.

Orange-and-Sunflower Rice Stuffing

SERVINGS: 4 ◆ 179 CALORIES PER ¾-CUP SERVING ◆ COOKING TIME: 9 TO 12 MINUTES

¾ **cup raw long-grain rice**
1½ **cups water**
2 **oranges, peeled, segmented with white membrane removed, and diced (1 cup), plus the juice**

2 **green onions, thinly sliced**
1 **tablespoon toasted sunflower seeds**
⅛ **teaspoon grated nutmeg**

Combine the rice and water in a 2-quart casserole. Cover tightly and cook on HIGH for 3 to 5 minutes, or until boiling; then on MEDIUM for 6 to 7 minutes, or until the water is absorbed.

Stir the remaining ingredients into the rice at the end of cooking. Let stand, covered, for 5 minutes.

◆ *For 2 Servings:* Combine ⅓ cup and 2 tablespoons rice with ¾ cup water in a 4-cup glass measure. Cover tightly and cook on HIGH for 2 to 3 minutes, or until boiling; then on MEDIUM for 4 to 6 minutes, or until the liquid is absorbed. Add 1 sliced green onion, ½ cup diced orange segments, 1½ teaspoons toasted sunflower seeds, and a pinch fresh nutmeg. Let stand, covered, for 3 to 6 minutes.

Harvest Vegetable Platter

SERVINGS: 4 ◆ 75 CALORIES PER SERVING ◆ COOKING TIME: 3 TO 5 MINUTES

This could serve as your Thanksgiving centerpiece, because the squash circles around the rim of the dish look like a gold and green doily.

1 medium acorn squash, halved, seeded, and cut into ¼-inch slices
1 cup broccoli flowerets
1 cup cauliflower flowerets
1 cup carrots, sliced into ¼-inch rounds
1 cup mushroom caps

1 tablespoon water
1 tablespoon lemon juice
1 tablespoon each finely chopped fresh parsley, dill, and chives
Dash freshly ground black pepper

Place the squash slices around the outer rim of a 10-inch dinner or serving plate. Arrange an alternating circle of broccoli and cauliflower inside the squash, with the stems facing the outer rim. Next, arrange a circle of carrots inside the broccoli and cauliflower. Spoon the mushrooms into the center. Sprinkle with water. Cover tightly and cook on HIGH for 3 to 5 minutes, or until the vegetables are tender-crisp or they have reached the desired doneness.

Meanwhile, combine the lemon juice, herbs, and pepper in a custard cup. Sprinkle them over the cooked vegetables.

◆ *For 1 Serving:* Seed and slice half a medium squash into ¼-inch slices. Place them around the rim of a microwaveproof plate to form a scalloped circle. Arrange ¼ cup each broccoli and cauliflower flowerets in a circle around the inside of the squash. Arrange ¼ cup sliced carrots in a circle inside. Place ¼ cup mushroom caps in the center. Sprinkle 1 teaspoon water over the top. Cover tightly and cook on HIGH for 1 to 3 minutes. Meanwhile, combine 1 teaspoon each lemon juice and finely chopped parsley with a pinch black pepper in a custard cup. Sprinkle over the cooked vegetables.

Nouvelle Waldorf Salad (Salad or Dessert)

SERVINGS: 4 ◆ 130 CALORIES PER ¾-CUP SERVING AS SALAD, 119 CALORIES AS DESSERT

You'll have to decide if you want to serve this as a dessert or salad. It is tasty either way.

2 **apples (10 ounces) cored and cut into ¼-inch cubes**
1 **cup sliced celery (optional)**
2 **tablespoons raisins**
2 **tablespoons chopped walnuts**
½ **cup low-fat plain yogurt**

2 **tablespoons cranberry juice concentrate**
   Lettuce leaves (optional)
½ **teaspoon vanilla extract (optional)**
   Ground cinnamon (optional)

For salad, place the apples, celery, raisins, and nuts in a medium mixing bowl. In another small bowl, combine the yogurt and cranberry concentrate. Fold into the fruit and nut mixture. Chill until serving time. Spoon onto plates lined with lettuce leaves.

For dessert, eliminate the celery and lettuce. Add the vanilla extract to the yogurt. Mound each serving into small bowls and top with a walnut half and a sprinkling of ground cinnamon.

◆ *For 1 Serving:* Rather than cutting this down to 1 serving, it might be more practical to make 2 servings, eliminating the celery, and serving one day as a dessert; the next day as a salad by adding ¼ cup chopped celery.

Combine ½ apple, cored and cut into ¼-inch cubes; ¼ cup sliced celery; and 1½ teaspoons each raisins and walnuts in a small bowl. In a custard cup, combine 2 tablespoons low-fat plain yogurt and 1½ teaspoons cranberry concentrate. (Add ¼ teaspoon vanilla for dessert.) Spoon this mixture over the apples and toss. Serve on lettuce leaves.

Menu
18
*416 calories
per serving
(without
vodka);
486 calories
with vodka*

Fall Brunch

TOMATO COCKTAIL

PUFFY PIPERADE ROLLED OMELET

PITA TOASTS

STEAMED PEARS WITH RASPBERRY SAUCE

Plan of action

25 MINUTES BEFORE SERVING

1. Cook the pears and leave them at room temperature or chill them.
2. Cook the raspberry sauce and leave it at room temperature or chill it.
3. While the pears and sauce are cooking, cut the vegetables up for

the piperade and mix the cocktails; chill them.
4. Cook the piperade.
5. Serve the cocktails.
6. Prepare the eggs and toast the pita.

Tomato Cocktail

SERVINGS: 1 ◆ 69 CALORIES (WITHOUT VODKA); 129 CALORIES WITH VODKA

1 cup tomato juice
  Juice from ¼ lemon
  Dash Worcestershire sauce
  Dash hot pepper sauce

Pinch freshly ground black pepper
1 ounce vodka (optional)
2 celery sticks

Combine all the ingredients, except the celery, in a shaker and chill. To serve: Pour over cracked ice in a tall glass and add celery sticks to glass.

196

Puffy Piperade Rolled Omelet

SERVINGS: 4 ◆ 147 CALORIES PER ¼ ROLL ◆ COOKING TIME: 9 TO 13 MINUTES

1 tablespoon plus 1 teaspoon full-flavored olive oil

1 garlic clove, minced

1 green bell pepper, seeded and sliced into ¼-inch strips

1 red bell pepper, seeded and sliced into ¼-inch strips

1 cup peeled and coarsely chopped ripe tomatoes

2 tablespoons chopped fresh basil, plus more for garnish

½ teaspoon chopped fresh oregano leaves, or ¼ teaspoon dried

Dash cayenne pepper (optional)

3 tablespoons grated Parmesan cheese

3 eggs, separated

⅛ teaspoon cream of tartar

1 tablespoon water

Combine 1 tablespoon oil and the garlic in a 9-inch pie plate. Cook on HIGH for 30 seconds. Add the peppers, tomatoes, basil, oregano, and cayenne. Cover with wax paper and cook on HIGH for 5 minutes; stir. Cover again and cook on HIGH for 2 to 5 minutes more, or until the vegetables are tender-crisp. Sprinkle with 2 tablespoons cheese and stir well. Cover and set aside.

Meanwhile, pour the remaining 1 teaspoon olive oil into the bottom of a 10-inch pie plate and brush it out with a pastry brush (this will facilitate removal of the omelet later). Combine the egg whites with cream of tartar in a small bowl and beat them until stiff but not dry. In a medium bowl, combine the egg yolks with the water and mix together well. Fold the whites into the yolks.

Pour the egg mixture into the prepared pie plate and spread to smooth the top. Cook on HIGH for 1½ to 2½ minutes, or until set but not hard. Spoon half of the filling (about 1¼ cup) into the center of the cooked eggs, and fold each side over the filling in twofold letter fashion. Cut into 4 equal serving pieces. Serve each piece with a generous ¼ cup of additional filling mixture and a sprinkling of basil. Divide remaining 1 tablespoon Parmesan between the servings, sprinkling on top.

◆ *For 1 Serving:* Combine 1 teaspoon olive oil and a small minced garlic clove in a 9-inch pie plate. Cook on HIGH for 15 seconds. Add ½ green or red bell pepper, cut into strips, ¼ cup peeled and chopped tomato, 1 teaspoon chopped fresh basil, and a pinch dry oregano and cayenne pepper. Cover with wax paper and cook on HIGH for 2 to 3 minutes, stirring once. Sprinkle with 2 teaspoons Parmesan cheese and stir. Set aside.

Combine 1 egg white with a pinch

cream of tartar in a small bowl and beat until stiff but not dry. In a separate small bowl combine the egg yolk with 1 teaspoon water and stir with a fork. Fold the white into the yolk. Spoon this into an 8-ounce ramekin (about 1 cup capacity). No oil is needed because it won't be unmolded. Cook on HIGH for 45 seconds to 1 minute. Spoon the vegetable filling on top, and serve without rolling.

Pita Toasts

SERVINGS: 4 ◆ 95 CALORIES PER 1 PITA

4 1-ounce whole wheat pitas

Toast and quarter each pita. Serve 4 quarters with each serving of Puffy Piperade Rolled Omelet.

Steamed Pears with Raspberry Sauce

SERVINGS: 4 ◆ 115 CALORIES PER PEAR AND 2 TABLESPOONS SAUCE
◆ COOKING TIME: 10 TO 12 MINUTES

4 firm ripe pears (1¼ pounds)
1 lemon, quartered
¼ cup water

½ cup Raspberry Sauce (see below)
Grated nutmeg (optional)

Keeping the stems in place, core the pears from the base with a grapefruit knife. Peel the pears and rub each with a quarter of the cut lemon to prevent discoloration.

Combine the lemon quarters and water in a 1½-quart casserole. Place the pears on their sides, positioning the thicker ends toward the outside of the casserole. Cover tightly and cook on HIGH for 6 minutes. Turn the pears over and baste. Cover again and continue to cook on HIGH for 4 to 6 minutes, or until tender. Let the pears cool in their liquid, turning them occasionally. Serve the pears warm or chilled. The pears may be kept refrigerated for 2 to 3 days.

To serve: Place each pear upright on a dessert plate. Spoon about 1 tablespoon cooking liquid over each pear. Sprinkle with nutmeg, if desired. Then drizzle with 2 tablespoons raspberry sauce.

◆ *For 1 Serving:* Keeping the stem in

place, peel and core 1 pear and rub it with a quarter of a lemon. Place the pear upright in a small microwave-proof bowl. Add the ¼ lemon and 1 tablespoon water. Cover tightly and cook on HIGH for 2½ to 4 minutes. Let the pear cool and serve it with its juices and a sprinkling of nutmeg, if desired. Drizzle with 2 tablespoons Raspberry Sauce.

Raspberry Sauce

MAKES: 1 CUP ◆ 15 CALORIES PER 1 TABLESPOON ◆ COOKING TIME: 4 TO 6 MINUTES

2 cups fresh or frozen raspberries
2 tablespoons sugar
1 tablespoon orange-flavored liqueur

Combine all the ingredients in a 2-quart casserole. Cook on HIGH for 4 to 6 minutes, or until the mixture is boiling, stirring after 3 minutes. Puree the mixture in a food processor. Serve warm or chilled.

Lunch Suggestions

Here are some ways to turn the leftovers from the Fall Menus into satisfying lunches that fit into your calorie plan. Where no beverage is suggested, select mineral water, sparkling soda with a twist of lemon, or black coffee or tea.

Chicken and Cranberry Salad

¾ cup Nouvelle Waldorf Salad (page 194)	130 calories
combined with 2 ounces cubed cooked chicken or hen	
without dressing (page 146 or 192)	108 calories
2 whole wheat melba toasts	30 calories
½ cup skim milk	44 calories
TOTAL	312 calories

Sliced Beef and Alfalfa Sprouts Sandwich

2 ounces thinly sliced Boiled Beef (page 169)	108 calories
with sliced radishes, alfalfa sprouts,	
mustard, and horseradish in	21 calories
1-ounce whole wheat pita bread, cut in half	95 calories
TOTAL	224 calories

Veal Loaf Sandwich with Sliced Apple

½ Veal and Vegetable Loaf (page 158) thinly sliced	123 calories
with mustard and lettuce in	10 calories
1-ounce whole wheat pita	95 calories
½ apple, sliced	40 calories
TOTAL	268 calories

Sliced Chicken Sandwich with Pear Slices

2 ounces sliced, cooked chicken (page 146)	108 calories
with lettuce in	2 calories
1-ounce whole wheat pita	95 calories
½ cup skim milk	44 calories
½ pear, sliced	49 calories
TOTAL	298 calories

Pear and Cheese Lunch

1 pear, thinly sliced	98 calories
1 ounce Swiss cheese or other hard cheese, sliced	100 calories
4 whole wheat melba toasts	60 calories
TOTAL	258 calories

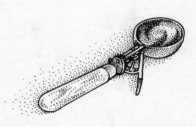

We have a friend who can take 30 minutes to eat one-half of a cantaloupe; 45 minutes for an apple. Her secret is to cut any fruit that she eats into thin pieces or small chunks. Then she arranges them beautifully on a plate and whittles away at the fruit, savoring each morsel before she reaches for another one.

When you're not in a hurry , take the time to eat a piece of fruit slowly. It will make your lunch or snack time more satisfying.

Cheeseless Banana Cheesecake Lunch

1 Cheeseless Banana Cheesecake (page 147)	102 calories
with 20 grapes	72 calories
2 whole wheat melba toasts	30 calories
½ cup low-fat cottage cheese	82 calories
TOTAL	286 calories

WINTER MENUS

Wintertime, especially around the holidays, is a time for entertaining, or being entertained at homes, at the office, or in restaurants. These situations can be the sure downfall of many dieters unless they are aware of the great temptations that await them. The best defense is a good offense, so be prepared in these ways:

▲▲▲▲▲▲▲▲▲▲▲▲

◆ Be especially conscious of everything you put in your mouth. One little potato chip may not seem like much, but 11 calories per chip can add up.
◆ Pack low-calorie snacks to take with you, and munch them on the way to the party to stave off hunger, especially at cocktail parties.
◆ If you are picking out a restaurant where you want to meet friends, choose one with "spa" cuisine or a salad bar.
◆ Avoid a lot of alcohol, for it not ony adds calories but lowers your willpower to resist food. Order club soda with lime on the rocks or sparkling apple cider. The hardest part about not having a drink may be answering people's questions as to why not. Club soda and cider will look to others like alcoholic drinks.

If you are drinking alcohol, stretch out your wine drinking with club soda in a red or white wine spritzer. Here are some alcoholic drinks that are lower in calories than others:

12 ounces "lite" beer	95 calories
3 ounces Liebfraumilch	68 calories
3 ounces champagne (Blancs de Blancs)	65 calories
3 ounces red Beaujolais, Moselle, Sancérre, Pouilly-Fumé	
	65 calories

Combine any of the wines with equal amounts of club soda or sparkling water for no additional calories. Even add some fruit juice for something different:

3 ounces pineapple or tangerine juice	45 calories
3 ounces grapefruit or orange juice	39 calories

◆ If you are going to a dinner party where everybody is bringing something, offer to bring a vegetable and dip for appetizers or a salad. That way you'll know there will be at least one low-calorie offering.

◆ If the plates are to be served to you and you're dining with close friends, indicate to the hostess discreetly beforehand that you would like a small portion. That includes dessert, especially.

◆ If you have been served more food than you'll ever eat, learn the fine art of pushing things around on your plate. Watch a two-year-old if you want to learn the technique. Spreading food out on your plate or hiding something under a roll or mashed potatoes gives you something to do with your hands, other than eating, and makes it look like you've eaten more.

Don't apologize for not finishing all that's on your plate, just thank the waiter or hostess profusely for the delicious meal, and he or she will never notice.

◆ Go to a restaurant or dinner party with a dress or pants that has a belt which will hold you snugly in place. In fact, tighten it one notch before you sit down to eat. It will be a constant reminder of everything that goes into your belly.

▼ ▼ ▼ ▼ ▼ ▼ ▼ ▼ ▼ ▼ ▼ ▼

Grocery shopping can sabotage your efforts to remain on a diet, too, so never shop right before lunch or dinner. Instead, go out early in the morning with a shopping list, and stick to it.

Make your first stop at the produce aisle and stock up on the beautiful winter fruit available: Mandarin oranges for snacks, fruit cups, salads, and accents for chicken dishes add only 33 calories per small orange. Another choice is pink, ruby, and white grapefruits. They adapt to any meal, and a rainbow salad of all three can be a first course, side dish, or dessert. Oranges fit in just as well as grapefruit do.

The salad is eaten first in this particular meal, because the stew takes much longer to make and is still cooking while you are eating the salad.

HEALTH SALAD WITH ZESTY YOGURT DRESSING

HOME-STYLE CHICKEN AND VEGETABLE STEW

BANANA MOUSSE

Menu

1

408 calories
per serving

Plan of action

30 MINUTES BEFORE SERVING

1. Cook the chicken part of the stew. Then make the banana mousse and speed chill it.

2. Make the salad.
3. Serve the salad while the vegetables are cooking in the stew broth.

Health Salad with Zesty Yogurt Dressing

SERVINGS: 4 ◆ 50 CALORIES PER 1-CUP SERVING

1 cup mixed greens
1 cup thinly sliced radishes
1 medium cucumber, thinly sliced

½ cup alfalfa sprouts
1 green pepper, seeded and thinly sliced

ZESTY YOGURT DRESSING:

½ cup low-fat plain yogurt
¼ cup chopped fresh parsley
1 teaspoon lemon juice
½ teaspoon dried oregano

2 chopped fresh mint leaves, or ¼ teaspoon dried
¼ teaspoon ground cuminseed
Dash cayenne pepper

Combine the salad ingredients in a medium salad bowl and toss.

Combine all the dressing ingredients together in a small mixing bowl. Toss with the salad.

◆ *For 1 Serving:* Combine ¼ cup mixed salad greens, 2 tablespoons grated carrot, ¼ cup thinly sliced cucumber, 2 tablespoons alfalfa sprouts, and ¼ thinly sliced green pepper in a small bowl. In another small bowl combine 2 tablespoons plain yogurt; 1 tablespoon chopped fresh parsley; ¼

207

teaspoon lemon juice; a dash dried oregano; and a pinch each dried mint leaves, cuminseed, and cayenne pepper. Pour the dressing on the salad and toss.

Home-Style Chicken and Vegetable Stew

SERVINGS: 4 WITH LEFTOVERS ◆ 280 CALORIES PER SERVING ◆ COOKING TIME: 35 TO 39 MINUTES

This home-style stew has just a touch of jalapeño pepper to zip it up.

1 whole 3½- to 4-pound chicken
1 garlic clove, minced
1 onion, quartered
1 carrot, coarsely chopped, plus 1 cup thinly sliced carrots
1 celery rib, thinly sliced
¼ cup chopped fresh parsley, plus more for garnish

½ jalapeño pepper, seeded and chopped, or ¼ teaspoon red pepper flakes
1 bay leaf, crushed
1 cup water
2 medium boiling potatoes, washed and quartered
1 cup thinly sliced parsnips
1 cup turnips, cut into ¼-inch cubes

Remove the giblets from the chicken. Place the chicken breast side down in a 3-quart casserole. Add the garlic, onion, coarsely chopped carrot, celery, parsley, hot pepper, bay leaf, and water. Cover tightly and cook on HIGH for 28 minutes, turning the chicken over after 14 minutes.

Remove the chicken from the cooking liquid and set it aside. Add the potatoes, thinly sliced carrots, parsnips, and turnips. Cover tightly and cook on HIGH for 7 to 11 minutes, or until tender, stirring after 4 minutes.

Meanwhile, remove the skin from the chicken and place 3 ounces of sliced chicken in each of 4 soup bowls. Add 2 quarters of a potato to each bowl and ¼ cup vegetables. Ladle ½ cup broth over the chicken and vegetables and sprinkle with fresh parsley.

◆ For 2 Servings: This recipe is difficult to reduce. Cook the whole chicken as directed and remove, but add only 1 medium boiling potato, quartered, ½ cup thinly sliced carrots and 1 cup thinly sliced parsnips. Save the leftover broth and chicken for another meal.

◆ Tip: After dinner, remove the remaining chicken meat and shred it for future meals. You should have about 2 cups.

Banana Mousse

SERVINGS: 4 ◆ 78 CALORIES PER 1-CUP SERVING

A frothy delight that is good chilled or frozen.

2 ripe bananas
1 tablespoon sugar
1 teaspoon lemon juice
1 teaspoon vanilla extract

¼ teaspoon grated nutmeg
2 egg whites, stiffly beaten
⅛ teaspoon cream of tartar

Combine the bananas, sugar, lemon juice, vanilla, and nutmeg in the bowl of a food processor or blender, or in a small bowl. Process, or mash with a fork until smooth.

In another bowl, beat together the egg whites and cream of tartar until stiff but not dry. Fold the egg whites into the bananas. Spoon into 4 dessert goblets. Speed chill in the freezer for 30 minutes.

◆ *For 2 Servings:* Combine 1 ripe banana, 1½ teaspoons sugar, ½ teaspoon each lemon juice and vanilla, and ⅛ teaspoon nutmeg in the bowl of

a food processor or blender or in a small bowl. Process or mash with a fork until smooth. In another bowl, beat together 1 egg white and a pinch of cream of tartar until stiff but not dry. Fold the egg whites into the banana. Spoon into 2 dessert goblets. Speed chill in the freezer for 30 minutes.

◆ *Tip:* Save the egg yolks for Egg Drop Soup (Menu #4) later in the week. To store egg yolks, place in an airtight plastic or glass container and keep refrigerated for up to 4 days.

209

Menu

2

*432 calories
per serving*

GREEN CHILE SOUP

SOFT CORN CHICKEN TORTILLAS WITH SALSA

BAHAMIAN ORANGES

Plan of action

20 MINUTES BEFORE SERVING

1. Prepare the oranges and chill them.
2. Prepare and cook the soup.
3. While the soup is cooking, prepare the chicken filling and salsa.

4. Serve the soup. Meanwhile, cook the chicken filling.
5. Heat the tortillas and serve the chicken tortillas.

Green Chile Soup

SERVINGS: 4 ◆ 36 CALORIES PER ¾-CUP SERVING ◆ COOKING TIME: 8 TO 10 MINUTES

> 4 green onions, thinly sliced
> 2 Anaheim chiles, coarsely chopped
> ½ jalapeño pepper, seeded and coarsely chopped, or ⅛ teaspoon red pepper flakes

> 1½ cups chicken broth
> 1 cup tomato juice
> 2 tablespoons chopped fresh cilantro

Combine all the ingredients, except the cilantro, in a 2-quart casserole. Cover tightly and cook on HIGH for 8 to 10 minutes, or until heated through.

To serve: Spoon the soup into 4 cups and sprinkle with cilantro.

◆ *For 1 Serving:* Combine 1 sliced green onion, ½ chopped Anaheim

chile, a couple of slices of jalapeño pepper or a pinch red pepper flakes, ½ cup chicken broth, and ¼ cup tomato juice in a microwaveproof soup bowl. Cover tightly and cook on HIGH for 1½ to 3 minutes. Sprinkle with 1½ teaspoons chopped cilantro before serving.

Soft Corn Chicken Tortillas with Salsa

SERVINGS: 4 ◆ 323 CALORIES PER 2 TORTILLAS WITH ½ CUP FILLING, ¼ CUP SALSA, AND
1 TABLESPOON GRATED CHEESE ◆ COOKING TIME: 7 TO 10 MINUTES

Soft corn tortillas can be purchased in the dairy case and are 50 calories per tortilla. Tomatillos are a variety of small green tomatoes from Mexico that add a wonderfully unique flavor; they have nothing in common with domestic unripe tomatoes.

If you have any filling left over, it is good reheated or served cold for lunch.

1 teaspoon vegetable oil
1 garlic clove, minced
2 tablespoons chopped onion
½ cup chopped tomatillos or tomatoes
1 teaspoon white vinegar
   Dash cayenne pepper
2 cups shredded chicken (page 208)

2 tablespoons chopped cilantro
8 soft corn tortillas
1 cup Simply Salsa (see below)
2 ounces low-fat mozzarella or Monterey
   Jack cheese, grated
½ cup shredded lettuce

Combine the oil, garlic, and onion in a 1-quart casserole. Cook on HIGH for 1 minute. Stir in the tomatillos, vinegar, cayenne, and chicken. Cover again and cook on HIGH for 4 to 6 minutes, or until heated through, stirring once. Stir in the cilantro. Set the mixture aside, covered.

Meanwhile, wrap the tortillas in a paper towel and place them in the microwave oven. Heat them on HIGH for 1½ to 2½ minutes, or until heated through.

To assemble the tortillas: Place ¼ cup chicken filling into each tortilla. Top each with 2 tablespoons salsa, 1 tablespoon cheese, and a little lettuce, then roll the tortillas around and serve.

◆ For 1 Serving: Combine a drop of oil, 1 small minced garlic clove, and 1½ teaspoons chopped onion in a pie plate. Cook on HIGH for 20 seconds. Stir in 2 tablespoons chopped tomatillos, ¼ teaspoon white vinegar, a pinch cayenne pepper, and ½ cup shredded chicken. Cover tightly and cook on HIGH for 1 to 2½ minutes, or until hot. Stir in 1½ teaspoons chopped cilantro. Wrap 2 soft corn tortillas in a paper towel. Place them in the microwave oven and heat them on HIGH for 20 seconds to 1 minute, or until hot. Spoon ¼ cup chicken filling into each tortilla, topped with 2 tablespoons salsa, 1 tablespoon grated low-fat Monterey Jack cheese, and a little lettuce. Roll the tortillas around this filling and serve.

Simply Salsa

MAKES: 1 CUP ◆ 16 CALORIES PER ¼ CUP

This mixture keeps in the refrigerator for 3 days, adds zing to soups, sandwiches, and even cooked eggs.

1 large ripe tomato
2 green onions

½ teaspoon white vinegar
1 jalapeño pepper, seeded

Combine all the ingredients in the bowl of a food processor or blender. Process until slightly chunky.

Unlimited quantities of most vegetables may be eaten with any meal and need not be added to the day's calorie count. You may eat these vegetables raw or steam them as with Summer Squash Salad (page 129), Steamed Vegetable Bowls (page 56), or Seasonal Vegetable Platter (page 112).

◆ Note: Unlimited means vegetables only, not dipping sauces or dressings. Here are some of those vegetables: asparagus, any greens, cabbage, celery, spinach, radishes, zucchini, watercress.

Bahamian Oranges

SERVINGS: 4 ◆ 57 CALORIES PER ½-CUP SERVING

2 cups naval oranges, peeled, segmented, and cubed
1 tablespoon rum
1 tablespoon grated unsweetened coconut

Combine all the ingredients in a bowl and chill them until serving time. Serve in long-stemmed goblets.

◆ For 1 Serving: Combine ½ cup cubed naval orange segments, 1 tea- spoon rum, and 1 teaspoon grated un- sweetened coconut in a small serving bowl. Chill and serve.

MUSHROOM MARSALA SOUP

TUNA STEAKS WITH PINK GRAPEFRUIT SAUCE

BROCCOLI SPEARS WITH LEMON

HONEYED PINEAPPLE RINGS WITH FROZEN VANILLA YOGURT

Menu

3

314 calories per serving

Plan of action

25 MINUTES BEFORE SERVING

1. Mix up the vanilla yogurt and speed chill it.
2. Make the soup. While it's cooking, prepare the fish, sauce and broccoli for cooking.
3. Serve the soup. Meanwhile, cook the fish.
4. Cook the broccoli, then allow it to stand, covered, while cooking the fish sauce.
5. Serve the fish with its sauce, and serve the broccoli.
6. Heat up the pineapple and serve it.

Mushroom Marsala Soup

SERVINGS: 4 ◆ 23 CALORIES PER ¾-CUP SERVING ◆ COOKING TIME: 4 TO 7 MINUTES

1 cup thinly sliced mushrooms
2 cups beef broth
1 tablespoon dry Marsala wine
½ teaspoon dried thyme leaves
¼ teaspoon dried mustard
¼ cup chopped fresh parsley

Combine all the ingredients, except the parsley, in a 2-quart casserole. Cover tightly and cook on HIGH for 4 to 7 minutes, or until heated through. Pour the soup into bowls and sprinkle with parsley.

◆ *For 1 Serving:* Combine ¼ cup thinly sliced mushrooms, ¼ cup beef broth, 1 teaspoon dry Marsala wine, a dash thyme leaves, and a pinch dried mustard in a microwaveproof soup bowl. Cover tightly and cook on HIGH for 1½ to 2 minutes. Sprinkle with 1 tablespoon chopped parsley to serve.

213

Tuna Steaks with Pink Grapefruit Sauce

SERVINGS: 4 ◆ 187 CALORIES PER SERVING ◆ COOKING TIME: 10 TO 13 MINUTES

2 *8-ounce tuna, sword, or salmon steaks, cut in half*
1 *tablespoon lemon juice*
   Dash freshly ground black pepper
2 *large pink grapefruit*
1 *garlic clove, minced*

2 *green onions, thinly sliced*
1 *teaspoon cornstarch*
½ *teaspoon dried thyme leaves*
   Dash cayenne pepper
¼ *cup chopped fresh parsley*

Place the fish steaks into a 10-inch pie plate, with the thicker edges toward the outside rim of the dish. Sprinkle with lemon juice and freshly ground pepper. Cover with wax paper and cook on MEDIUM for 7 to 9 minutes, or until the fish flakes under the pressure of a fork. Let the fish stand, covered, until serving time.

Meanwhile, squeeze the juice from 1 grapefruit and pour it into a glass measure. Segment the other grapefruit and set the segments aside. While segmenting the grapefruits, save any of the juices from the membranes and squeeze them into the same glass measure. You should have about ½ cup grapefruit juice. Set the juices aside.

Combine the garlic, green onions, and 1 tablespoon grapefruit juice in a 4-cup glass measure. Cook on HIGH for 1 minute. In a custard cup combine the cornstarch and 1 tablespoon grapefruit juice. Add the cornstarch mixture, along with the thyme, cayenne pepper, and remaining grapefruit juice to the garlic and green onions. Cook on HIGH for 1 minute;

stir. Cook on HIGH for 1 to 2 minutes more, or until the mixture boils and is slightly thickened.

To serve: Arrange each tuna steak on a dinner plate with about 3 grapefruit segments fanned out beside it and spoon 2 tablespoons sauce over the top. Sprinkle the steaks with parsley. Place the broccoli with lemon on the other side of the plate.

◆ *For 2 Servings:* It will be necessary to purchase at least one steak for a single serving, so cook the whole steak and make a salad with the remaining cooked half.

Cut one 8-ounce fish steak in half and place the halves, with the thicker portion to the outside, on a microwaveproof plate. Sprinkle with 1 teaspoon lemon juice and a dash black pepper. Cover with wax paper and cook on MEDIUM for 3 to 4 minutes. Let the fish stand, covered, until serving time.

Meanwhile, segment ½ grapefruit (saving half the segments for breakfast the next day) and squeeze any of the juices from the membrane into a cup (about 2 tablespoons). Combine 1 small minced garlic clove, 1 sliced green onion, and 1 tablespoon grapefruit juice in a 2-cup glass measure. Cook on HIGH for 30 seconds. In a custard cup combine ½ teaspoon cornstarch with 1 tablespoon grapefruit juice in a custard cup. Add the corn-

starch mixture to the garlic and green onion, along with the remaining grapefruit juice, ¼ teaspoon thyme, and a dash of cayenne pepper. Cook the mixture on HIGH for 1 to 2 minutes, or until bubbling and slightly thickened, stirring once. Spoon the sauce over the fish. Sprinkle with parsley.

When *you eat is as important as* what *you eat, so try not to eat too late at night.* "The No Diet, No Willpower Way to Weight Loss" by the editors of Prevention magazine, a study documented in Chrono-biologica (Vol. 3, No. 1, 1976), showed that when seven volunteers ate 2,000 calories a day at breakfast, they lost weight. But when the same people ate the same amount at an evening meal, they lost less weight, or even gained it.

Broccoli Spears with Lemon

SERVINGS: 4 ◆ 26 CALORIES PER 2 STALKS BROCCOLI ◆ COOKING TIME: 6 TO 8 MINUTES

1 pound broccoli, trimmed and cut into 8 long spears
1 lemon, thinly sliced
2 tablespoons water

Place the broccoli wagon wheel fashion, with the stalk ends toward the outside of a 10-inch round serving dish. Place the lemon slices over the stalks. Sprinkle with water. Cover tightly and cook on HIGH for 6 to 8 minutes, or until the desired doneness is reached, rotating the dish halfway through cooking. Let the broccoli stand, covered, for 3 minutes.

◆ *For 1 Serving:* Trim 4 ounces broccoli and cut it into spears. Place the broccoli in an 8-ounce ramekin. Add 2 lemon slices and 1 teaspoon water. Cover tightly and cook on HIGH for 1 to 3 minutes.

Honeyed Pineapple Rings with Frozen Vanilla Yogurt

SERVINGS: 4 ◆ 78 CALORIES PER SERVING ◆ COOKING TIME: 2 TO 4 MINUTES

½ cup low-fat plain yogurt
1 teaspoon vanilla extract
½ teaspoon ground cinnamon

4 fresh pineapple rings (3½" x ¾" thick),
center core removed; or 4 canned rings
packed in their own juices, drained
4 teaspoons honey

Combine the yogurt, vanilla, and cinnamon in a small bowl and place it in the freezer to speed chill until serving time, at least 30 minutes.

Right before serving, place the pineapple rings on a 10-inch microwaveproof plate and drizzle 1 teaspoon honey over each. Cover with wax paper and cook on HIGH for 2 to 4 minutes, or until heated through.

To serve: Place 1 warm pineapple ring on each of 4 dessert plates and spoon 2 tablespoons of the frozen vanilla yogurt into the center of each ring. Sprinkle with additional cinnamon, if desired.

◆ For 1 Serving: Combine 2 tablespoons yogurt with ¼ teaspoon each vanilla and cinnamon in a custard cup and place in the freezer for at least 30 minutes. Right before serving, place 1 pineapple ring on a microwaveproof serving plate and drizzle it with 1 teaspoon honey. Cook on HIGH for 30 seconds to 1 minute. Spoon the frozen yogurt into the center of the warm pineapple ring.

EGG DROP SOUP

PITA PIZZA

CARROT AND CELERY STICKS (1 CARROT, 21 CALORIES)

PEARS IN ORANGE SAUCE

Plan of action

30 MINUTES BEFORE SERVING

1. Cook the pears and refrigerate them, or leave them at room temperature.
2. Make the tomato sauce. While the sauce is cooking, cut the carrots and celery into sticks.

3. Prepare and cook the soup. While the soup is cooking, prepare the pizza.
4. Serve the soup, and meanwhile cook the pizza.

Egg Drop Soup

SERVINGS: 4 ◆ 64 CALORIES PER 1-CUP SERVING ◆ COOKING TIME: 9 TO 13 MINUTES

This recipe makes use of the 2 egg yolks from the Banana Mousse (Menu #1).

4 cups chicken broth
1 teaspoon lemon juice
2 green onions, thinly sliced
⅛ teaspoon grated nutmeg
2 egg yolks

1 tablespoon flour
1 tablespoon water
2 tablespoons chopped fresh parsley
Dash freshly ground black pepper

Combine the broth, lemon juice, green onions, and nutmeg in a 2-quart casserole. Cover tightly and cook on HIGH for 8 to 10 minutes, or until boiling.

Meanwhile, combine the egg yolks, flour, and water in a custard cup and beat with a fork until smooth. Remove the soup from the microwave oven and force the egg mixture through a small sieve into the soup to make egg drops. Place the soup back into the microwave and cook it on HIGH for 1 to 3 minutes, or until the soup comes to a boil again. Spoon the soup into bowls and top it with parsley and black pepper.

217

◆ *For 2 Servings:* It isn't practical to make 1 serving, so make 2 servings, and serve some the next day. Combine 2 cups chicken broth, ½ teaspoon lemon juice, 1 thinly sliced green onion, and a dash nutmeg in a 1-quart casserole. Cook on HIGH for 4 to 5 minutes, or until boiling. Meanwhile, combine 1 egg yolk and 1½ teaspoons each flour and water into a custard cup and beat with a fork until

smooth. Remove the soup from the microwave and force the egg mixture through a small sieve into the soup to make egg drops. Place the soup back into the microwave and cook it on HIGH for 30 seconds to 1½ minutes, or until the soup comes to a boil again. Spoon the soup into 2 bowls and top each with 1½ teaspoons chopped fresh parsley and a dash black pepper.

Pita Pizza

SERVINGS: 4 ◆ 276 CALORIES PER SERVING ◆ COOKING TIME: 6 TO 11 MINUTES

1 tablespoon full-flavored olive oil
2 garlic cloves, minced
1 cup tomato puree (we like Progresso)
1 teaspoon dried oregano
¼ teaspoon black pepper, plus extra for garnish

¼ teaspoon red pepper flakes (optional)
2 large (7-inch-diameter) pita rounds, cut in half horizontally
8 ounces grated low-fat mozzarella cheese

Combine the oil and garlic in a 4-cup glass measure. Cook on HIGH for 35 seconds. Add the tomato puree, oregano, and black and red pepper. Cook on HIGH for 2 or 3 minutes, or until boiling, stirring once. Set aside.

Place 2 pita halves, cut side up, on each of 4 paper plates or paper towel–lined paper plates (the paper will absorb the excess moisture). Spread each round with ¼ cup tomato sauce. Sprinkle 2 ounces cheese on each round. Sprinkle with pepper. Place 2 plates at a time in the microwave oven and cook on MEDIUM for 2 to 4 minutes, or until the cheese is melted. Repeat the process and, meanwhile, cut the cooked pitas in quarters.

◆ *For 1 Serving:* Combine ½ teaspoon olive oil, ½ minced garlic clove, ¼ cup tomato puree, ⅛ teaspoon dried oregano, a dash each black and red pepper in a 1-cup glass measure. Cook on HIGH for 30 seconds. Cut one 7-inch pita in half horizontally. Place one half on a paper plate or paper towel–lined plate. Spread with tomato sauce and sprinkle with 2 ounces low-fat cheese. Cook on MEDIUM for 1 to 2 minutes. Cut into quarters and serve.

◆ *For 2 Servings:* Combine 1 teaspoon olive oil, 1 small minced garlic clove, ½ cup tomato puree, ¼ teaspoon dried oregano, and a dash black and red pepper in a 1-cup glass measure. Cook on HIGH for 1 minute, or until boiling. Cut one 7-inch pita in half horizontally, and place both halves on a paper plate or paper towel—lined plate. Divide ½ cup tomato sauce between the 2 pita halves. Divide 4 ounces low-fat mozzarella cheese between the two. Cook on MEDIUM for 1½ to 2½ minutes. Cut into quarters and serve.

Variations:

Mushroom Pita Pizza: To each pizza add 2 small, thinly sliced mushrooms with the cheese. 6 calories.
Artichoke Pita Pizza: To each pizza add 3 canned drained artichoke hearts, split in half, with the cheese. 22 calories.
Olive Pita Pizza: To each pizza, add 5 small green olives, cut into 3 pieces each, with the cheese. 21 calories.

Pears in Orange Sauce

SERVINGS: 4 ◆ 97 CALORIES PER SERVING ◆ COOKING TIME: 10 TO 12 MINUTES

4 firm ripe pears (1¼ pounds)
½ cup unsweetened orange juice
1 teaspoon vanilla extract

½ teaspoon ground cinnamon
¼ teaspoon grated nutmeg

Keeping the stems intact, core the pears from the base so that they retain their shape.

Combine the remaining ingredients in a 1½-quart casserole. Place the pears on their sides, positioning the thicker ends toward the outside of the casserole. Cover tightly and cook on HIGH for 6 minutes; turn the pears over and baste. Cover again and cook on HIGH for 4 to 6 minutes, or until the pears are tender when pierced with a knife. Let the pears stand, covered, or cool in refrigerator in their juices until serving time, turning them over occasionally.

To serve: Place each pear standing upright in a dessert dish and spoon about 2 tablespoons cooking liquid over each one.

◆ *For 1 Serving:* Core 1 firm, ripe pear, keeping the shape of the pear and the stem intact. Place the pear upright in a small microwaveproof bowl. Add 2 tablespoons unsweetened orange juice, ¼ teaspoon vanilla, a dash cinnamon, and a pinch nutmeg. Cover tightly and cook on HIGH for 2½ to 3 minutes. Let the pear stand, covered, and serve warm, or place in refrigerator to chill until serving time (10 to 20 minutes).

These flavors were inspired when visiting an Indian restaurant, and we discovered that a touch of steamy, hot India was a terrific antidote for mid-winter blues.

CHUNKY TOMATO-BUTTERMILK SOUP WITH MINT

CURRIED SCROD

MINTED POTATOES AND PEAS

FLAMING BANANAS

Plan of action

30 MINUTES BEFORE SERVING

1. Prepare and cook the soup. While the soup cooks, prepare the fish, sauce and vegetables.
2. Serve the soup, and meanwhile cook the fish.
3. Cook the vegetables.
4. Cook the sauce.
5. Serve the fish and vegetables.
6. Make the dessert and serve it.

Chunky Tomato-Buttermilk Soup with Mint

SERVINGS: 4 ◆ 63½ CALORIES PER 1-CUP SERVING ◆ COOKING TIME: 8 TO 10 MINUTES

3 *cups tomato juice*
1 *cup buttermilk*
2 *green onions, sliced*
1 *teaspoon chopped fresh mint leaves*

¼ *teaspoon dried cilantro*
⅛ *teaspoon cayenne pepper*
1 *cup peeled, seeded, and chopped cucumber*

Combine all the ingredients, except the cucumber, in a 2-quart casserole. Cover tightly and cook on HIGH for 8 to 10 minutes, until heated through.

To serve: Place ¼ cup chopped cucumber into each of 4 soup bowls and pour 1 cup soup into each bowl. Serve.

◆ *For 1 Serving:* Combine ⅔ cup tomato juice, ¼ cup buttermilk, ½ sliced green onion, ¼ teaspoon chopped mint leaves, a dash cilantro, and a pinch cayenne pepper in a microwaveproof serving bowl. Cook on HIGH for 2 to 3 minutes. Spoon in ¼ cup peeled, seeded, and chopped cucumbers. Serve.

Curried Scrod

SERVINGS: 4 ◆ 144 CALORIES PER SERVING ◆ COOKING TIME: 11 TO 14 MINUTES

4 4-ounce scrod or cod fillets
1 tablespoon lemon juice

Sauce:

1 teaspoon vegetable oil
1 tablespoon chopped onion
2 tablespoons curry powder

1 teaspoon cuminseed
½ teaspoon ground cinnamon
1 cup low-fat plain yogurt

Place the fish fillets around the outer rim of a 9- or 10-inch pie plate with the center open. Sprinkle with lemon juice. Cover with wax paper. Cook on MEDIUM for 9 to 11 minutes, or until the fish tests done. Let the fish stand, covered.

To make the sauce, combine the oil, onion, curry powder, cuminseed, and cinnamon in a 4-cup glass measure. Cook on HIGH for 1 minute. Transfer the fish from the cooking liquid to individual serving plates. Stir the cooked onion mixture and yogurt into the cooking liquid from the fish. Cook on HIGH for 1 to 2 minutes, or until heated through; stir.

To serve: Spoon ⅓ cup of sauce over each fish fillet. Serve the potatoes and peas on the same plate with the fish.

◆ *For 1 Serving:* Place a 4-ounce fish fillet in an 8-ounce ramekin with 1 teaspoon lemon juice. Cover with wax paper and cook on MEDIUM for 2 to 4 minutes. Let stand, covered, while cooking the sauce.

Combine ¼ teaspoon oil, 1¼ teaspoons chopped onion, 1½ teaspoons curry powder, ¼ teaspoon cuminseed, and a dash cinnamon in a 4-cup glass measure. Cook on HIGH for 20 to 30 seconds. Transfer the fish fillet to a serving plate. Stir the onion mixture into the cooking liquid from the fish and add ¼ cup low-fat plain yogurt. Cook on HIGH for 30 seconds, or until hot; stir well. Spoon over the fish.

Minted Potatoes and Peas

SERVINGS: 4 ◆ 76 CALORIES PER ½ POTATO AND ¼ CUP PEAS ◆ COOKING TIME: 5 TO 9 MINUTES

2 boiling potatoes, washed and cut into 8 chunks
1 cup fresh or frozen peas
1 teaspoon dried mint
1 green onion, thinly sliced
¼ cup water

Combine all the ingredients in a 1½-quart casserole. Cover tightly and cook on HIGH for 5 to 9 minutes, or until the vegetables are tender, stirring once.

◆ *For 1 Serving:* Combine 1 small (2 ounces) quartered potato, ¼ cup fresh or frozen peas, ¼ teaspoon dried mint, ½ sliced green onion, and 1 tablespoon water in an 8-ounce ramekin. Cover tightly and cook on HIGH for 2 to 4 minutes, stirring once.

Flaming Bananas

SERVINGS: 4 ◆ 110 CALORIES PER SERVING ◆ COOKING TIME: 2 TO 4 MINUTES

Diet desserts are anything but boring when they are flamed before serving, as with these brandied bananas.

¼ cup orange juice
2 tablespoons brown sugar
1 teaspoon lemon juice
1 teaspoon vanilla extract
½ teaspoon ground cinnamon
2 bananas, peeled and cut in half lengthwise
2 tablespoons brandy (80 proof for flaming)

Combine the orange juice, brown sugar, lemon juice, vanilla, and cinnamon in a 9-inch pie plate. Cook on HIGH for 1 minute; stir.

Place the bananas in the sauce, turning them over to coat and positioning them with flat sides up. Cover with wax paper and cook on HIGH for 1 to 3 minutes, or until the bananas are heated through. Pour the brandy into a 1-cup glass measure and heat on HIGH for 15 seconds. Pour the mixture over the bananas and ignite with a match.

◆ *For 1 Serving:* Combine 1 tablespoon orange juice, 1½ teaspoons brown sugar, ¼ teaspoon each lemon juice and vanilla, and a pinch cinnamon in an 8-ounce ramekin. Cook on HIGH for 30 seconds. Place ½ banana, halved lengthwise, in the sauce, turning it over to coat and positioning it with the flat side up. Cover with wax paper and cook on HIGH for 30 seconds, or until the banana is heated through. Pour 1½ teaspoons brandy into a 1-cup glass measure and heat on HIGH for 10 seconds. Pour over the bananas and ignite.

We recommend that you buy a 1½-pound round steak (London broil) and cut it in half. Freeze the other half for Menu #14 and the Beef Teriyaki. Freezing the beef will make it easier to slice.

Menu

6

363 calories
per serving

SHERRIED MUSHROOM-BEEF BROTH

GRILLED ROUND STEAK
WITH TOMATO-ORANGE SALSA

WARM CORN TORTILLAS

MIXED GREENS WITH DRESSING

APPLE-APRICOT CREAM

Plan of action

1. Cook the dessert. Meanwhile, prepare the ingredients for the soup.
2. Chill the dessert.
3. Cook the soup and, meanwhile, prepare the ingredients for the salsa.

30 MINUTES BEFORE SERVING

4. Cook the salsa, serve the soup.
5. Meanwhile, heat the browning dish, and toss the salad.
6. Cook the steak.
7. Warm the tortillas and serve with the steak, salsa, and salad.

Sherried Mushroom-Beef Broth

SERVINGS: 4 ◆ 28 CALORIES PER ½-CUP SERVING ◆ COOKING TIME: 4 TO 6 MINUTES

2 cups beef broth
1 tablespoon dry sherry
4 large mushrooms, thinly sliced

2 green onions, thinly sliced
4 thin lemon slices

Pour the broth and sherry into a 4-cup glass measure. Cook on HIGH for 4 to 6 minutes, until heated through. Divide the mushrooms, green onions, and lemon slices between 4 microwaveproof soup bowls. Pour the heated broth into each bowl.

and 1 teaspoon sherry in a 2-cup glass measure. Heat on HIGH for 1 to 1½ minutes. Place 1 thinly sliced mushroom, ½ thinly sliced green onion, and 1 lemon slice into a microwaveproof soup bowl. Pour the hot broth into the bowl.

◆ *For 1 Serving:* Pour ½ cup broth

Grilled Round Steak

SERVINGS: 4 ◆ 131 CALORIES PER SERVING OF STEAK ◆ COOKING TIME: 9 TO 15 MINUTES, INCLUDING HEATING THE BROWNING DISH

¾ pound round steak, 1 to 1½ inches thick
1 teaspoon vegetable oil

Place the browning dish in the microwave on HIGH for 5 to 9 minutes, or according to the manufacturer's instructions for steak.

Rub the steak with oil and press it down onto the hot browning dish. Cook on HIGH for 2 minutes; turn the steak over. Cook on HIGH for 2 to 4 minutes for medium rare, or until the desired doneness is reached. Thinly slice the steak on the diagonal. Place 3 ounces (3 to 4 strips) of steak onto each plate along with ¼ cup salsa and a warm corn tortilla.

◆ *For 1 Serving:* Place the browning dish in the microwave on HIGH for 5 to 9 minutes, or according to the manufacturer's instructions for steak. Rub 3 ounces round steak, 1 to 1½ inches thick, with ¼ teaspoon oil and press it down on the hot browning dish. Cook on HIGH for 1 minute; turn over. Cook on HIGH for 1 minute more for medium rare, or until the desired doneness is reached. Serve with ¼ cup salsa and a warm tortilla.

Tomato-Orange Salsa

MAKES: 1 CUP ◆ 40 CALORIES PER ¼-CUP SERVING ◆ COOKING TIME: 2 TO 3 MINUTES

1 teaspoon full-flavored olive oil
1 garlic clove, minced
¼ teaspoon cuminseed
1 cup peeled, chopped, and seeded fresh or
canned tomatoes, drained

½ cup chopped orange segments
1 jalapeño pepper, seeded and chopped
2 green onions, thinly sliced

Combine the oil, garlic, and cumin-seed in a 4-cup glass measure and cook on HIGH for 35 seconds. Stir in the remaining ingredients. Cook on HIGH for 2 to 3 minutes, or until heated through, stirring once. Set aside until the steak is cooked.

Warm Corn Tortillas

SERVINGS: 4 ◆ 63 CALORIES PER TORTILLA ◆ COOKING TIME: 1 MINUTE

4 corn tortillas

Loosely wrap 4 corn tortillas with a paper towel. Place the tortillas in the microwave and heat them on HIGH for 30 seconds to 1 minute.

◆ *For 1 Serving:* Wrap 1 corn tortilla in a paper towel and place it in the microwave. Heat on HIGH for 15 seconds.

Mixed Greens with Dressing

SERVINGS: 4 ◆ 36 CALORIES PER 1-CUP SERVING

4 cups salad greens
½ cup dressing of your choice (pages 287–
291)

Combine the ingredients in a salad bowl and toss.

Apple-Apricot Cream

MAKES: 2⅔ CUPS ◆ 65 CALORIES PER ⅓ CUP ◆ COOKING TIME: 6 TO 10 MINUTES

You are making a double amount of this dessert; 4 servings for this meal and 4 servings for a frozen dessert later.

5 whole or 10 halves dried apricots, coarsely chopped
½ cup unsweetened apple juice
4 MacIntosh apples, peeled, cored, and thickly sliced

¼ cup low-fat plain yogurt
1 teaspoon vanilla extract

Combine the apricots and apple juice in a 1½-quart casserole. Cover tightly and cook on HIGH for 2 to 3 minutes. Add the apples. Cover again and cook on HIGH for 4 to 7 minutes, or until the apples are tender.

Pour the mixture into the bowl of a food processor or blender. Add the yogurt and vanilla and process the mixture until smooth.

To serve: Divide 1⅓ cup of the mixture between 4 individual dessert cups. Speed chill them in the freezer for 30 minutes.

◆ *For 1⅓ Cup (4 Servings):* Halve the recipe ingredients and cooking times. Serve half the amount immediately, making two ⅓-cup servings, and freeze the remainder in two 3-ounce paper cups to be served as Frozen Apple-Apricot Cream.

Variation:

Frozen Apple-Apricot Cream: Spoon the remaining 1⅓ cup mixture into four 3-ounce paper cups. Freeze them for a later meal.

CARROT SOUP WITH CINNAMON
SESAME-TOPPED SCALLOPS
PARMESAN BRUSSELS SPROUTS
WINTER FRUIT SALAD

Plan of action

1. Prepare the fruit salad and chill it.
2. Prepare and cook the soup. Meanwhile, prepare the scallops and Brussels sprouts for cooking.

25 MINUTES BEFORE SERVING

3. Put the scallops in to cook. Meanwhile, serve the soup.
4. Cook the Brussels sprouts during the standing time of the scallops.

Carrot Soup with Cinnamon

SERVINGS: 4 ◆ 27 CALORIES PER ½-CUP SERVING ◆ COOKING TIME: 5 TO 8 MINUTES

1 cup grated carrots
2 tablespoons finely chopped onions
2 cups chicken broth

½ teaspoon ground cinnamon
½ teaspoon black pepper
Dash cayenne pepper

Combine the carrots, onions, and 2 tablespoons broth in a 1½-quart casserole. Cover tightly and cook on HIGH for 2 minutes. Stir in the remaining ingredients. Cover again and cook on HIGH for 3 to 6 minutes, or until heated through.

◆ *For 1 Serving:* Combine ¼ cup grated carrots and 1½ teaspoons

chopped onion in a microwaveproof soup bowl. Cover tightly and cook on HIGH for 45 seconds. Stir in ½ cup broth, ⅛ teaspoon cinnamon, a dash black pepper, and a pinch cayenne. Cover again and cook on HIGH for 1 to 2 minutes.

Sesame-Topped Scallops

SERVINGS: 4 ◆ 126 CALORIES PER SERVING ◆ COOKING TIME: 5 TO 7 MINUTES

This scallop dish is extremely fresh tasting, but for the best results it is necessary to use very fresh scallops and steam them for the minimum time. We find the scallops absorb more of the flavors of the surrounding ingredients when they are cooked in individual ramekins.

1 cup thinly sliced celery
1 cup thinly sliced mushrooms
4 green onions, thinly sliced
1 pound bay scallops or sea scallops (quarter the sea scallops)
4 teaspoons lemon juice

4 teaspoons dry white wine
4 teaspoons toasted sesame seeds
1 teaspoon paprika
   Dash freshly ground black pepper

Layer the above ingredients in the order that they appear, dividing them among four 8-ounce ramekins. Place them in a circle in the microwave with at least a 1-inch space between them. Cover them loosely with wax paper. Cook on MEDIUM for 5 to 7 minutes, or until the scallops are opaque. Let them stand, covered, while the Brussels sprouts are cooking.

◆ *For 1 Serving:* Assemble 1 ramekin as described above, using ¼ of all the ingredients. Cover with wax paper and cook on MEDIUM for 2 to 3 minutes.

◆ *For 2 Servings:* Assemble two ramekins as described above, and cook on MEDIUM for 3 to 5 minutes.

◆ *For 3 Servings:* Assemble 3 ramekins and cook on MEDIUM for 4 to 6 minutes.

Parmesan Brussels Sprouts

SERVINGS: 4 ◆ 63 CALORIES PER SERVING ◆ COOKING TIME: 4 TO 8 MINUTES

1 pound Brussels sprouts
¼ cup water
2 tablespoons grated Parmesan cheese

Dash freshly ground black pepper
Pinch grated nutmeg
4 lime wedges

Trim the Brussels sprouts and cut an X in the bottom of each. Place them in a 1-quart casserole with the water.

Cover tightly and cook on HIGH for 4 to 8 minutes, stirring once.

To serve: Place 6 sprouts on each serving plate and sprinkle each with 1½ teaspoons cheese, pepper, and nutmeg. Serve with a lime wedge.

◆ *For 1 Serving:* Combine 6 Brussels sprouts with 1 tablespoon water in an 8-ounce ramekin. Cover tightly and cook on HIGH for 1½ to 2½ minutes, or until tender. Drain the sprouts and sprinkle with 1½ teaspoons Parmesan cheese, a pinch pepper and nutmeg. Serve with a lemon wedge.

Winter Fruit Salad

SERVINGS: 4 ◆ 101 CALORIES PER 1-CUP SERVING

1 large naval orange, segmented and cubed
1 banana, sliced
1 apple, cored and cut into ½-inch pieces

1 cup seedless grapes
2 tablespoons Kirsch

Combine all the ingredients in a bowl and chill. Serve in goblets.

◆ *For 1 Serving:* If you want only 1 serving, make the whole recipe anyway and serve the rest for breakfast. Sprinkle it with 1 tablespoon granola or Grape-Nuts Flakes and 2 tablespoons low-fat plain yogurt. Or serve for desserts the next 3 days, or for lunches, mixed with ½ cup low-fat plain yogurt and 1 tablespoon walnuts.

The dessert has already been made for today's meal from menu #6.

WARMED SPICED CRANBERRY COCKTAIL

VEGETARIAN CHILI

FROZEN APPLE-APRICOT CREAM

Plan of action

30 MINUTES BEFORE SERVING

1. Make and chill the Frozen Apple-Apricot Cream.
2. Heat the cranberry cocktail. Meanwhile, begin to chop up the ingredients for the chili.
3. Cook the chili and serve the cranberry cocktail while you relax.

Warm Spiced Cranberry Cocktail

SERVINGS: 4 ◆ 83 CALORIES PER ½ CUP ◆ COOKING TIME: 4 TO 6 MINUTES

Take your time to sip this hot drink and as you do, you'll take the chill out of winter.

2 cups cranberry cocktail
½ teaspoon ground cinnamon
¼ teaspoon grated nutmeg

¼ teaspoon ground cloves
4 orange slices
4 lemon slices

Pour all the ingredients into a 4-cup measure. Heat on HIGH for 4 to 6 minutes, or until very hot.

To serve: Pour ½ cup cocktail into each mug and serve with a floating orange and lemon slice.

◆ *For 1 Serving:* Combine ½ cup cranberry cocktail with a dash of cinnamon, and a pinch each of nutmeg and cloves in a serving cup. Heat on HIGH for 1 to 2 minutes. Garnish with 1 slice each of lemon and orange.

MOLDED SHIMMERING CRANBERRY COCKTAIL

SERVINGS: 4 ◆ 87 CALORIES PER ½-CUP SERVING ◆ COOKING TIME: ABOUT 1 MINUTE

This may be a refreshing snack or dessert substitute in any menu and can be made with any fruit except fresh or frozen pineapple.

A beautiful way to serve this dessert is to divide the mixture between 8 small individual molds. To serve them, unmold them onto individual serving plates and surround them with ¼ cup fresh berries. This makes an elegant dessert for 8 at 58 calories per serving.

2 cups cranberry cocktail
1 envelope unflavored gelatin

Pour ¼ cup juice into a 1-quart bowl. Stir in the gelatin. Heat on HIGH for 45 seconds to 1 minute; stir well to dissolve the gelatin.

If not thoroughly dissolved, continue to heat it on HIGH for 10 to 20 seconds more. Stir in the remaining juice and mix well. Pour into molds or chill as is until firm.

Variation:

Shimmering Cranberry Cocktail with Berries: Chill the mixture about 1 hour until it is the consistency of an unbeaten egg white. Fold in 1 cup fresh strawberries, raspberries, or blueberries. 104 calories per ¾-cup serving.

Vegetarian Chili

SERVINGS: 4 ◆ 175 CALORIES PER 1¼-CUP SERVING ◆ COOKING TIME: 23 TO 29 MINUTES

Even to us chili lovers, this vegetarian version is so delicious no one even misses the meat or the salt. You may want to add some optional toppings to vary each serving.

1 teaspoon full-flavored olive oil
2 garlic cloves, minced
1 medium onion, chopped
1½ tablespoons chili powder
1½ teaspoons cuminseed
1½ teaspoons dried oregano
½ teaspoon dried thyme leaves
¼ teaspoon black pepper
¼ teaspoon red pepper flakes (optional)

1 green bell pepper, coarsely chopped
2 cups chopped canned tomatoes, undrained
½ to 1 jalapeño pepper, seeded and finely chopped
1 15½-ounce can red kidney beans, undrained
½ cup water
½ cup bulgur wheat

Combine the oil, garlic, onion and seasonings in a 3-quart casserole. Cover tightly and cook on HIGH for 1 minute; stir well. Stir in the remaining ingredients. Cover again and cook on HIGH for 5 to 8 minutes, or until boiling; stir. Cover again and cook on MEDIUM for 15 to 20 minutes, or until the flavors have developed.

Some Optional Toppings for Vegetarian Chili: Low-fat plain yogurt, 19 calories per 2 tablespoons; 1 lime wedge, squeezed, 4 calories; finely chopped fresh onion, 1½ calories per 1 teaspoon; sunflower seeds, 17 calories per 1 teaspoon.

For Fewer Servings: It makes the most sense to prepare the entire recipe rather than to cut it down to 1 or 2 servings. By having some servings left over, you'll save in preparation time later in the week. In fact, the flavors actually improve upon refrigeration. Freeze any remaining portions after 1 week and reheat them for Chili Tater (page 298).

Chile peppers, unlike sweet peppers, gain their fiery bite from a chemically hot compound called "capsaicin." This organic compound is present in the white tissue that holds the seeds, so the more tissue that you leave in, the hotter the pepper will be.

And most of us know that hot feeling: Our mouth burns; our eyes water; and it is even possible that capsaicin causes our body to secrete endorphins, the body's own opiate, which can give a sensation similar to a runner's "high." Small amounts of the compound also stimulate digestion.

When looking for peppers, choose those that are bright and shiny. You'll generally find that the pointier the variety of pepper, the hotter it will be. When removing that white tissue, handle with care and watch any cuts you might have on your hands. Above all, wash your hands immediately afterward, and don't be tempted to rub your eyes before you do this.

Frozen Apple-Apricot Cream

SERVINGS: 4 ◆ 65 CALORIES PER ⅓-CUP SERVING

See the recipe for Apple-Apricot Cream (page 226).

HORSERADISH-SPIKED TOMATO SOUP

CELERY RIBS (2 INNER CELERY RIBS, 7 CALORIES)

ACORN SQUASH WITH SUNFLOWER-VEAL STUFFING

GRAPEFRUIT SALAD WITH RASPBERRY VINEGAR

WARM BRANDIED APPLE SLICES
WITH FROZEN YOGURT CREAM

Menu

9

*367 calories
per serving*

Plan of action

1. Cook the acorn squash before stuffing it.
2. Mix up and freeze the yogurt cream.
3. Prepare the stuffing for the squash.
4. Cook the stuffing. Meanwhile, prepare the soup and salad.
5. Cook the soup. Meanwhile, pre-

30 TO 35 MINUTES BEFORE SERVING

pare the celery ribs and spoon the stuffing into the squash.
6. Serve the soup with the celery. If the squash are not warm enough, cover them and cook them on HIGH for 2 minutes.
7. Cook the apples right before serving them with the yogurt cream.

Horseradish-Spiked Tomato Soup

SERVINGS: 4 ◆ 27 CALORIES PER ½-CUP SERVING ◆ COOKING TIME: 4 TO 6 MINUTES

2 cups tomato juice
1 tablespoon lemon juice
4 teaspoons prepared horseradish

1 teaspoon Worcestershire sauce
¼ teaspoon hot pepper sauce

Combine all the ingredients in a 4-cup glass measure. Cover tightly and cook on HIGH for 4 to 6 minutes, or until heated through. Serve with the celery.

◆ *For 1 Serving:* Pour ½ cup tomato juice into a microwaveproof bowl. Add

1 teaspoon each lemon juice and horseradish, ¼ teaspoon Worcestershire sauce, and a drop hot pepper sauce. Cook on HIGH for 1 to 1½ minutes.

Acorn Squash with Sunflower-Veal Stuffing

SERVINGS: 4 ◆ 202 CALORIES PER SERVING ◆ COOKING TIME: 19 TO 24 MINUTES

2 1-pound acorn squash
1 garlic clove, minced
2 tablespoons chopped onion
½ pound ground veal
1 cup peeled, seeded, and chopped fresh or canned tomatoes, drained
2 tablespoons raisins

2 tablespoons sunflower seeds
¼ teaspoon dried thyme leaves
¼ teaspoon grated nutmeg
⅛ teaspoon cayenne pepper
½ teaspoon ground cinnamon

Pierce the squash on each side with a fork. Place the squash on a paper towel in the microwave oven, leaving at least a 1-inch space between them. Cook on HIGH for 12 to 15 minutes, or until the squash are fork tender, turning them over after 5 minutes. Let them stand for 5 to 10 minutes.

During the standing time, combine the garlic and onion in a 9-inch pie plate. Break up the veal and spread it evenly over the garlic and onion. Cover with wax paper and cook on HIGH for 3 minutes (the veal will still be slightly pink). Stir in the tomatoes, raisins, sunflower seeds, thyme, nutmeg, and cayenne pepper, pushing the mixture to the outer rim of the dish. Cover again and cook on HIGH for 2 to 3 minutes, or until no pink color remains in the meat. Let the meat stand, covered, while preparing the squash for stuffing.

To serve: Cut the cooked squash in half and remove the seeds. Place the squash halves, cut side up, on a 12-inch microwaveproof platter. Sprinkle lightly with cinnamon. Spoon ½ cup filling into each cavity. Cover with wax paper and heat on HIGH for 2 to 3 minutes, right before serving.

◆ *For 1 Serving:* Cut 1 raw squash in half. Place the cut side of one-half down on a microwaveproof dish. Pierce with a fork. Cook on HIGH for 3 to 5 minutes or until tender. Let the squash stand, 5 minutes, before scooping out the seeds.

Combine 1 small minced garlic clove and 1½ teaspoons chopped onion in a 1-quart casserole. Break up 2 ounces ground veal and spread it evenly over the garlic and onions. Cover with wax paper and cook on HIGH for 1 minute. Stir in ¼ cup peeled, seeded, and chopped tomatoes or canned, undrained; 1½ teaspoons each raisins and sunflower seeds; a dash each thyme and nutmeg; and a pinch cayenne pepper. Cover again and cook on HIGH for 1 to 3 minutes.

Meanwhile, remove the seeds from the squash. Place it, cut side up, on a microwaveproof plate. Sprinkle it lightly with cinnamon and spoon in the filling. Cover with wax paper and heat it on HIGH for 30 seconds to 1 minute.

Grapefruit Salad with Raspberry Vinegar

SERVINGS: 4 ◆ 44 CALORIES PER SERVING

2 cups romaine lettuce leaves
2 medium, pink grapefruit, segmented

4 teaspoons raspberry vinegar
Freshly ground black pepper

Line each salad plate with ½ cup romaine leaves. Arrange the grapefruit segments on top of the romaine, dividing them evenly between the 4 plates. Drizzle 1 teaspoon vinegar over the grapefruit on each plate. Sprinkle with black pepper.

◆ *For 1 Serving:* Place ½ cup romaine leaves on a salad plate. Arrange the segments from ½ grapefruit (save the other half for breakfast). Sprinkle with 1 teaspoon raspberry vinegar, and then pepper.

Warm Brandied Apple Slices with Frozen Yogurt Cream

SERVINGS: 4 ◆ 87 CALORIES PER SERVING ◆ COOKING TIME: 3 TO 4 MINUTES

½ cup low-fat plain yogurt
1 teaspoon vanilla extract
½ teaspoon grated nutmeg
1 tablespoon brown sugar
1 tablespoon brandy

1 teaspoon lemon juice
¼ teaspoon ground cinnamon
2 MacIntosh apples, peeled, cored, and thinly sliced

Combine the yogurt, vanilla, and nutmeg in a small bowl and place it in the freezer until serving time.

Combine the sugar, brandy, lemon juice, and cinnamon in a 9-inch pie plate. Heat on HIGH for 1 minute. Stir the apple slices into this mixture. Cover with wax paper and cook on HIGH for 2 to 3 minutes, or until the apples are tender, stirring once. Stir again to coat the apple slices.

To serve: Place 2 tablespoons frozen yogurt onto each dessert plate and top with ¼ cup apples and juices.

◆ *For 1 Serving:* Combine 2 tablespoons plain yogurt, ¼ teaspoon vanilla, and a grating of nutmeg in a custard cup. Freeze until serving time. Place 1 teaspoon each brown sugar and brandy, ¼ teaspoon lemon juice, and a dash cinnamon into a small microwaveproof dessert bowl. Heat on HIGH for 20 seconds. Stir in ½ apple that has been thinly sliced. Cover with wax paper and cook on HIGH for 30 seconds.

Menu

10

471 calories
per serving

In this menu a variety of exotic flavors combine to excite your taste buds.

CURRIED APPLE-TOMATO SOUP

CHINA ROAD SHRIMP

LEMON RICE

CREAMY CABBAGE AND CUCUMBER SALAD

TANGERINES WITH SPIKED ORANGE CREAM

Plan of action

30 MINUTES BEFORE SERVING

1. Mix up the orange cream and chill.
2. Cook the rice. While the rice is cooking prepare the shrimp and soup for cooking.
3. Cook the soup, and let the rice stand, covered (it will stay warm for up to 1 hour).
4. Meanwhile, chop up the ingredients for the salad.
5. Serve the soup.
6. Cook the shrimp, and serve it with the rice and salad.

Curried Apple-Tomato Soup

SERVINGS: 4 ◆ 57 CALORIES PER ⅔-CUP SERVING ◆ COOKING TIME: 4 TO 6 MINUTES

1 large apple, coarsely chopped
1 cup tomato juice
1 cup chicken broth

2 green onions, thinly sliced
2 teaspoons curry powder
4 teaspoons grated unsweetened coconut

Combine all the ingredients in a 4-cup glass measure or microwaveproof bowl. Cover tightly and cook on HIGH for 4 to 6 minutes, or until heated through.

◆ *For 1 Serving:* Combine ¼ coarsely chopped apple, ¼ cup tomato juice, ¼ cup chicken broth, ½ thinly sliced green onion, ½ teaspoon curry powder, and 1 teaspoon grated unsweetened coconut in a microwaveproof serving bowl. Cover tightly and cook on HIGH for 45 seconds to 1 minute.

China Road Shrimp

SERVINGS: 4 ◆ 160 CALORIES PER ¼ POUND SHRIMP AND SAUCE
◆ COOKING TIME: 4 TO 6 MINUTES

1 tablespoon full-flavored olive oil
1 garlic clove, minced
4 green onions, thinly sliced
½ teaspoon cuminseed
⅛ teaspoon cayenne pepper
⅛ teaspoon ground cinnamon
⅛ teaspoon ground cloves

1 pound peeled large shrimp
1 tablespoon chopped fresh dill, or 1 teaspoon dried
2 tablespoons white vinegar
1 long sweet red pepper and 1 long sweet green pepper, seeded and cut lengthwise into thin slices
    Lemon wedges

Combine the oil, garlic, green onion, and seasonings in a 9- or 10-inch pie plate. Cook on HIGH for 1 minute. Stir well. Add the shrimp, dill, and vinegar. Stir well to coat. Push the shrimp to the outer rim of the dish, leaving the center open. Cover with wax paper and cook on HIGH for 2 minutes; stir well, making sure to move the lesser cooked shrimp to the outer rim. Cover again and cook on HIGH for 1 to 3 minutes, or until the shrimp have just turned opaque and pink.

To serve: Spoon onto a serving plate with lemon wedges and sprinkle the shrimp with pepper slices.

◆ *For 1 Serving:* Combine 1 teaspoon olive oil, 1 small minced garlic clove, 1½ teaspoons chopped onion, a dash cuminseed, a pinch each cayenne, cinnamon, and cloves. Cook on HIGH for 20 seconds. Add 1 teaspoon chopped fresh dill, 1½ teaspoons vinegar, and ¼ pound peeled shrimp. Cover with wax paper and cook on HIGH for 1 minute; stir well. Cover again and cook on HIGH for 30 seconds to 1 minute or until the shrimp have just turned opaque and pink. Sprinkle with 1 tablespoon chopped parsley and serve with a lemon wedge garnish.

Lemon Rice

SERVINGS: 4 ◆ 136 CALORIES PER ½-CUP SERVING ◆ COOKING TIME: 10 TO 15 MINUTES

1 recipe cooked Basic Rice (page 294)
1 tablespoon lemon juice
1 teaspoon grated lemon peel

After the rice is cooked, stir in the remaining ingredients. Let stand, covered, for 5 minutes.

Creamy Cabbage and Cucumber Salad

SERVINGS: 4 ◆ 32 CALORIES PER 1-CUP SERVING

½ cup grated red cabbage
½ cup mixed salad greens
½ cup sliced radishes

½ cup thinly sliced cucumbers
½ cup Creamy Herb Dressing I or II (page 288)

Combine all the ingredients in a salad bowl and toss right before serving.

Tangerines with Spiked Orange Cream

SERVINGS: 4 ◆ 86 CALORIES PER SERVING

½ cup low-fat plain yogurt
1 tablespoon Grand Marnier or other orange-flavored liqueur
1 tablespoon sugar
½ teaspoon vanilla extract

1 teaspoon grated tangerine peel, plus extra cut into thin strips for garnish
4 small tangerines, segmented
12 fresh raspberries (optional)
Pinch mace (optional)

Combine the yogurt, orange liqueur, sugar, vanilla, and grated tangerine peel in a small bowl. Chill until serving time.

To serve: Fan out the tangerine segments onto 4 serving plates. Place 2 tablespoons cream at the base of each fan. Garnish with raspberries if desired, plus peel strips, and sprinkle the cream with a little mace, if desired.

SPINACH THREAD SOUP

CHICKEN PARMIGIANA

SLICED MUSHROOMS WITH PARSLEY

MIXED GREENS WITH MUSTARD VINAIGRETTE

FRESH GRAPES

Menu

11

392 calories
per serving

Plan of action

30 MINUTES BEFORE SERVING

1. Cook the tomato sauce. Meanwhile, prepare and chill the salad.
2. Prepare and cook the chicken. Meanwhile, prepare the soup.
3. Cook the soup. Meanwhile, assemble the chicken.

4. Serve the soup. Meanwhile, do the final heating of the chicken.
5. Cook the mushrooms during the standing time of the chicken.

Spinach Thread Soup

SERVINGS: 4 ◆ 18 CALORIES PER ½-CUP SERVING ◆ COOKING TIME: 4 TO 6 MINUTES

2 cups chicken broth
1 cup thinly sliced spinach
2 green onions, thinly sliced

½ teaspoon white vinegar
⅛ teaspoon black pepper
⅛ teaspoon grated nutmeg

Combine all the ingredients in a 4-cup glass measure. Cover tightly and cook on HIGH for 4 to 6 minutes, or until heated through.

◆ *For 1 Serving:* Combine ½ cup broth, 2 tablespoons thinly sliced spinach, ½ thinly sliced green onion, a drop of vinegar, and a dash each black pepper and nutmeg. Cook on HIGH for 45 seconds to 1½ minutes.

Chicken Parmigiana

SERVINGS: 4 ◆ 216 CALORIES PER SERVING (INCLUDING SAUCE)
◆ COOKING TIME: 8 TO 10 MINUTES

This recipe works best when the chicken is cooked individually in ramekins, because the chicken soaks in the sauce, and it is easier to get every last drop when it is served.

If you have a compact oven that does not hold 4 ramekins, place all the chicken in one 10-inch pie plate.

4 3-ounce boneless, skinless chicken breasts
2 cups Tomato Sauce (see below)
4 ounces low-fat mozzarella, thinly sliced

Flatten the chicken cutlets between 2 pieces of wax paper with a meat pounder to about ¼-inch thickness. Place the chicken in individual ramekins or a 10-inch pie plate. Cover with wax paper and cook on HIGH for 4 to 5 minutes, or until cooked through. Remove the cutlets and set them aside. Drain any excess liquid from the cooking dishes.

Spoon 1 cup tomato sauce into the bottom of 4 ramekins (¼ cup each) or into a pie plate. Return the cutlets to the dishes, on top of the sauce; spoon the remaining 1 cup tomato sauce on top of the chicken. Top each cutlet with 1 ounce cheese.

Cover the assembled chicken with wax paper and heat it on MEDIUM for 4 to 5 minutes, or until the cheese is melted and all is heated through. Let is stand, covered, while the Sliced Mushrooms with Parsley are cooking.

◆ *For 1 Serving:* Flatten a 3-ounce boneless, skinless chicken breast to ¼-inch thickness between wax paper with a meat pounder. Place it in an 8-ounce ramekin. Cover with wax paper and cook on HIGH for 1 to 1½ minutes. Drain the ramekin and lift up the chicken cutlet to spoon ¼ cup tomato sauce into the bottom. Replace the cutlet and top it with the remaining ¼ cup tomato sauce. Top with 1 ounce thinly sliced low-fat mozzarella cheese. Cover the dish with wax paper and heat it on MEDIUM for 1 to 1½ minutes.

Tomato Sauce

MAKES: 2 CUPS ◆ 51 CALORIES PER ½ CUP ◆ COOKING TIME: 9 TO 10 MINUTES

1 teaspoon full-flavored olive oil

2 garlic cloves, minced

2 cups chopped canned plum tomatoes, undrained

2 tablespoons chopped fresh parsley

2 tablespoons grated Parmesan cheese

1 tablespoon chopped fresh basil, or 1 teaspoon dried

⅛ teaspoon red pepper flakes

Dash freshly ground black pepper

Combine the oil and garlic in a 2-quart casserole. Cook on HIGH for 35 seconds. Add the tomatoes and parsley. Cover with wax paper and cook on HIGH for 5 minutes, stirring after 3 minutes. Add the cheese, basil, and red and black pepper. Cover again and cook on MEDIUM for 4 minutes, or until heated through and somewhat thickened.

◆ For 1 Serving: Combine ¼ teaspoon olive oil and 1 small minced garlic clove in a 1-quart casserole. Cook on HIGH for 20 seconds. Add ½ cup chopped canned undrained tomatoes and 1½ teaspoons chopped parsley. Cover with wax paper and cook on HIGH for 1 minute. Stir in 1½ teaspoons grated Parmesan cheese, 1 teaspoon chopped fresh basil or ¼ teaspoon dried, and a pinch each black and red pepper. Cover again and cook on MEDIUM for 1 to 2 minutes.

Sliced Mushrooms with Parsley

SERVINGS: 4 ◆ 32 CALORIES PER 1-CUP SERVING ◆ COOKING TIME: 3 TO 4 MINUTES

1 pound mushrooms, trimmed and thinly sliced

Dash cayenne

¼ cup chopped fresh parsley

Place the mushrooms and cayenne in a 2-quart casserole. Cook on HIGH for 3 to 4 minutes, or until tender, stirring once. Sprinkle with parsley.

◆ For 1 Serving: Place ¼ pound mushrooms in an individual serving dish. Cook on HIGH for 1 to 2 minutes, or until tender, stirring once. Sprinkle with 1 tablespoon chopped parsley.

241

Mixed Greens with Mustard Vinaigrette

SERVINGS: 4 ◆ 22 CALORIES PER ½-CUP GREENS WITH 1 TABLESPOON DRESSING

2 cups mixed greens
¼ cup Mustard Vinaigrette (page 288)

Combine the greens and vinaigrette in a salad bowl and toss right before serving.

Fresh Grapes

53 CALORIES PER SERVING

A mixture of red and green grapes is nice; two little bunches of 10 to 12 each make eating more pleasurable.

LEMON-SAGE BROTH

CARROT STICKS (12 CALORIES)

SEAFOOD MARINARA OVER WHOLE WHEAT PASTA

FRUIT AND CHEESE

Plan of action

30 MINUTES BEFORE SERVING

1. Prepare the soup ingredients.
2. Begin cooking the soup. Meanwhile, chop the ingredients for the pasta sauce. Allow the soup to steep until serving time, then reheat it for a minute or two, if needed.

3. Cook the pasta on top of the stove, and the tomato sauce in the microwave.
4. While the sauce is cooking, cut up the carrot sticks.
5. Serve the soup while the tomato sauce is standing.

Lemon-Sage Broth

SERVINGS: 4 ◆ 18 CALORIES PER ½-CUP SERVING ◆ COOKING TIME: 4 TO 6 MINUTES

This is a good winter broth because fresh sage can survive year-round in many areas of the country.

In the Middle Ages, sage was believed to be a cure-all and to impart wisdom and improve the memory, and that is where the Old English word *sage*, meaning a wise man, comes from. We don't know how wise this soup will make you , but it will warm you up on a winter night.

2 cups chicken broth
2 teaspoons lemon juice
*2 chopped fresh sage leaves, or
½ teaspoon dried*

4 green onions, thinly sliced
Freshly ground black pepper

Pour the broth into a 4-cup measure. Cover tightly and cook on HIGH for 4 to

6 minutes, or until it comes to a boil. Stir in the remaining ingredients and

let the soup steep for at least 5 minutes. If necessary, reheat on HIGH for 1 or 2 minutes before serving.

◆ *For 1 Serving:* Pour ½ cup broth into a microwaveproof cup. Cook it on HIGH for 1 to 2 minutes, or until it comes to a boil. Stir in ½ teaspoon lemon juice, ½ chopped sage leaf, ½ sliced green onion, and freshly ground pepper. Let the soup steep, covered, for 3 minutes. Reheat on HIGH for 30 seconds, if necessary.

Seafood Marinara over Whole Wheat Pasta

SERVINGS: 4 ◆ 366 CALORIES PER SERVING ◆ COOKING TIME: 8 TO 12 MINUTES

2 **quarts water**
4 **ounces dry thin whole wheat pasta**
1 **tablespoon full-flavored olive oil**
2 **garlic cloves, minced**
1 **onion, chopped**
10 **medium black olives, minced**
2 **cups chopped canned plum tomatoes, undrained**
2 **tablespoons tomato paste (see Tip)**
¼ **pound fresh mushrooms, sliced**

¼ **teaspoon dried thyme leaves**
¼ **cup chopped fresh basil leaves, or 1 teaspoon dried**
¼ **cup chopped fresh parsley, or 1 teaspoon dried**
⅛ **teaspoon red pepper flakes**
    Freshly ground black pepper
1 **pound tuna or any other firm fish, cut into ½-inch chunks, or scallops or shrimp, peeled**

Bring the water to a boil on top of the conventional stove and cook the pasta until al dente.

Meanwhile, combine the oil, garlic, and onion in a 2-quart casserole. Cook on HIGH for 1 minute. Add the olives, tomatoes, and tomato paste. Cover with wax paper and cook on HIGH for 3 to 5 minutes, or until boiling; stir. Add the remaining ingredients, except the pasta. Cover again and cook on HIGH for 4 to 6 minutes, or until the fish is cooked through. Let stand for 5 minutes.

To serve: Drain the pasta and spoon ½ cup into each of 4 bowls. Spoon ½ cup tomato sauce with fish on top.

◆ *For 1 Serving:* Boil 1 quart water on top of the conventional stove and cook 1 ounce whole wheat pasta until it is al dente.

Meanwhile, combine 1 teaspoon olive oil; 1 small minced garlic clove; 1 tablespoon chopped onion; ½ cup chopped canned tomatoes, undrained; and 1½ teaspoons tomato paste in a 1-quart casserole. Cover with wax paper and cook on HIGH for 1 to 2 minutes, or until boiling. Add 2 chopped black olives; ½ cup sliced mushrooms; a pinch thyme; 1 tablespoon each chopped fresh basil and parsley; a pinch each of red and black pepper; and ¼ pound firm fish, cut into ½-inch chunks, or scallops or shrimp, peeled. Cover again and cook on HIGH for 1 to 3 minutes. Drain the pasta and spoon it into a bowl, topping it with the tomato sauce.

◆ *Tip:* Tomato paste that comes in a tube is convenient when you want to use small amounts.

We find kitchen shears a great help in chopping up canned tomatoes, especially when you are trying to retain the juices. Measure the tomatoes into your measuring cup, along with the juices, and then just snip away at the pulp.

The shears are also helpful in cutting up individual pizza rounds of pita bread for sandwiches.

Fruit and Cheese

SERVINGS: 4 ◆ 189 CALORIES

This is a perfect ending for this menu. The cheese runs about 64 calories. Choose one fruit or serve each person ¼ apple and ¼ pear, or 10 grapes with ¼ apple or ¼ pear.

4 compressed rice cakes or crackers
2 ounces Gorgonzola, blue, or Roquefort cheese (1-inch square)
2 apples or pears, thinly sliced, or 80 seedless grapes

Serve 1 cracker and ½ ounce cheese on each plate. Divide one fruit choice between plates.

Menu

13

358 calories
per serving

GERMAN DUMPLING AND SPINACH SUPPE

MOTHER EARTH VEGETABLE SALAD

INDIVIDUAL APPLE CRISPS

Plan of action

30 MINUTES BEFORE SERVING

1. Prepare the salad and chill it.
2. Prepare and cook the soup.
3. While the soup is cooking, prepare the dessert for cooking.
4. Cook the dessert during the standing time of the soup.
5. Serve the soup, and then the salad.

German Dumpling and Spinach Suppe

SERVINGS: 4 ◆ 185 CALORIES PER 1¼-CUP SERVING (ABOUT 6 DUMPLINGS)
◆ COOKING TIME: 14 TO 19 MINUTES

Liver is one of the best sources of iron, but for many it is almost impossible to get it past the palate. This is a delicious and soothing way to do it.

4 cups beef broth
   Dash hot pepper sauce
½ pound beef or calf liver
2 pieces whole wheat bread, made into crumbs (½ cup) (see Notes)
1 tablespoon flour
1 egg, lightly beaten

¼ cup finely chopped fresh parsley
1 tablespoon finely chopped green onion
¼ teaspoon black pepper
⅛ teaspoon grated nutmeg
1 pound fresh spinach leaves, cut into ¼-inch strips, or 1 10-ounce package frozen chopped spinach (see Notes)

Combine the broth and hot pepper sauce in a 3-quart casserole. Cover tightly and cook on HIGH for 8 to 10 minutes, or until boiling.

Meanwhile, remove the outer membrane of the liver and discard it. Cut the liver into chunks and grind it up or chop it finely in a food processor. Combine the liver, bread crumbs, flour, egg, parsley, green onion, pepper, and nutmeg in a bowl to make the mixture for the dumplings. To form

246

the dumplings, dip 2 teaspoons into the hot broth and then, using one spoon, scoop a heaping teaspoon of liver mixture and push it into the broth with the other spoon. Continue this process until the mixture is gone and you have about 24 dumplings.

Cover the broth and dumplings tightly and cook them on HIGH for 3 minutes. Stir in the spinach. Cover again and cook on HIGH for 3 to 6 minutes, or until the dumplings are set and the spinach is tender. Let the soup stand, covered, for 5 minutes.

◆ *For 1 Serving:* Pour 1 cup beef broth and a dash hot pepper sauce into a 1-quart casserole. Cover tightly and cook on HIGH for 2 to 3 minutes. Combine ¼ pound finely ground liver, 2 tablespoons bread crumbs, ¾ teaspoon flour, 1 egg white, 1 tablespoon chopped fresh parsley, 1 teaspoon chopped green onion, and a dash

each pepper and nutmeg. Form 6 dumplings using 2 teaspoons, and drop them into the hot broth. Cover the broth and dumplings tightly and cook on HIGH for 2 minutes. Add ¼ pound thinly sliced spinach leaves. Cover again and cook on HIGH for 1 to 2 minutes, or until the dumplings are set and the spinach is tender.

◆ *Variation:* Chicken livers and chicken broth may be substituted.

◆ *Notes:* Make bread crumbs in a food processor or blender by quartering the bread before adding to the bowl.

If using frozen spinach, defrost it slightly first so as not to cool down the soup. Place it in a 1-quart casserole. Cook on HIGH for 3 minutes, stirring every minute to break up the pieces. Let the spinach stand, covered, until you are ready to use it.

Mother Earth Vegetable Salad

SERVINGS: 4 ◆ 51 CALORIES PER 1-CUP SERVING

You can mix up this salad and store it, tightly covered, in the refrigerator for up to 4 days. For this reason, even if you just want a single serving, it makes sense to prepare the whole amount for later meals.

1 medium carrot, peeled and grated
1 medium cucumber, thinly sliced
½ cup alfalfa sprouts

2 green onions, thinly sliced
½ cup radishes, thinly sliced
½ cup green pepper, thinly sliced

Dressing:

½ cup low-fat plain yogurt
¼ cup chopped fresh parsley
1 teaspoon lemon juice
½ teaspoon paprika
½ teaspoon dried dill

¼ teaspoon dried tarragon leaves
¼ teaspoon dry mustard powder
Dash freshly ground black pepper
Dash cayenne pepper

Combine the vegetables in a large bowl.

In a smaller bowl, combine the dressing ingredients. Add the dressing to the vegetables and toss. Chill until serving time.

Individual Apple Crisps

SERVINGS: 4 ◆ 100 CALORIES PER SERVING, PLUS 22 CALORIES WITH 2 TABLESPOONS YOGURT ◆ COOKING TIME: 5 TO 8 MINUTES

These are nice for breakfast if you have any left over.

2 apples, peeled, cored, and thinly sliced
1 teaspoon grated lemon peel
1 teaspoon vanilla extract
4 teaspoons brown sugar
¼ cup old-fashioned oatmeal flakes

4 teaspoons finely chopped walnuts
½ teaspoon ground cinnamon
½ cup low-fat plain yogurt mixed with 1 teaspoon vanilla extract (optional)

Place ½ sliced apple in each of 4 custard cups. Divide the lemon rind and vanilla among the apples.

Top each custard cup of apples with 1 teaspoon packed brown sugar, 1 tablespoon oatmeal, 1 teaspoon walnuts, and a sprinkling of cinnamon. Place the custard cups in the microwave oven in a circle, leaving at least a 1-inch space between them. Cover them with wax paper and cook on HIGH for 5 to 8 minutes, or until the apples are tender. Let them stand at room temperature, or until serving time.

If desired, top the crisps with the yogurt and vanilla at serving time.

◆ *For 1 Serving:* Follow the instructions for assembling a single custard cup. Cover with wax paper and cook on HIGH for 1½ to 2½ minutes, or until the apples are tender. If desired, combine 2 tablespoons low-fat plain yogurt and ¼ teaspoon vanilla in a custard cup and spoon it on top.

◆ *For 2 Servings:* Follow the instructions for assembling 2 custard cups. Cover with wax paper and cook on HIGH for 3 to 5 minutes, or until the apples are tender. If desired, combine ¼ cup low-fat plain yogurt and ½ teaspoon vanilla in a custard cup and divide it between the crisps.

Variation:

Individual Pear Crisps: Substitute pears for apples.

◆ *Tip:* For ease of handling, place the custard cups on a 12-inch glass plate or tray.

MISO SOUP WITH BEAN SPROUTS

BEEF TERIYAKI WITH BROCCOLI

WHOLE WHEAT SOBA NOODLES

ORANGE AND PINEAPPLE COCKTAIL

Menu

14

*421 calories
per serving*

Plan of action

1. Marinate the meat.
2. Prepare the fruit and chill it.
3. Cook the soup. While the soup is cooking, cut up the vegetables for the teriyaki.
4. Bring the water to boil on top of the stove to cook the noodles.

25 MINUTES BEFORE SERVING

5. Serve the soup.
6. Cook the noodles on top of the stove, and the teriyaki in the microwave oven.
7. Serve the teriyaki and noodles, then the fruit.

Miso Soup with Bean Sprouts

SERVINGS: 4 ◆ 31 CALORIES PER 1-CUP SERVING ◆ COOKING TIME: 8 TO 10 MINUTES

Nourishing miso is made from soybean paste and is one of East Asia's most important food products.

2 6-ounce packets natural, instant miso (see Tip)
4 cups water
1 cup bean sprouts

Combine the miso and water in a 2-quart casserole. Cover tightly and cook on HIGH for 8 to 10 minutes, or until boiling.

To serve: Place ¼ cup bean sprouts into each soup bowl and pour the broth over them.

◆ *For 1 Serving:* Combine ½ packet instant miso, 1 cup water, and ¼ cup sprouts. Cover tightly and cook on HIGH for 2 to 3 minutes.

◆ *Tip:* Instant miso is available in health food stores and many vegetable stores. If you are unable to find it, you may substitute beef or chicken broth with an added ¼ teaspoon low-sodium soy sauce for each cup.

Beef Teriyaki with Broccoli

SERVINGS: 4 ◆ 249 CALORIES PER SERVING ◆ COOKING TIME: 5 TO 7 MINUTES

If you have frozen the other half of the round steak from Menu #6, you are ready to defrost it in the microwave. Unwrap it and place it on a microwave roasting rack or a dish and heat it on DEFROST for 5 to 8 minutes, or until still slightly frozen. It is much easier to cut the meat into thin strips while it is still frozen.

¾ pound round steak, cut into ¼-inch strips
2 tablespoons low-sodium soy sauce
1 tablespoon orange juice
1 tablespoon white vinegar
1 teaspoon cornstarch
1 teaspoon sesame oil
1 garlic clove, minced

2 teaspoons grated fresh ginger
1 pound broccoli, trimmed and cut into 1-inch pieces (about 4 cups)
4 green onions, trimmed and cut into 2-inch pieces
1 recipe Whole Wheat Soba Noodles (see below)

250

Cut the beef strips into 3-inch pieces. Combine the soy, orange juice, vinegar, and cornstarch in a medium bowl. Stir in the beef. Let it marinate for 10 to 15 minutes at room temperature.

Combine the garlic and ginger in a 10-inch pie plate. Cook on HIGH for 35 seconds. With a slotted spoon, remove the meat from the marinade and stir it into the ginger-garlic mixture. Push the meat to the outer rim of the dish, leaving the center open. Cover tightly and cook on HIGH for 1½ minutes, or until the meat is still slightly pink.

Add the broccoli and onions to the meat. Cover again and cook on HIGH for 2 minutes; stir. Cook on HIGH for 1 to 3 minutes, or until the broccoli is tender-crisp.

To serve: Place ½ cup cooked soba noodles on each plate and spoon 1½ cups broccoli and beef over it.

◆ *For 1 Serving:* Thinly slice 3 ounces frozen bottom round steak, and cut it into 3"- × -¼" pieces. Combine 1½ teaspoons soy sauce, 1 teaspoon each orange juice and white vinegar, and ¼ teaspoon cornstarch in a small bowl. Add the beef and stir to coat.

Combine ¼ teaspoon sesame oil, 1 small minced garlic clove, and ½ teaspoon grated ginger in a 1-quart casserole. Cook on HIGH for 20 seconds. Stir in the beef. Cover tightly and cook on HIGH for 1 minute. Stir in 1 cup trimmed broccoli, cut into 1-inch pieces, and 1 green onion, cut into 2-inch pieces. Cover again and cook on HIGH for 1 to 2 minutes.

Serve with ½ cup cooked soba noodles.

Whole Wheat Soba Noodles

SERVINGS: 4 ◆ 100 CALORIES PER ½-CUP SERVING

2 quarts water
4 ounces whole wheat soba noodles or fettuccine

Bring the water to a boil on top of a conventional stove. Boil the noodles until al dente. Drain and serve.

◆ *For 1 Serving:* Bring 1 quart water to a boil on top of a conventional stove, and boil 1 ounce whole wheat soba until al dente. Drain.

Orange and Pineapple Cocktail

SERVES: 4 ◆ 41 CALORIES PER ½-CUP SERVING

1 cup cubed orange segments
1 cup diced fresh pineapple or pineapple
 packed in its own juices, drained

Combine the fruit in a small bowl and chill it. Spoon it into goblets and serve.

Menu

15

361 calories
per serving

CHUNKY TOMATO SOUP

MELBA TOASTS (2, 32 CALORIES)

FLOUNDER WITH CARAWAY CABBAGE

DILLED BABY POTATOES

RUMMY TANGERINE ROLL

Plan of action

25 MINUTES BEFORE SERVING

1. Segment the tangerines and sprinkle them with rum. Refrigerate them until later.
2. Cook the cabbage. Meanwhile, prepare the soup.
3. Cook the soup. Meanwhile, finish the preparations for the fish, cabbage, and potatoes.

4. Put the potatoes in to cook. Meanwhile, serve the soup.
5. Cook the fish during the standing time of the potatoes.
6. Serve the fish, cabbage, and potatoes.
7. Cook and serve the dessert.

Chunky Tomato Soup

SERVINGS: 4 ◆ 52 CALORIES PER ¾-CUP SERVING ◆ COOKING TIME: 6 TO 9 MINUTES

3 cups tomato juice

2 fresh tomatoes, coarsely chopped, or ½ cup
seeded and coarsely chopped canned
tomatoes

2 tablespoons dry vermouth or Marsala wine

1 teaspoon lemon juice

½ teaspoon dried mint leaves, or 1 teaspoon
chopped frozen or fresh

½ teaspoon celery seeds

⅛ teaspoon cayenne pepper

Combine all the ingredients in a 2-quart casserole. Cover tightly and cook on HIGH for 6 to 9 minutes, or until heated through. Serve each ¾-cup portion with 2 melba toasts.

◆ For 1 Serving: Combine ¾ cup tomato juice, ½ chopped tomato, 1½ teaspoons dry vermouth, ¼ teaspoon lemon juice, a dash each dried mint leaves and celery seeds, and a pinch cayenne pepper in a microwaveproof soup bowl. Cover tightly and cook on HIGH for 1½ to 2½ minutes.

Flounder with Caraway Cabbage

SERVINGS: 4 ◆ 120 CALORIES PER SERVING ◆ COOKING TIME: 10 TO 14 MINUTES

4 cups shredded Savoy or other cabbage

1 tablespoon cider vinegar

3 tablespoons water

2 teaspoons caraway seeds

¼ teaspoon black pepper

4 4-ounce flounder fillets

2 tablespoons grated Parmesan cheese

½ teaspoon paprika
    Lemon or lime wedges

Combine the cabbage, vinegar, water, caraway, and pepper in a 1½-quart casserole. Cover tightly and cook on HIGH for 5 to 7 minutes, or until the cabbage is tender-crisp, stirring once. Divide the cabbage between four 8-ounce ramekins.

Place the fish fillets on top of the cabbage. Sprinkle each fillet with 1½ teaspoons Parmesan cheese and ⅛ teaspoon paprika. Cover with wax paper. Arrange the ramekins in a circle in the microwave, leaving at least a 1-inch space between them. Cook on HIGH for 5 to 7 minutes, or until the fish flakes under the pressure of a fork. Serve with a lemon or lime wedge.

◆ For 1 Serving: Combine 1 cup shredded cabbage with 1 teaspoon cider vinegar, 1 tablespoon water, ½ teaspoon caraway seeds, and a dash black pepper in an 8-ounce ramekin. Cover tightly and cook on HIGH for 2 to 4 minutes. Place a 4-ounce flounder fillet on top and sprinkle it with ½ tea-spoon grated Parmesan cheese and ⅛ teaspoon paprika on top. Cover with wax paper and cook on HIGH for 2 to 4 minutes, or until the fish tests done. Top with a lemon or lime wedge.

Dilled Baby Potatoes

SERVINGS: 4 ◆ 67 CALORIES PER TWO 2-OUNCE POTATOES ◆ COOKING TIME: 6 TO 9 MINUTES

1 pound (about 8) small red or white potatoes, washed and peeled around the center
¼ cup water
1 tablespoon chopped fresh dill, or 1 teaspoon dried

Combine the potatoes and water in a 1½-quart casserole. Cover tightly and cook on HIGH for 6 to 9 minutes, or until tender, stirring once. Let stand, covered, while cooking the fish. Sprinkle with dill and serve.

◆ For 1 Serving: Combine 2 small (1 ounce each) potatoes in an 8-ounce ramekin with 1 tablespoon water. Cover tightly and cook on HIGH for 3 to 4 minutes, or until tender. Sprinkle with ¼ teaspoon chopped fresh dill, or ⅛ teaspoon dried, to serve.

Rummy Tangerine Roll

SERVINGS: 4 ◆ 90 CALORIES PER SLICE WITH ¼ CUP TANGERINES ◆ COOKING TIME: 2 TO 3 MINUTES

1 cup cubed tangerine segments (from 2 or 3 tangerines)
2 tablespoons rum
2 eggs, separated
¼ teaspoon cream of tartar
1 teaspoon grated orange peel

1 tablespoon sugar
1 tablespoon water
Long thin pieces of orange or tangerine peel for garnish (optional)
Grated nutmeg

Combine the tangerines and rum in a small bowl. Set aside until dessert time.

Just before serving, combine the egg whites and cream of tartar in a medium mixing bowl and beat until stiff but not dry. In another small bowl combine the yolks, grated orange peel, sugar, and water, beating well with a fork until slightly foamy and lemon-colored. Gently fold the yolks into the egg whites.

Pour the mixture into a 9-inch pie plate and smooth the top lightly. Cook on HIGH for 1½ to 2½ minutes, or until set. Spoon the tangerine segments in

a 3-inch row down the center of the cooked egg mixture. Fold each side over the oranges in envelope fashion. Cut this into 4 servings and place onto a serving plate with a spatula. Garnish with the long orange or tangerine peel and a grating of fresh nutmeg.

◆ *For 1 Serving:* It is difficult to cut this recipe down. If you can spare a few extra calories today, eat half the recipe (154 calories), and save the second half for breakfast or tomorrow's dessert. It is equally good warm or cold.

If time doesn't allow you to make the sorbet, serve half a chilled pink grapefruit at 49 calories.

Menu

16

374 calories
per serving

JULIENNED TURNIP IN CLEAR BROTH

CHICKEN POACHED IN GINGER SAUCE

BOK CHOY PILAF

PINK GRAPEFRUIT SORBET

Plan of action

10 MINUTES THE NIGHT BEFORE
20 TO 25 MINUTES BEFORE SERVING

1. The night before, segment the grapefruit and freeze them.
2. The next day, mix the marinade for the chicken and stir in the chicken.
3. Prepare and cook the soup. Mean-

while, prepare the bok choy and bulgur.

4. Serve the soup. Meanwhile, place the bulgur in to cook.
5. Cook the chicken. While the

255

chicken is cooking, finish the grapefruit sorbet in the food processor and place it back in the freezer.
6. During the standing time of the

chicken, cook the bok choy.
7. Stir the bok choy into the bulgur and serve it with the poached chicken.

Julienned Turnip in Clear Broth

SERVINGS: 4 ◆ 22 CALORIES PER ¾-CUP SERVING ◆ COOKING TIME: 4 TO 6 MINUTES

1 cup thinly julienned turnip
2 cups chicken broth
1 teaspoon low-sodium soy sauce

1 teaspoon white vinegar
1 green onion, thinly sliced
    Dash freshly ground black pepper

Combine the turnip, broth, soy sauce, and vinegar in a 4-cup casserole. Cover tightly and cook on HIGH for 4 to 6 minutes, or until heated through.

To serve: Spoon the soup into 4 individual soup bowls and sprinkle the tops with green onion and black pepper.

◆ For 1 Serving: Combine ¼ cup julienned turnip, ½ cup broth, and ¼ teaspoon each soy sauce and white vinegar in a microwaveproof bowl. Cover tightly and cook on HIGH for 1 to 2 minutes, or until heated through. Sprinkle with ¼ thinly sliced green onion and a pinch black pepper.

Chicken Poached in Ginger Sauce

SERVINGS: 4 ◆ 154 CALORIES PER SERVING ◆ COOKING TIME: 4 TO 6 MINUTES

Marinating, cooking, and serving are easier, and the flavors become more concentrated, when the chicken is cooked in individual ramekins. If your oven doesn't hold four 8-ounce ramekins, try a 9-inch pie plate.

4 4-ounce boneless, skinless chicken breasts
4 green onions, thinly sliced
¼ cup grated fresh ginger
4 teaspoons low-sodium soy sauce

4 teaspoons brown sugar
4 teaspoons water
1 teaspoon dry sherry

Slice each chicken cutlet diagonally into ¼-inch slices.

In each of four 8-ounce ramekins combine 1 tablespoon each sliced green onion and grated ginger; 1 tea-spoon each soy sauce, sugar, and water; and ¼ teaspoon dry sherry, stir-ring well to mix. Divide the chicken pieces into 4 equal portions, then stir into the marinade. Let stand at room temperature for 10 to 15 minutes.

When you are ready to cook them, cover each ramekin tightly and place them in a circle in the microwave, leaving a 1-inch space between them. Cook on HIGH for 4 to 6 minutes, or until the chicken is cooked through.

◆ *For 1 Serving:* Diagonally slice one 4-ounce boneless, skinless chicken breast into ¼-inch slices. Combine 1 tablespoon each sliced green onion and freshly grated ginger; 1 teaspoon each soy sauce, brown sugar, and water; and ¼ teaspoon sherry into an 8-ounce ramekin, stirring well to mix. Add the chicken pieces and stir to coat. Let stand at room temperature for 10 minutes, or until ready to cook. When ready to cook, cover tightly and cook on HIGH for 1 to 2 minutes.

Complex carbohydrates—barley, wheat, rice, corn, oats, potatoes, peas, beans, and lentils—may seem to be the antithesis of light eating, but studies show that they will help you to feel full longer and cause your body to absorb fewer calories. The U.S. De-partment of Agriculture together with the University of Maryland examined people who ate a moderate amount of high-fiber foods and found that they absorbed 5 per-cent fewer calories than those eating a low-fiber diet.

Bok Choy Pilaf

SERVINGS: 4 ◆ 140 CALORIES PER 1-CUP SERVING ◆ COOKING TIME: 10 TO 18 MINUTES

Chopsticks are appropriate eating utensils for this slightly sticky bulgur pilaf.

1 teaspoon full-flavored olive oil
2 tablespoons finely chopped onion
½ cup bulgur
1 cup chicken broth

1 pound bok choy, cut into ¼-inch slices (about 4 cups)
1 tablespoon rice wine or dry sherry
⅛ teaspoon red pepper flakes

257

Combine the oil and onion in a 4-cup glass measure or 1-quart casserole. Cook on HIGH for 1 minute. Stir in the bulgur. Add the broth. Cover tightly and cook on HIGH for 2 to 3 minutes, or until boiling; stir. Cover again and cook on MEDIUM for 5 to 10 minutes, or until all the liquid is absorbed. Let the bulgur stand, covered.

Combine the bok choy, rice wine or sherry, and red pepper flakes in a 2-quart casserole. Cover tightly and cook on HIGH for 1 minute; stir. Cover again and cook on HIGH for 1 to 3 minutes more, or until the bok choy is tender-crisp.

To serve: Stir the bulgur into the bok choy and mix well. Spoon the mixture into individual serving bowls and spoon on the chicken and cooking juices. Eat with a fork or chopsticks.

◆ *For 2 Servings:* Combine ½ teaspoon oil and 1 tablespoon finely chopped onion in a 2-cup glass measure. Cook on HIGH for 30 seconds. Stir in ¼ cup bulgur and ½ cup chicken broth. Cover tightly and cook on HIGH for 1 to 2 minutes, or until boiling; stir. Cover again and cook on MEDIUM for 2½ to 5 minutes, or until all the liquid is absorbed.

Combine ½ pound sliced bok choy, ½ tablespoon rice wine, and a dash red pepper flakes in a 1-quart casserole. Cover tightly and cook on HIGH for 1 minute; stir. Cover again and cook on HIGH for 30 seconds to 1 minute.

To serve: Stir the bulgur into the bok choy and mix well. Spoon the mixture into individual bowls. This makes 1 serving as a main course when topped with cheese or yogurt, for around 300 calories.

Pink Grapefruit Sorbet

SERVINGS: 4 ◆ 58 CALORIES PER ½-CUP SERVING ◆ COOKING TIME: 1 MINUTE

The success of this wonderful dessert depends on perfectly ripened grapefruit.

2 large ripe pink grapefruit, peeled
¼ cup low-fat plain yogurt

2 teaspoons superfine sugar
1 teaspoon vanilla extract

Segment the grapefruit and squeeze as much juice as possible from the membranes. Cut the segments into 1-inch pieces. Place the grapefruit and juice in a single layer in a 9-inch pie plate or other microwaveproof flat dish. Cover and freeze for at least 2 hours or overnight.

When you are ready to make the sorbet, place the plate of frozen grapefruit in the microwave and heat on DEFROST for 35 seconds to 1 minute, or until you can break the pieces apart. Place the grapefruit pieces into the bowl of a food processor or blender. Process until granular.

Add the remaining ingredients and process until smooth and creamy. Serve it in this creamy state, or scoop into dessert bowls and freeze for later.

◆ *For 2 Servings:* It is difficult to make less than 2 servings. Because this dessert is so delicious, you will probably not have any left over. Cut the ingredients in half and proceed as above, heating on DEFROST for only 20 to 40 seconds before processing.

The hearty soup is the main course.

FISHERMAN'S CHOWDER

WHOLE WHEAT MELBA TOAST (4, 64 CALORIES)

HOT CABBAGE AND APPLE SLAW

ORANGE-PINEAPPLE SORBET

Menu

17

422 calories per serving

Plan of action

10 MINUTES THE NIGHT BEFORE
30 MINUTES BEFORE SERVING

1. The night before, freeze the orange and pineapple segments. If you didn't do this, serve ¾ cup fresh pineapple chunks each as an alternate dessert.
2. The next day, prepare the chowder and cook it. While the chowder is cooking, prepare the slaw and mix up the sorbet and place in freezer until serving time.
3. Heat up the slaw during the standing time of the chowder.
4. Serve the chowder and slaw.

Fisherman's Chowder

SERVINGS: 4 ◆ 218 CALORIES PER SERVING ◆ COOKING TIME: 17 TO 21 MINUTES

If you don't have fresh parsley, see our suggestions for freezing parsley on page 144. Frozen parsley has much more flavor than dried.

1 teaspoon full-flavored olive oil
2 garlic cloves, minced
1 cup sliced leeks
½ cup diced carrots
½ cup thinly sliced celery
1 cup peeled and diced potatoes
1 cup peeled and chopped fresh or canned tomatoes, undrained
½ cup dry white wine
2 cups chicken broth
¾ pound halibut, haddock, or scrod, cut into 1-inch cubes

¼ pound scallops
¼ cup chopped fresh or frozen basil leaves, or 1 tablespoon dried
¼ cup chopped fresh or frozen parsley, plus extra for garnish
½ teaspoon dried thyme leaves
½ jalapeño pepper, seeded and finely chopped, or ⅛ teaspoon red pepper flakes
1 bay leaf, crushed
Dash freshly ground black pepper, plus extra for garnish

Combine the oil, garlic, and leeks in a 3-quart casserole. Cover tightly and cook on HIGH for 1 minute; stir. Add the carrots, celery, potatoes, and tomatoes. Cover again and cook on HIGH for 8 to 10 minutes, or until the vegetables are tender, stirring once.

Stir in the remaining ingredients. Cover tightly and cook on HIGH for 8 to 10 minutes, or until the fish pieces are cooked and the soup is heated through, stirring after 5 minutes. Let the soup stand, covered, for 5 minutes.

To serve: Spoon 1½ cups each into large soup bowls. Garnish with additional parsley and black pepper. Serve with melba toast.

◆ *For 1 Serving:* Combine a drop of olive oil, 1 small minced garlic clove, and ¼ cup sliced leeks in a 1-quart casserole. Cover tightly and cook on HIGH for 1 minute. Add 2 tablespoons each diced carrot and sliced celery, ¼ cup each diced potatoes and peeled and chopped tomatoes. Cover tightly and cook on HIGH for 2 to 4 minutes, or until the vegetables are tender.

Add 2 tablespoons dry white wine, ½ cup chicken broth, ¼ pound scallops or fish chunks, 1 tablespoon chopped fresh basil or ½ teaspoon dried, 1 tablespoon chopped fresh parsley, ⅛ teaspoon dried thyme, a slice of jalapeño pepper or a dash red pepper flakes, ½ crushed bay leaf, and a dash black pepper. Cover tightly and heat on HIGH for 3 to 5 minutes, or until the fish pieces are cooked and the chowder is heated through. Let stand, covered, for 3 minutes.

Hot Cabbage and Apple Slaw

SERVINGS: 4 ◆ 75 CALORIES PER 1-CUP SERVING ◆ COOKING TIME: 4 TO 6 MINUTES

2 cups thinly sliced red cabbage
2 cups thinly sliced green cabbage
1 Granny Smith or Jonathan apple, thinly
   sliced
1 tablespoon full-flavored olive oil
2 tablespoons chopped onion

1 teaspoon freshly ground ginger
3 tablespoons water
1 tablespoon cider vinegar
1 tablespoon lemon juice
1 teaspoon caraway seeds
1 teaspoon low-sodium soy sauce (optional)

Combine the cabbage and apple in a 2-quart casserole; set aside.

Combine the oil, onion, and ginger in a 1-cup glass measure. Cook on HIGH for 1 minute. Add the remaining ingredients and cook on HIGH for 1 minute more, or until boiling.

Pour over the cabbage and apple mixture and toss to coat. Cover tightly and cook on HIGH for 2 to 4 minutes, or until the vegetables are tender-crisp, stirring after 1 minute. Serve in bowls.

◆ For 1 Serving: Combine 1 cup sliced cabbage and ¼ sliced apple in a 1-quart bowl; set aside. In a 1-cup glass measure combine 1 teaspoon oil, 1½ teaspoons chopped onion, and ¼ teaspoon grated ginger. Cook on HIGH for 35 seconds. Add 1 tablespoon water, 1 teaspoon each cider vinegar and lemon juice, ¼ teaspoon caraway seeds, and ¼ teaspoon low-sodium soy sauce, if desired. Cook on HIGH for 1 minute. Pour over the cabbage and apples and toss well. Cover tightly and cook on HIGH for 1 minute, or until tender, stirring after 35 seconds.

Orange-Pineapple Sorbet

SERVINGS: 4 ◆ 65 CALORIES PER ½-CUP SERVING ◆ COOKING TIME: 1 MINUTE

As with all of our fruit sorbets, the success lies in the ripeness of the fruit, so be very choosy.

1 cup diced orange segments with juice
1 cup fresh pineapple chunks (½ inch)
2 tablespoons low-fat plain yogurt

2 tablespoons orange-flavored liqueur
   Grated orange peel

Place the orange and pineapple pieces in a single layer in a 10-inch pie plate and freeze them early in the day or the night before serving.

261

Right before you make the sorbet, place the pie plate in the microwave and heat it on DEFROST for 35 seconds to 1 minute, or until you can break up the pieces. Place the frozen chunks into the bowl of a food processor and whir until chopped into small chunks. Add the remaining ingredients and process until smooth. Eat as is, or freeze until serving time.

◆ *Tip:* Contrary to popular belief, pineapples don't become sweeter by ripening a few days at home. You must select a ripe and tasty one at the store. To test for ripeness, sniff the base of the pineapple; you should get a whiff of a heady, winelike pineapple aroma. Grasp a leaf firmly and give it a tug; it should pull out easily. The color will be orangey-yellow with some green.

Menu

18

Winter Brunch
386 calories
per serving

GLAZED PINK GRAPEFRUIT

SAVORY VEAL SAUSAGE PATTIES

CHEESE POLENTA

APRICOTS POACHED IN WHITE WINE

SPICED COFFEE

Plan of action

5 MINUTES THE NIGHT BEFORE
25 MINUTES BEFORE SERVING

1. The night before, mix up the sausage patties.
2. The next day, poach the apricots and set them aside.
3. Cook the polenta and spoon it into custard cups. While the polenta is cooking, prepare the grapefruit and brew the coffee.
4. Heat the grapefruit. While the grapefruit is heating, form the sausage patties.

5. Serve the grapefruit and, meanwhile, preheat the browning dish.
6. Cook the sausage. While the sausage is cooking, arrange the plates. While arranging and serving the plates, heat the pitcher of coffee with spices.
7. Serve together the sausage, polenta, apricots, and coffee.

Glazed Pink Grapefruit

SERVINGS: 4 ◆ 55 CALORIES PER ½ GRAPEFRUIT ◆ COOKING TIME: 2 MINUTES

**2 medium pink grapefruit, cut in half,
    segments loosened**
4 teaspoons brown sugar

Place each grapefruit half, cut side up, on an individual microwaveproof serving plate. If 4 plates don't fit into your microwave, place all the grapefruit on a 10-inch plate and then transfer them to individual serving plates. Sprinkle each grapefruit half with 1 teaspoon brown sugar. Place the dishes in the microwave oven and heat them on HIGH for 1½ to 2 minutes, or until the sugar is melted and the top is glazed.

◆ *For 1 Serving:* Loosen the segments of 1 pink grapefruit half. Place it cut side up on a microwaveproof serving plate. Sprinkle the top with 1 teaspoon brown sugar. Heat it on HIGH for 35 to 45 seconds, or until the sugar is melted and the top is glazed.

Savory Veal Sausage Patties

SERVINGS: 4 ◆ 165 CALORIES PER SERVING ◆ COOKING TIME: 9 TO 13 MINUTES, INCLUDING HEATING THE BROWNING DISH

It is important to assemble the sausage the night before, because the flavors develop by standing in the refrigerator for 12 hours.

1 pound ground veal
¼ cup chopped fresh parsley
¼ teaspoon dried basil
¼ teaspoon freshly grated nutmeg
¼ teaspoon paprika

¼ teaspoon dried sage
¼ teaspoon dried thyme
¼ teaspoon freshly ground black pepper
**4 fresh purple or green basil leaves for
    garnish (optional)**

In a medium bowl blend all the ingredients together. Cover and refrigerate overnight.

Right before cooking, place the browning dish in the microwave and heat it on HIGH for 5 to 9 minutes, or according to the manufacturer's instructions for grilled sausage or hamburgers. Meanwhile, form the sausage mixture into four 4-ounce patties, about ¾ inch thick. Press the patties down firmly on the skillet and cook them on HIGH for 2 minutes; turn over. Cook them on HIGH for 2 minutes more, or until they test done.

◆ *For 1 Serving:* Combine ¼ pound ground veal, 1 tablespoon chopped parsley, and a dash each dried basil, freshly grated nutmeg, paprika, dried sage, dried thyme, and black pepper in a small bowl. Refrigerate overnight.

No matter what meal you are serving, whether for yourself or your family, serve it with style. Arrange the food on the plates with care, and use your own personal artistry to garnish them with flower blossoms, small green leaves, or lemon slices. Set the table with cloth napkins and goblets. Dieting should be as pleasant as possible and with these touches you help to make dining a soothing and elegant experience.

Right before serving, place the browning dish in the microwave and heat it on HIGH for 5 to 9 minutes, or according to the manufacturer's instructions for grilled sausage or hamburgers. Meanwhile, form a patty out of the sausage mixture, about ¾ inch thick. Press the patty firmly down on the hot browning dish and cook on HIGH for 1½ minutes. Turn over and cook on HIGH for 1½ minutes, or until the patty tests done.

Cheese Polenta

SERVINGS: 4 ◆ 121 CALORIES PER ½-CUP SERVING ◆ COOKING TIME: 5 TO 6 MINUTES

½ cup cornmeal
1¾ cups skim milk
　2 tablespoons low-fat plain yogurt
　2 tablespoons grated Parmesan cheese

¼ teaspoon freshly ground black pepper
⅛ teaspoon freshly grated nutmeg
　Dash cayenne pepper

Place the cornmeal in a 2-quart casserole. Stir in the milk. Cover tightly and cook on HIGH for 1 minute; stir well to prevent lumping. Cover again and

cook on HIGH for 4 to 5 minutes more, stirring every minute until all the liquid is absorbed. Stir in the remaining ingredients.

Divide the mixture between 4 custard cups. Cover and set aside until serving time.

To serve: Invert the custard cups onto the plates, releasing the polenta. Place the sausage patties beside the polenta along with 2 poached apricots, spooning the apricot juices over the top.

◆ *For 1 Serving:* Place 2 tablespoons cornmeal in a 1-quart casserole. Stir in ½ cup milk. Cover tightly and cook on HIGH for 1 minute; stir. Cook, uncovered, on HIGH for 1 to 2 minutes more, stirring every 30 seconds until all the liquid is absorbed. Stir in 1½ teaspoons each low-fat plain yogurt and grated Parmesan cheese, a dash black pepper, and a pinch each nutmeg and cayenne. Spoon into a custard cup and cover until serving time.

Apricots Poached in White Wine

SERVINGS: 4 ◆ 42 CALORIES PER 2 APRICOTS ◆ COOKING TIME: 2 MINUTES

3 tablespoons water
2 tablespoons dry white wine
1 teaspoon lemon juice

1 teaspoon brown sugar
½ teaspoon ground cinnamon
8 whole dried apricots, or 16 halves

Combine all the ingredients except the apricots in a 1-quart casserole; mix together well. Stir in the apricots and push them into the liquid to cover. Cover tightly and cook on HIGH for 1 minute; stir. Cook on HIGH for 1 minute more. Let the apricots stand, covered, at room temperature until serving time (most of the liquid will be absorbed by the apricots during this time).

◆ *For 1 Serving:* Combine 1 tablespoon water, 1½ teaspoons white wine, ½ teaspoon each lemon juice and brown sugar, and ⅛ teaspoon cinnamon in a custard cup; stir. Add 2 whole or 4 halves dried apricots. Cover tightly and cook on HIGH for 45 seconds. Let stand until serving time.

Spiced Coffee

SERVINGS: 4 ◆ 3 CALORIES ◆ COOKING TIME: 1 TO 3 MINUTES

4 cups brewed coffee
1 teaspoon grated orange peel

½ teaspoon ground cinnamon
¼ teaspoon ground allspice

Right before serving the coffee, pour it into a microwaveproof pitcher. Stir in the orange peel, cinnamon, and allspice. Heat the coffee on HIGH for 1 to 3 minutes, or until heated through.

◆ *For 1 Serving:* Pour 1 cup brewed coffee into a microwaveproof cup. Add ¼ teaspoon grated orange peel, ⅛ teaspoon cinnamon, and a dash allspice. Heat on HIGH for 30 seconds to 1 minute.

SWEET POTATO—APPLE SOUP

SERVINGS: 4 ◆ 164 CALORIES PER ¾-CUP SERVING ◆ COOKING TIME: 10 TO 16 MINUTES

This is a deliciously spiced and flavorful soup. It would be nice served around the holidays.

1½ **pounds sweet potatoes**
2 **tablespoons chopped onion**
1 **medium apple, peeled, cored, and thinly sliced**
2 **cups chicken broth**
½ **teaspoon chopped fresh rosemary, or ¼ teaspoon dried, plus 4 sprigs for garnish**

½ **teaspoon ground cinnamon**
⅛ **teaspoon freshly grated nutmeg, plus extra for garnish**
⅛ **teaspoon cayenne pepper**

Pierce the potatoes on the top and bottom. Place the potatoes on a paper towel in the microwave. Cook on HIGH for 4 to 6 minutes, or until slightly tender when squeezed. Let stand for 5 minutes.

Meanwhile, combine the onion and apple in a 2-quart casserole. Cover tightly and cook on HIGH for 3 to 5 minutes, or until tender. Spoon into the bowl of a food processor or blender.

Peel the cooked potatoes and cut them into 1-inch cubes. Add the potatoes to the processor. Pour in ½ cup broth and process until a smooth puree. Add the remaining 1½ cups broth and process to blend well.

Pour the mixture back into the casserole. Stir in the remaining ingredients. Cover tightly and cook on HIGH for 3 to 5 minutes, or until heated through.

To serve: Spoon the soup into 4 bowls and top each with nutmeg and a sprig of rosemary if you have it.

◆ *For Fewer Servings:* It isn't practical to cut this recipe in half. Instead, plan to serve it for lunches later in the week. Top it with ¼ cup low-fat plain yogurt and add 38 calories, with 1 tablespoon sunflower seeds and add 51 calories more.

Lunch Suggestions

You may wish to take warm soup to the office for lunch on these cold winter days. If your employer has a microwave oven on the premises, heat approximately 1 cup of soup, covered with wax paper, on HIGH for 3 to 4 minutes, or until hot, stirring once. (If the soup has cheese or yogurt in it, heat it on MEDIUM for 3 to 5 minutes instead.)

If there is no microwave oven where you work, heat the soup in the morning and store it in a Thermos until lunchtime.

German Dumpling Soup and Apfel Lunch

1 cup German Dumpling and Spinach Suppe (page 246)	148 calories
2 melba toasts	30 calories
½ apple, sliced	40 calories
Seltzer or mineral water	
	TOTAL 218 calories

Fisherman's Lunch

¾ cup Fisherman's Chowder (page 260)	109 calories
2 melba toasts	30 calories
1 medium orange	62 calories
½ cup skim milk	44 calories
	TOTAL 245 calories

Chicken Pocket

2 ounces sliced chicken (page 256)	108 calories
in 1-ounce pita	95 calories
½ cup skim milk	44 calories
½ apple, sliced	40 calories
	TOTAL 287 calories

Veal Sausage Sandwich

½ Savory Veal Sausage Patty (page 263)	105 calories
in 1-ounce pita	95 calories
with lettuce	2 calories
½ cup skim milk	44 calories
20 seedless grapes	72 calories
TOTAL	**318 calories**

Healthy Beef Sandwich

2 ounces thinly sliced Grilled Round Steak (page 224)	108 calories
in 1-ounce pita	95 calories
with lettuce, radishes, mustard, and horseradish	10 calories
Seltzer	
TOTAL	**213 calories**

Hot Cheese and Tomato on Bagel

½ bagel	82 calories
Topped with 1 ounce grated partially skim milk cheese	80 calories
1 tomato slice	4 calories
TOTAL	**166 calories**

Place the bagel, cheese, and tomato on a paper towel and put in the microwave. Heat it on MEDIUM for 1 minute, or until the cheese is melted. You can substitute 1 piece of toast (60 calories) or a 1-ounce pita (95 calories).

BREAKFASTS

*B*reakfast is no less important than any meal of the day. If you skip it, you're likely to have less energy during the day and more likely to overeat. If you choose one of these menus, the average time you will spend in cooking will be about 1 minute. Now really, is that too much time to spend?

Each menu is approximately 200 calories, which fits into the initial 800-to-900-calories-per-day plan.

As your diet successfully continues, add a fruit or ½ cup skim milk or low-fat yogurt to your daily regime in the morning or as an afternoon pick-me-up.

GRAPEFRUIT (½, 43 CALORIES), SEGMENTED
GARNISHED WITH BERRIES

CHEESE MELT

Cheese Melt

SERVINGS: 1 ◆ 172 CALORIES ◆ COOKING TIME: ABOUT 1 MINUTE

1 ounce hard cheese, sliced (Cheddar, Swiss, or Fontina)
1 slice whole wheat bread, toasted
1 tablespoon Fresh Tomato Salsa (page 43) (optional)

Place the cheese on top of the toasted bread on a microwaveproof plate. Heat on MEDIUM for 35 seconds to 1½ minutes. Serve with salsa.

271

Menu

2

178 calories
per serving

This is for when you are in a real hurry.

BANANA (½, 50 CALORIES)

SCRAMBLED EGG ON THE RUN

MELBA TOAST (3 SLICES, 48 CALORIES)

Scrambled Egg on the Run

SERVINGS: 1 ◆ 80 CALORIES ◆ COOKING TIME: ABOUT 1 MINUTE

Break 1 egg into a Styrofoam cup and
beat it with a fork. Cook on HIGH for 35
to 45 seconds; stir.

Menu

3

234 calories
per serving

HERBED SCRAMBLED EGG
IN WHOLE WHEAT PITA POCKET

ORANGE (74 CALORIES)

Herbed Scrambled Egg in Whole Wheat Pita Pocket

SERVINGS: 1 ◆ 187 CALORIES ◆ COOKING TIME: ABOUT 1 MINUTE

Wrap this breakfast in foil and take it with you to eat in the car, on the train, or at
your desk.

1 _egg, beaten_
1 _tablespoon chopped mixed fresh herbs_
   (parsley, chives, tarragon)
1 _1-ounce whole wheat pita, cut in half_

Combine the egg and herbs in a 5- or 6-ounce custard cup. Cook on HIGH for 35 to 50 seconds, or until slightly puffed up. Stir and break the egg up with a fork and spoon it into the pita pockets.

WATERMELON SLICES WITH STAR FRUIT GARNISH (1-INCH WEDGE, 25 CALORIES)

PIMENTO AND TARRAGON–FLECKED SCRAMBLED EGGS

TOAST (1 SLICE, 65 CALORIES)

TROPICAL PINEAPPLE JAM (PAGE 299)
(1 TABLESPOON, 11 CALORIES)

Menu

4

*186
calories
per
serving*

Pimento and Tarragon–Flecked Scrambled Eggs

SERVINGS: 1 ◆ 100 CALORIES ◆ COOKING TIME: ABOUT 1 MINUTE

1 egg, beaten
1 tablespoon chopped fresh tarragon
1 tablespoon thinly sliced pimento

Combine the egg and tarragon in a 5- or 6-ounce custard cup. Cook on HIGH for 35 to 50 seconds, or until slightly puffed up. Stir and break the egg up with a fork and spoon onto a serving plate. Garnish with sliced pimento.

Menu

5

236 calories
per serving

GRAPEFRUIT (½, 40 CALORIES)

BAKED EGG IN A CUP

WHOLE WHEAT TOAST (1 SLICE, 65 CALORIES)

TROPICAL PINEAPPLE JAM (PAGE 299)
(1 TABLESPOON, 11 CALORIES) (OPTIONAL)

SKIM MILK (½ CUP, 40 CALORIES)

O R

T E A

Baked Egg in a Cup

SERVINGS: 1 ◆ 80 CALORIES ◆ COOKING TIME: ABOUT 1 MINUTE

Break the egg into a 6- or 7-ounce custard cup. Prick the membrane of the yolk with a toothpick or fork. Cover with plastic wrap, turning back one corner slightly. Cook on MEDIUM for 45 seconds to 1 minute 20 seconds, or until set.

Menu

6

177 calories
per serving

ORANGE SEGMENTS (½ CUP, 46 CALORIES)

COOKED WHEATENA CEREAL WITH RAISINS

SKIM MILK (½ CUP, 40 CALORIES)

Cooked Wheatena Cereal with Raisins

SERVINGS: 1 ◆ 98 CALORIES ◆ COOKING TIME: 2 TO 3 MINUTES

2 tablespoons Wheatena cereal
⅓ cup water
1 tablespoon raisins

274

Combine the Wheatena and water in a 1½-cup microwaveproof cereal bowl. Cook on HIGH for 2 to 3 minutes, or until the cereal is thickened, stirring once. Stir in the raisins and serve.

Menu

7

153 to 163 calories per serving

SLICED PEACHES (½ CUP, 33 CALORIES), BERRIES FOR GARNISH (OPTIONAL)

BROWN SUGARED OATMEAL

SKIM MILK (½ CUP, 40 CALORIES)

Brown Sugared Oatmeal

SERVINGS: 1 ◆ 92 CALORIES WITH SUGAR, 90 WITH RAISINS ◆ COOKING TIME: 2 MINUTES

3 tablespoons old-fashioned oatmeal
½ cup water
1 teaspoon brown sugar, or 1 tablespoon raisins

Combine the oatmeal and water in a 1½-cup microwaveproof cereal bowl. Cook on HIGH for 1 minute, or until it boils; stir. Cook on MEDIUM for 1 minute to reach the desired consistency. Stir in the brown sugar or raisins.

Meal-in-One

Fiber and Fruit Breakfast

SERVINGS: 4 ◆ 133 CALORIES PER ½-CUP SERVING ◆ COOKING TIME: 6 TO 13 MINUTES

¼ cup bulgur
½ cup skim milk
¼ cup low-fat plain yogurt
¼ cup raisins

1 apple, cored and chopped
1 tablespoon brown sugar
Ground cinnamon

Combine the bulgur and milk in a 4-cup glass measure. Cover tightly and cook on HIGH for 1 to 3 minutes, or until the mixture boils; stir. Cover again and cook on MEDIUM for 5 to 10 minutes, or until the liquid is absorbed. Stir in the remaining ingredients, except cinnamon. Cover again and let stand for 2 minutes. Sprinkle with cinnamon before serving.

◆ *For 1 Serving:* Combine 1 tablespoon bulgur and 2 tablespoons milk in a 2-cup glass measure. Cover tightly and cook on HIGH for 45 seconds to 1 minute, or until the mixture boils, then on MEDIUM for 2 to 4 minutes, or until the liquid is absorbed. Stir in 1 tablespoon each yogurt and raisins; ¼ apple, cored and chopped; and ¾ teaspoon brown sugar. Cover and let stand for 1 minute.

◆ *For 2 Servings:* Combine 2 tablespoons bulgur with ¼ cup milk in a 4-cup glass measure. Cover tightly and cook on HIGH for 1 minute, or until the mixture boils, then on MEDIUM for 3 to 4 minutes, or until the liquid is absorbed. Stir in 2 tablespoons each yogurt and raisins; ½ apple, cored and chopped; and 1½ teaspoons brown sugar. Cover and let stand for 1 minute.

Banana Muffins

MAKES: 12 ◆ 104 CALORIES PER MUFFIN ◆ COOKING TIME: 3 TO 6 MINUTES

Think about making these the night before you plan to eat them, for they will be a pleasant surprise at breakfast time and the flavor improves overnight. Split the muffins and spread them with Tropical Pineapple Jam at 11 calories per tablespoon (page 299) or Apple-Apricot Cream (page 226) at 16 calories per tablespoon.

1 cup bran flakes
1 cup wheat flour
1½ teaspoons baking powder
2 tablespoons brown sugar
1 teaspoon ground cinnamon
1 teaspoon grated lemon peel

½ teaspoon grated nutmeg
2 medium bananas, peeled and mashed (1 cup)
2 tablespoons vegetable oil
1 egg, slightly beaten
1 teaspoon vanilla extract

Combine the dry ingredients in a large bowl. Add the remaining ingredients and stir until just moistened. Place 2 paper cupcake liners in one or up to six 5- or 6-ounce custard cups, depending on the amount you want to cook (six is the maximum number for best results). Spoon about 2 tablespoons batter into each cup, filling them about one-third of the way.

Place the custard cups in a circle in the microwave with at least a 1-inch space between them. Follow these cooking instructions until a toothpick inserted in the center comes out clean:

▲ ▲ ▲ ▲ ▲ ▲ ▲ ▲ ▲ ▲

1 muffin	HIGH	30 seconds
2 muffins	HIGH	1 minute
4 muffins	HIGH	1½ minutes
6 muffins	HIGH	1½ to 3 minutes

▼ ▼ ▼ ▼ ▼ ▼ ▼ ▼ ▼ ▼

Remove the muffins and papers immediately from the cups and cool them on a cake rack.

◆ Tip: For ease of handling you may wish to position the cups on a 12-inch microwaveproof tray.

You may keep the batter for up to 1 week in the refrigerator, stirring each time before use. You may also bake all of the batter and freeze the extra muffins.

To reheat 1 frozen muffin, wrap it in a paper towel and heat it on HIGH for 15 to 25 seconds: 2 muffins will take 30 to 40 seconds. To reheat a room-temperature muffin, wrap it in a paper towel and heat it on HIGH for only 10 seconds.

Variations:

Banana Muffins with Raisins: Add ¼ cup raisins with the dry ingredients. 114 calories per muffin.

Banana Muffins with Walnuts: Add ¼ cup chopped walnuts with the dry ingredients. 120 calories per muffin.

MUFFIN LUNCH

Bake 1 muffin and cut it in half, spreading it with 1 tablespoon cream cheese (50 calories) for a total of 154 calories. Add a piece of fresh fruit (about 70 calories) and ½ cup skim milk (44 calories) and you've got a skinny 268-calorie lunch.

SNACKS

Snacks are for a change of pace, a dose of comfort, or a reward for a valiant and successful effort, perhaps in your dieting. Some people have a specific and even biological hunger for carbohydrates, so they would be best satisfied by popcorn or baked potato (page 295). Others want something slightly salty; for instance, something dipped into low-sodium soy sauce. Still others go for something creamy or simply can't resist a certain cookie that they have enjoyed since childhood.

Whatever your particular urge, we give a variety of snack choices. Healthwise, some are better than others, but all are 100 calories or less. It is best not to have more than one of these once every other day. And how do you know when it is right to have a snack? Follow these three steps:

1. Make sure you are not choosing it strictly in a moment of weakness, but that the snack will really have a beneficial effect on your mood and not just make you feel guilty later. Ask yourself: "Do I really want this treat? How will I feel after I've eaten it?"

2. Sit down and do something with your hands for a few minutes while you decide; knit, clip coupons, or shine your shoes.

3. If you decide "Yes!", eat your snack leisurely and enjoy it. Make sure that you only choose one snack at a sitting.

	CALORIES
1 rice cake spread with 1 tablespoon cream cheese mixed with 1 teaspoon brown sugar	99
3 to 4 shelled Brazil nuts	97
½ ounce pine nuts	95
½ cantaloupe	94
2 dozen grapes	86
½ ice cream sandwich	84
½ pear topped with 2 teaspoons blue cheese	81
3 chocolate Kisses	77
10 shelled almonds	75
½ cup blueberries with 2 tablespoons unsweetened whipped cream	72
1 s'more (1 graham cracker, 5 chocolate bits on top, and 1 marshmallow on top of that, placed on a paper plate, and cook on HIGH for 20 seconds)	65
1 cup popcorn tossed with 1 teaspoon melted butter	58
½ grapefruit with 1 teaspoon brown sugar on top	57
Ice pop made with 4 ounces orange juice	56
1 Oreo cookie	51
2 Girl Scout shortbread cookies	46
Jello-O gelatin pop	35
2 vanilla wafers	34
10 pretzel sticks (2¼" x 8")	12

282

Basic Popcorn

AMOUNT: 2 CUPS ◆ 23 CALORIES PER 1 CUP ◆ COOKING TIME: 3 TO 5 MINUTES

Popcorn is not an "empty-calorie" snack. It is high in fiber, and that is something that nutritionists say is good for you. Can you think of a more blissful way to add fiber to your diet? . . . And at 23 calories per cup, you can really enjoy!

⅓ cup popping corn

Place the popcorn in a brown sandwich-size paper bag (an unrecycled bag is best). *Do not add oil.* Fold down the top of the bag twice, gently, to close lightly but firmly.

Only in a 500-watt oven or more, cook on HIGH for 3 minutes, or until the popping begins to slow down but is not completely stopped. Watch closely the last minute. Popping may take less time, but never more.

Note: Without at least a 500-watt oven, there won't be enough power to pop corn.

Variations:

Parmesan Popcorn: Sprinkle 1 cup popped corn with 1 teaspoon grated Parmesan cheese. Add 8 calories.

Pop and Spicy Corn: Stir in a few drops of Tabasco and/or a pinch chili powder or cayenne to each cup.

Creamy Fruit Drinks

Here are drinks under 100 calories that make great snacks, are good for you, and can be quickly made in a blender or food processor. These are for 1 serving.

½ cup skim milk + 1 whole fresh peach, pitted, or ½ cup frozen slices + pinch ground cardamon (82 calories)

½ cup skim milk + ½ banana + pinch grated nutmeg (99 calories)

½ cup skim milk + ½ cup fresh or frozen strawberries, trimmed + 2 drops vanilla extract (69 calories)

CATCHALL

*T*his chapter is just what its name states—a collection of recipes that don't fit into the other chapters but which will help to make dieting more pleasant. You'll find low-calorie dressings and dips, delicious diet jams, and instructions for cooking everyday basics such as rice and potatoes, some broths and a bean stew.

Ginger Oriental Dressing

MAKES: ¼ CUP ◆ 6 CALORIES PER 1 TABLESPOON

This is more than just a delicious salad dressing. It can be stirred into cooked rice, cooked vegetables, or served as a dipping sauce for quickly steamed vegetables. Or try pouring 1 tablespoon dressing over the top of a fish fillet, scallops, or boneless chicken breast before cooking.

   You may find that you use this recipe so often that you'll want to double or triple it. It will keep, refrigerated, for at least a month in a sealed jar.

1 teaspoon freshly grated ginger
¼ teaspoon minced garlic
2 tablespoons low-sodium soy sauce

2 tablespoons water
2 teaspoons orange juice
1 teaspoon white vinegar

Combine all the ingredients into a small jar and shake well to mix.

Variations:

Gingered Oriental Dressing with Mustard: Add ¼ teaspoon dry mustard to the mixture. 7 calories.

Very Gingery Oriental Dressing: Add 1 additional tablespoon freshly grated ginger. This will set your taste buds aglow. 7 calories.

Creamy Herb Dressing I

MAKES: 1½ CUPS ◆ 10 CALORIES PER 1 TABLESPOON

½ cup low-fat cottage cheese
1 cup low-fat plain yogurt
1 tablespoon prepared horseradish
1 tablespoon chopped fresh parsley

1 tablespoon chopped fresh dill
1 tablespoon chopped fresh chives or green onion tops
1 tablespoon fresh lemon juice

Combine all the ingredients in a bowl or food processor and blend well. Chill. Keeps in the refrigerator for 1 week.

Creamy Herb Dressing II

MAKES: ¼ CUP ◆ 11 CALORIES PER 1 TABLESPOON

¼ cup Mock Sour Cream (see below)
1 teaspoon chopped fresh chives
1 teaspoon chopped fresh parsley, dill, tarragon, basil, oregano, or thyme

¼ teaspoon grated lemon peel
Freshly ground pepper to taste

Combine all the ingredients in a small bowl. Chill.

Mustard Vinaigrette

MAKES: ⅔ CUP ◆ 17 CALORIES PER 1 TABLESPOON

1 tablespoon olive oil
2 tablespoons thinly sliced green onion
2 tablespoons Dijon-style mustard
3 tablespoons cider or wine vinegar

¼ cup water
2 tablespoons chopped fresh parsley
Pinch freshly grated nutmeg
Freshly ground black pepper

Combine all the ingredients in a bowl or food processor, beating with the addition of each ingredient until the mixture is well blended. Chill. Keeps in the refrigerator for 2 weeks.

Curry-Herb Dip

MAKES: 1 CUP ◆ 11 CALORIES PER 1 TABLESPOON

This is a tantalizing dip for raw vegetable crudités, Confetti Veal Meatballs or Svelte Terrine de Poisson.

1 cup low-fat plain yogurt
1 tablespoon Dijon mustard
1 tablespoon thinly sliced fresh chives or green onion

1 tablespoon chopped fresh dill, or 1 teaspoon dried
½ to 1 teaspoon curry powder

Combine all the ingredients in a bowl or food processor and blend well. Chill. Keeps in the refrigerator for 1 week.

Mock Sour Cream

MAKES: 1¼ CUPS ◆ 10 CALORIES PER 1 TABLESPOON

Make this sour cream on the weekend and vary it through the week with the recipes that follow. We think you'll find it invaluable to zip up baked potatoes or salads.

1 cup low-fat cottage cheese
¼ cup low-fat plain yogurt
2 tablespoons fresh lemon juice (see Note)

Place all the ingredients in a blender or food processor and blend until very smooth. Refrigerate for up to 2 weeks.

Note: It is important to use fresh lemon juice in this recipe, because the flavor is far superior to the frozen or jarred.

Creamy Mustard Dressing

MAKES: ¼ CUP ◆ 11 CALORIES PER 1 TABLESPOON

¼ cup Mock Sour Cream (see above)
1 teaspoon Dijon mustard
   Dash hot pepper sauce

Combine all the ingredients in a small bowl. Chill.

Creamy Horseradish

MAKES: ¼ CUP ◆ 11 CALORIES PER 1 TABLESPOON

¼ cup Mock Sour Cream (see above)
1 teaspoon prepared horseradish

Dash hot pepper sauce
Freshly ground pepper to taste

Combine all the ingredients in a small bowl. Chill.

Creamy Oriental Dressing

MAKES: ¼ CUP ◆ 12 CALORIES PER 1 TABLESPOON

¼ cup Mock Sour Cream (see above)
1 teaspoon freshly grated ginger
1 teaspoon low-sodium soy sauce

1 teaspoon orange juice
1 tablespoon chopped green onion
¼ teaspoon minced garlic

Combine all the ingredients in a small bowl. Chill.

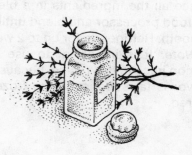

Creamy Orange Dressing

MAKES: 1 CUP ◆ 16 CALORIES PER 1 TABLESPOON

You may want to make more of this dressing than any other because it can be combined into many salads. It is even unusually delicious on fruit salads and as a dip for fresh fruits.

1 cup Mock Sour Cream (see above)
1 tablespoon orange-flavored liqueur or orange juice
1 tablespoon confectioner's sugar

1 teaspoon grated orange peel
Pinch freshly grated nutmeg, ground cinnamon, or cardamom

Combine all the ingredients in a small bowl. Chill.

Chicken Broth

MAKES: 4½ TO 5 CUPS ◆ 22 CALORIES PER 1 CUP ◆ COOKING TIME: 1¼ HOURS

By making your own broths, you can eliminate any salt and grease found in store-bought brands. And the flavor will be better.

1 3-pound chicken, cut up, or backs, necks, and wings
1 leek, sliced
1 onion, sliced
1 celery rib with leaves, sliced
1 carrot, peeled and sliced

¼ cup coarsely chopped fresh parsley, or 2 tablespoons dried
4 peppercorns
2 whole cloves
1 bay leaf, crushed
5 cups water

Combine all the ingredients in a 4-quart casserole. Cover tightly and cook on HIGH for 15 to 20 minutes, or until boiling. Uncover and turn the chicken pieces over. Cover again and cook on MEDIUM for 1 hour. Let stand, covered, for 10 minutes. Strain and degrease. Refrigerate for up to 1 week, or freeze for up to 2 months.

Quick Brown Broth

MAKES: ABOUT 5 CUPS ◆ 31 CALORIES PER 1 CUP ◆ COOKING TIME: 1 HOUR

1½ pounds lean ground beef
2 onions, thinly sliced
2 carrots, sliced
1 leek, trimmed and white stalk sliced
1 celery rib with leaves
¼ cup chopped fresh parsley with stems

1 tablespoon sherry (optional)
4 black peppercorns
3 sprigs thyme, or ½ teaspoon dried
2 whole cloves
1 bay leaf, crushed
5 cups water

Combine all the ingredients in a 4-quart casserole. Cover tightly and cook on HIGH for 10 to 15 minutes, or until boiling; stir and skim if necessary. Cover again and cook on MEDIUM for 45 minutes. Let stand, covered, for 10 minutes. Strain and degrease before serving or cooking in soups.

Fish Stock

MAKES: 3 CUPS ◆ 22 CALORIES PER 1 CUP ◆ COOKING TIME: 28 TO 35 MINUTES

1 cup coarsely chopped onion
2 leeks, trimmed and white stalk sliced
1 celery rib, chopped
1 carrot, scraped and chopped
1 tablespoon lemon juice
6 parsley stems, or 1 tablespoon dried

½ teaspoon dried thyme
¼ teaspoon black pepper
3 cups water
½ cup dry white wine
1 pound bones and trimmings from non-oily fish (no gills)

Combine the vegetables and seasonings in a 3-quart casserole. Cover tightly and cook on HIGH for 5 minutes. Stir in the water, wine, and bones. Cover again and cook on HIGH for 8 to 10 minutes, or until boiling; stir. Cook on MEDIUM for 15 to 20 minutes to develop flavor. Let it stand, covered, for 10 minutes. Strain and degrease.

Thick Lentil Stew

SERVINGS: 4 ◆ 221 CALORIES PER 1 CUP (132 CALORIES WHEN SERVED WITH ½ CUP BROWN RICE) ◆ COOKING TIME: 25 TO 30 MINUTES

When this lentil stew is coupled with brown rice, it makes a high-fiber dish that makes a complete protein.

1 teaspoon full-flavored olive oil
2 garlic cloves, minced
2 tablespoons chopped onion
1 cup thinly sliced celery
1 carrot, thinly sliced
½ jalapeño pepper, seeded and thinly sliced, or ¼ teaspoon red pepper flakes

3 cups chicken broth, tomato juice, or water
1 cup dry lentils
2 tablespoons lime juice
1 teaspoon low-sodium soy sauce
¼ cup chopped fresh parsley or cilantro

Combine the oil, garlic, onion, celery, carrot, and pepper in a 3-quart casserole. Cover tightly and cook on HIGH for 5 minutes. Stir in the remaining ingredients, except the parsley or cilantro. Cover again and cook on MEDIUM for 20 to 25 minutes, or until the lentils are tender. Let stand, covered, for 5 minutes. Sprinkle with the parsley or cilantro.

Some Optional Toppings: yogurt, add 19 calories per 2 tablespoons; chopped raw onions, add 4 calories per 1 tablespoon; chopped raw green pepper, 1 calorie per 1 tablespoon.

Soaking and Cooking Dry Beans

MAKES: 2 CUPS ◆ 343 CALORIES PER 1 CUP ◆ COOKING TIME: 47 TO 72 MINUTES (INCLUDES PRESOAKING)

These beans may be prepared in advance for the Pasta e Fagioli (page 174) or the Vegetarian Chili (page 231). We think they will bring a slightly better texture to the finished product.

Presoaking:

1 cup kidney or northern beans
2 cups water

293

Combine the beans and water in a 3-quart casserole. Cover tightly and cook on HIGH for 5 to 10 minutes to boil; stir. Cover again and cook on MEDIUM for 2 minutes. Let them stand, covered, for 1 hour. Makes 2 cups presoaked beans.

Cooking:

2 cups presoaked kidney or northern beans, drained
3 cups water

Combine the beans and water in a 3-quart casserole. Cover tightly and cook on HIGH for 10 to 15 minutes, or until boiling; stir. Cover again and cook on MEDIUM for 30 to 45 minutes, or until the beans are tender, stirring after 15 minutes. Let stand, covered, for 5 minutes. Drain, degrease, and serve with chopped onion or use in cooking.

Basic Rice

MAKES: 2 CUPS ◆ 134 CALORIES PER ½ CUP ◆ COOKING TIME: 10 TO 15 MINUTES

¾ cup long-grain rice
1¼ cups water

Combine the ingredients in a 2-quart casserole. Cover tightly and cook on HIGH for 3 to 5 minutes, or until boiling; then on MEDIUM for 7 to 10 minutes, or until most of the water is absorbed. Stir and let stand, covered, for 3 minutes.

◆ *For 2 Servings:* It is not practical to cook 1 serving, so it is best to save the other for another meal later in the week.

Combine ⅓ cup and 2 tablespoons long-grain rice and ¾ cup water in a 4-cup glass measure or 1-quart casserole. Cover tightly and cook on HIGH for 2 to 3 minutes to boil. Cook on MEDIUM for 4 to 6 minutes, until the liquid is absorbed. Let stand, covered, for 3 minutes.

Brown Rice

MAKES: 2 CUPS ◆ 132 CALORIES PER ½ CUP ◆ COOKING TIME: 25 TO 33 MINUTES

Brown rice is not part of our menu plans because it takes longer to cook than 30-minute menu guidelines. We do, however, appreciate the fact that it is richer in fiber, protein value, and potassium than polished white rice, so we suggest that you plan in advance if you want brown rice to be a part of your menu.

    You can even make it the night before, while you are eating dinner, and then reheat it the next evening following the instructions given below.

¾ cup brown rice
1¾ cups water

Combine the rice and water in a 3-quart casserole. Cover tightly and cook on HIGH for 5 to 8 minutes to bring it to a boil; then cook on MEDIUM for 20 to 25 minutes, or until most of the liquid is absorbed and the rice is tender. Let it stand, covered, for 5 minutes.

◆ *For Fewer Servings:* Cooking only 1 or 2 servings of rice in the microwave doesn't save much time. We suggest that you make the whole amount and refrigerate (for up to 1 week) or freeze it to be reheated later.

To Reheat Refrigerated Rice:

2 Cups: Cover tightly and heat on HIGH for 2 to 3 minutes, stirring once.

½ Cup: Cover tightly and heat on HIGH for 35 seconds to 1 minute.

Frozen Rice:

2 Cups: Cover tightly and heat on HIGH for 4 to 6 minutes, stirring twice to break up the frozen kernels.

½ Cup: Cover tightly and heat on HIGH for 1½ to 2½ minutes, stirring once to break up the frozen kernels.

Baked Potato

SERVING: 1 ◆ 88 CALORIES ◆ COOKING TIME: 3 TO 5 MINUTES

1 medium baking potato

Pierce the potato on the top and bottom and place it on a paper towel in the microwave. Cook it on HIGH for 3 to 5 minutes, turning over once. Test for doneness by holding the potato in a cloth kitchen towel and squeezing it; the outside should give slightly. Let it stand for 5 minutes. (You may wrap it in a cloth to absorb some moisture.)

Variations:

For 2 Potatoes: Pierce 2 potatoes on the top and bottom and place them on a paper towel in the microwave oven, leaving a 1-inch space between them.

Cook on HIGH for 5 to 9 minutes, or until they give slightly when squeezed, turning them over once. Let them stand for 5 to 10 minutes.

For 4 Potatoes: Pierce 4 potatoes on the top and bottom and place them in a circle on a paper towel in the microwave oven, leaving a 1-inch space between them. Cook on HIGH for 10 to 13 minutes, or until they give slightly when squeezed, turning over once. Let stand for 5 to 10 minutes.

Potato Meals

Here are some suggestions for concocting "potato meals." Check your refrigerator and choose any topping you like. If the topping is something like a stew or chili that needs to be heated first, do that during the standing time of the potato.

The Simple Potato

1 warm baked potato, cut in half,	88 calories
topped with 2 tablespoons low-fat plain yogurt	20 calories
and freshly ground black papper	
TOTAL	120 calories

Broccoli and Melted Cheese Potato

1 warm baked potato, cut in half,	88 calories
topped with ½ cup cooked chopped broccoli	20 calories
and 1 ounce grated partially skim milk cheese	80 calories

Heat on MEDIUM for 1 to 2 minutes or until the cheese is melted.

TOTAL	188 calories

Potatoes Parisian

1 warm baked potato, cut in half,	88 calories
topped with 1 cup Sliced Mushrooms with Parsley (page 241)	32 calories
Heat on MEDIUM for 1 to 2 minutes.	
TOTAL	120 calories

Chicken and Cheese Potatoes

1 warm baked potato, cut in half,	88 calories
topped with 1 ounce poached and thinly sliced chicken	54 calories
and 1 ounce grated partially skim milk cheese	80 calories
Heat on MEDIUM for 1 to 2 minutes, or until the cheese is melted.	
TOTAL	222 calories

Garden Variety Potatoes

1 warm baked potato, cut in half,	88 calories
topped with ½ cup Seasonal Vegetable Platter (page 112)	29 calories
and 1 ounce grated partially skim milk cheese	80 calories
Heat on MEDIUM for 1 to 2 minutes, or until cheese is melted.	
TOTAL	197 calories

Uptown Veal Potatoes

1 warm baked potato, cut in half,	88 calories
topped with ½ cup Veal Cubes with Vegetables Printemps (page 65)	130 calories
Heat on HIGH for 1 minute.	
TOTAL	218 calories

Seaside Spud

1 baked potato, cut in half,	88 calories
topped with ½ cup Scallops Provençale (page 149)	100 calories
and 1 ounce grated partially skim milk cheese	80 calories
Heat on MEDIUM for 2 minutes, or until the cheese is melted.	
TOTAL	268 calories

Chili Tater

1 warm baked potato, cut in half,   88 calories
topped with ½ cup Vegetarian Chili (page 231)   70 calories
   Heat on MEDIUM for 2 minutes.

                             TOTAL 158 calories

Jams

Here are a trio of jams from the ordinary to the exotic. As with any dish made with fruit, choose those ones that are perfectly ripened and flavorful.

Make sure that these recipes are cooked in a large casserole or you will be cleaning boilovers from your oven.

These will keep for 1 month in the refrigerator, though I doubt they will be around that long. Use 1 tablespoon of jam in place of 1 tablespoon butter and save yourself a lot of calories.

Strawberry Jam

MAKES: ¾ CUP ◆ 8 CALORIES PER 1 TABLESPOON ◆ COOKING TIME: 4 TO 6 MINUTES

1½ cups sliced strawberries
  1 teaspoon grated lemon peel

1 teaspoon vanilla extract
1 teaspoon unflavored gelatin

Puree the strawberries in a blender or food processor to make about 1 cup. Combine the strawberry puree and lemon peel in a 2-quart casserole. Cover with wax paper and cook on HIGH for 4 to 6 minutes, or until the mixture has reached a rolling boil, stirring once after 2 minutes. Stir in the vanilla.

Transfer ¼ cup of the cooked puree into a small bowl. Stir in the gelatin to dissolve it. Return this mixture to the casserole and stir well to blend. Pour the warm jam into a jar and refrigerate it.

298

Tropical Pineapple Jam

MAKES: ¾ CUP ◆ 12 CALORIES PER 1 TABLESPOON ◆ COOKING TIME: 4 TO 6 MINUTES

This has to be our favorite. It is especially good spooned over the small Banana Cheesecakes (page 147).

1½ cups fresh pineapple chunks
1 teaspoon grated orange peel

1 teaspoon vanilla extract
1 teaspoon unflavored gelatin

Puree the pineapple chunks in a food processor or blender to make about 1 cup. Combine the pineapple puree and orange peel in a 2-quart casserole. Cover with wax paper and cook on HIGH for 4 to 6 minutes, or until it reaches a rolling boil, stirring after 2 minutes. Stir in the vanilla.

Remove ¼ cup of the warm fruit to a small bowl and combine it with the gelatin to dissolve it. Return this mixture to the casserole and stir well to blend. Pour the warm jam into a jar to refrigerate it.

Gingered Fresh Fig Jam

MAKES: ¾ CUP ◆ 23 CALORIES PER 1 TABLESPOON ◆ COOKING TIME: 4 TO 6 MINUTES

4 figs (about 12 ounces)
1 teaspoon grated lemon peel
¼ teaspoon ground ginger

1 teaspoon vanilla extract
1 teaspoon unflavored gelatin

Puree the figs in a food processor or blender to make about 1 cup. Combine the fig puree and lemon peel in a 2-quart casserole. Cover with wax paper and cook on HIGH for 4 to 6 minutes, or until the mixture reaches a rolling boil, stirring after 2 minutes. Stir in the vanilla.

Remove ¼ cup of the cooked fruit to a small bowl and combine it with the gelatin to dissolve it. Return this mixture to the casserole. Stir well to blend. Pour the warm jam into a jar to refrigerate.

INDEX

313

About the Authors

Thelma Snyder was born in Chicago but grew up in Connecticut. She holds a Master's in Education from Hunter College, New York. Thelma is an award-winning oil painter, who approaches cooking as she would a canvas. She now lives on Long Island with her husband, Dave, and their two children, David and Suzanne.

Marcia Cone was born in Connecticut and grew up in New York and Pennsylvania. She holds a Bachelor of Science (Foods and Nutrition) from Purdue University and a certificate from Le Cordon Bleu in Paris. Travel is an avocation that she has pursued on six continents and it has been a major influence in her food tastes. Marcia is married to Koji Esaki and they live with their daughter Hana in Illinois.

Thelma and Marcia met in 1976 while working for a microwave manufacturer. In the past few years they have authored *The Microwave French Cookbook* and *The Microwave Italian Cookbook*. They have contributed to articles that have appeared in *Ladies' Home Journal, Redbook,* and *Woman's Day.* Much of their inspiration comes from their food tastings in restaurants and markets in this country and beyond.